USING

microsoft®

word

2010

Tim Huddleston
with Michael Miller

800 East 96th Street, Indianapolis, Indiana 46240 USA

Using Microsoft® Word 2010

Copyright © 2011 by Pearson Education, Inc.

ISBN-13: 978-0-7897-4298-8

ISBN-10: 0-7897-4298-5

Library of Congress Cataloging-in-Publication Data

Huddleston, Tim, 1959-

  Using Microsoft word 2010 / Tim Huddleston with Michael Miller.

      p. cm.

  ISBN 978-0-7897-4298-8

  1. Microsoft Word. 2. Word processing. I. Miller, Michael, 1958- II. Title.

  Z52.5.M52H83 2011

  005.52—dc22

                    2010040174

Printed in the United States of America

First Printing: November 2010

Trademarks

Warning and Disclaimer

Bulk Sales

Que Publishing offers excellent discounts on this book when ordered in quantity for bulk purchases or special sales. For more information, please contact

U.S. Corporate and Government Sales

1-800-382-3419

corpsales@pearsontechgroup.com

For sales outside of the U.S., please contact

International Sales

international@pearson.com

Associate Publisher
Greg Wiegand

Acquisitions Editor
Katherine Bull

Development Editor
Julie Bess

Managing Editor
Kristy Hart

Senior Project Editor
Lori Lyons

Copy Editor
Apostrophe Editing Services

Indexer
Lisa Stumpf

Proofreader
Water Crest Publishing

Technical Editor
Vince Averello

Publishing Coordinator
Cindy Teeters

Interior Designer
Anne Jones

Cover Designer
Anna Stingley

Compositor
Nonie Ratcliff

Contents at a Glance

Introduction 1

Part I **The Basics of Using Word 2010**

1   Creating, Saving, and Printing Documents 7

2   Editing Documents 27

3   Proofing a Document 57

Part II **Formatting Characters and Paragraphs**

4   Character Formatting 90

5   Paragraph Formatting 111

6   Formatting Text with Styles 136

Part III **Organizing Text into Lists, Tables, and Columns**

7   Setting Up Lists 158

8   Creating Tables 174

9   Setting Text in Columns 210

Part IV **Formatting Pages and Documents**

10   Laying Out a Document's Pages 224

11   Formatting Documents with Themes and Templates 249

12   Adding Headers and Footers to a Document 269

Part V **Taking Your Documents to the Next Level**

13   Adding Graphics to Your Documents 284

14   Working with Charts and Diagrams 310

Note: Chapters 15-22 can be found online in your Free Web Edition by going to quepublishing.com/using.

15   Online Only—Using Advanced Text Features 335

16   Online Only—Citing Your Sources in a Word Document 355

17   Online Only—Generating Outlines, Tables of Contents,
     and Indexes 370

Part VI **Online Only—Using Word Like a Pro**

18   Online Only—Performing Mail Merges 388

19   Online Only—Collaborating with Others 399

20   Online Only—Sharing Word Documents Online 412

21   Online Only—Adding Components That Work Only
     on the Screen 435

22   Online Only—Making Word Your Own 452

Index 473

Media Files Table of Contents

To register this product and gain access to the Free Web Edition and the audio and video files, go to quepublishing.com/using.

Chapter 1:   **Creating, Saving, and Printing Documents**
Show Me **Media 1.1**—Working with Word Templates 12
Tell Me More **Media 1.2**—Understanding Word's .docx Format 14
Show Me **Media 1.3**—Saving a Word Document 15
Show Me **Media 1.4**—Printing a Word Document 25

Chapter 2:   **Editing Documents**
Tell Me More **Media 2.1**—The Dangers of Overtype Mode 32
Show Me **Media 2.2**—Browsing a Word Document 41
Show Me **Media 2.3**—Dragging and Dropping Text in a
Word Document 49
Show Me **Media 2.4**—Inserting Building Blocks in a
Word Document 53

Chapter 3:   **Proofing a Document**
Tell Me More **Media 3.1**—The Truth About Word's Proofreading 58
Show Me **Media 3.2**—Working with Word's Spelling Checker 69
Show Me **Media 3.3**—Creating an AutoCorrect Entry 82
Show Me **Media 3.4**—Using Word's Research Pane 88

Chapter 4:   **Character Formatting**
Show Me **Media 4.1**—Character Formatting in Word 92
Show Me **Media 4.2**—Using Word's Format Painter 107
Show Me **Media 4.3**—Setting AutoFormat As You Type Options
in Word 108
Tell Me More **Media 4.4**—Formatting: Is More Always Better? 110

Chapter 5:   **Paragraph Formatting**
Show Me **Media 5.1**—Aligning Paragraphs in Word 115
Show Me **Media 5.2**—Indenting Paragraphs in Word 119
Show Me **Media 5.3**—Using Word's Ruler to Set Tab Stops 124
Tell Me More **Media 5.4**—Tabs versus Spaces in Word Processing 124

Chapter 6:   **Formatting Text with Styles**
Tell Me More **Media 6.1**—Using Word's Styles to Get
Professional-Looking Documents in Less Time 139
Show Me **Media 6.2**—Seeing Word's Styles in Action 139
Show Me **Media 6.3**—Creating a New Style in Word 152
Show Me **Media 6.4**—Modifying a Style in Word 156

Chapter 7:   **Setting Up Lists**
Tell Me More **Media 7.1**—Enhancing a Document's Readability
with Lists 158
Show Me **Media 7.2**—Choosing a Different Bullet Character 164

Show Me **Media 7.3**—Keeping a List's Numbering on Track
in Word 171
Show Me **Media 7.4**—Using Word's Ruler to Set Spacing and
Indents in a List 173

Chapter 8: **Creating Tables**
Show Me **Media 8.1**—Drawing a Table in Word 182
Show Me **Media 8.2**—Merging and Splitting Cells in a Word Table ... 197
Tell Me More **Media 8.3**—The Best Ways NOT to Format a Table 203
Show Me **Media 8.4**—Formatting a Word Table by Hand 203

Chapter 9: **Setting Text in Columns**
Tell Me More **Media 9.1**—Columns: A Simple Way to Get
Professional Results 211
Show Me **Media 9.2**—Applying Column Formatting to
Existing Text 216
Show Me **Media 9.3**—Creating a Custom Column Layout in Word 219
Show Me **Media 9.4**—Using Column Breaks to Balance
Multicolumn Content 222

Chapter 10: **Laying Out a Document's Pages**
Tell Me More **Media 10.1**—Word as a Desktop Publishing Tool 224
Show Me **Media 10.2**—Setting Margins in Word 229
Show Me **Media 10.3**—Using Section Breaks to Insert a Multicolumn
Page in a One-Column Document 232
Show Me **Media 10.4**—Hyphenating a Document in Word 242

Chapter 11: **Formatting Documents with Themes and Templates**
Tell Me More **Media 11.1**—The Truth About Themes and Templates .. 249
Show Me **Media 11.2**—Modifying a Theme in Word 257
Show Me **Media 11.3**—Locating Word Templates on Your PC
and Finding Others Online 262
Show Me **Media 11.4**—Modifying and Creating Templates in Word ... 268

Chapter 12: **Adding Headers and Footers to a Document**
Tell Me More **Media 12.1**—Why Bother with Headers or Footers? 271
Show Me **Media 12.2**—Adding a Header to a Word Document 274
Show Me **Media 12.3**—Editing a Footer in a Word Document 280

Chapter 13: **Adding Graphics to Your Documents**
Tell Me More **Media 13.1**—Graphics in Word: The Good, The Bad..... 284
Show Me **Media 13.2**—Finding Clip Art in Word 290
Show Me **Media 13.3**—Mastering the Art of Text Wrapping
in Word 295
Show Me **Media 13.4**—Inserting and Modifying a Photo in Word 304
Show Me **Media 13.5**—Drawing Geometric Shapes in Word 309

Chapter 14: **Working with Charts and Diagrams**
Tell Me More **Media 14.1**—Using Charts and Diagrams to Add
Depth to a Document 314
Show Me **Media 14.2**—Creating a Chart in Word 316

Show Me **Media 14.3**—Changing a Chart's Appearance in Word 326
Show Me **Media 14.4**—Creating a SmartArt Diagram in Word 330

Chapter 15:   **Using Advanced Text Features**

Tell Me More **Media 15.1**—Using Linked Text Boxes to Create
a Newsletter 343
Show Me **Media 15.2**—Creating and Formatting a Text Box
in Word 345
Show Me **Media 15.3**—Working with WordArt 350
Show Me **Media 15.4**—Addressing Envelopes in Word 354

Chapter 16:   **Citing Your Sources in a Word Document**

Tell Me More **Media 16.1**—The Importance of Citing Your Sources 356
Show Me **Media 16.2**—Adding a Source to a Word Document 360
Show Me **Media 16.3**—Adding a Bibliography to a Word
Document 364
Show Me **Media 16.4**—Creating a Footnote in Word 369

Chapter 17:   **Generating Outlines, Tables of Contents, and Indexes**

Tell Me More **Media 17.1**—Understanding Outlines, TOCs,
and Indexes 370
Show Me **Media 17.2**—Using Word's Outlining Tools 377
Show Me **Media 17.3**—Creating a Table of Contents in Word 382
Show Me-- **Media 17.4**—Generating and Updating an Index
in Word 386

Chapter 18:   **Performing Mail Merges**

Tell Me More **Media 18.1**—Why Would Anyone Need to Do
a Mail Merge? 388
Show Me **Media 18.2**—Preparing a Letter for a Mail Merge 394
Show Me **Media 18.3**—Adding Merge Fields to a Document 395
Show Me **Media 18.4**—Performing a Simple Mail Merge in Word 398

Chapter 19:   **Collaborating with Others**

Tell Me More **Media 19.1**—Document Collaboration in a
Networked World 400
Show Me **Media 19.2**—Working with Comments in a
Word Document 405
Show Me **Media 19.3**—Tracking Changes in a Word Document 408
Show Me **Media 19.4**—Restricting Editing Privileges to a
Word Document 411

Chapter 20:   **Sharing Word Documents Online**

Tell Me More **Media 20.1**—Online Collaboration and the
World of Work 412
Show Me **Media 20.2**—Attaching a Word Document to
an Email Message 417
Show Me **Media 20.3**—Saving a Word Document to a
SkyDrive Folder 424
Show Me **Media 20.4**—Using Word Web App to View a
File on SkyDrive 429

Chapter 21: **Adding Components That Work Only on the Screen**

Tell Me More **Media 21.1**—If It Won't Show Up in Print,
Why Bother? 435
Show Me **Media 21.2**—Adding a Hyperlink to a Word Document 440
Show Me **Media 21.3**—Adding a Bookmark to a Word Document 445
Show Me **Media 21.4**—Adding a Cross-Reference to a
Word Document 451

Chapter 22: **Making Word Your Own**

Tell Me More **Media 22.1**—The Advantage of Quick-and-Dirty
Customization 452
Show Me **Media 22.2**—Personalizing Word's Quick Access Toolbar 459
Show Me **Media 22.3**—Customizing Word's Ribbon 469
Show Me **Media 22.4**—Creating a Keyboard Shortcut in Word 471

Table of Contents

Introduction 1

How This Book Is Organized 1

Using This Book 3

Special Features 4

About the USING Web Edition 5

Bonus Chapters 5

Part I: The Basics of Using Word 2010

1   Creating, Saving, and Printing Documents 7

Starting a Document from Scratch 7

Starting a Document from a Template 8

Using a Local Template 10
Finding a Template Online 10

Saving a Document 12

Saving a New Document to a Disk 13
Resaving an Existing Document 14
Saving a File with a Different Name, Location, or File Type 16

Opening an Existing Document 17

Opening a Document from the Recent Documents List 18
Opening a Document from the Open Dialog Box 19
Searching for a Document in the Open Dialog Box 20

Printing a Document 22

Quick-Printing a Document 22
Printing the (Not-so-Much) Harder Way 22

Closing a Document 26

2   Editing Documents 27

Adding Text to a Document 27

Understanding Lines and Paragraphs 28
Viewing Hidden (Nonprinting) Characters 29
Using Insert Mode and Overtype Mode 30
Using Click and Type 33
Inserting Nonalphanumeric Characters 35
Deleting Text 37

Moving Around in a Document 38
  Browsing a Document 38
  Using the Go To Command 40
Selecting Text 41
Copying and Moving Text 44
  Copying and Pasting Text 45
  Moving Text 45
  Working Directly with the Clipboard 45
  Using Paste Options 47
  Using Drag-and-Drop 49
Undoing, Redoing, and Repeating an Action 49
Working with Building Blocks 50
  Inserting a Building Block 51
  Creating a New Building Block 53
Inserting a Blank Page 55
Inserting One Word Document into Another 55

3   Proofing a Document **57**
Viewing a Document's Statistics 57
  Finding Document Statistics 57
Evaluating a Document's Readability 58
  Activating Readability Statistics 60
Checking Your Spelling and Grammar 60
  Finding and Fixing Errors While You Type 61
  Changing Options for Checking Spelling and Grammar
    as You Type 65
  Checking Spelling and Grammar in an Entire Document 66
Finding and Replacing Text 69
  Finding Text 69
  Finding Text with the Find and Replace Dialog Box 72
  Replacing Text 76
Working with AutoCorrect 78
  Rejecting a Change Made by AutoCorrect 78
  Changing AutoCorrect Settings 79
  Adding and Deleting AutoCorrect Entries 82
  Disabling AutoCorrect 84
Using Word's Research Tools 84
  Finding Definitions and Synonyms 84
  Looking Up Information in the Research Pane 87

Part II: Formatting Characters and Paragraphs

4   Character Formatting **90**

Accessing Word's Character-Formatting Tools 90

The Mini Toolbar 90

The Font Dialog Box 91

Changing the Font, Size, and Color of Text 92

Selecting a Different Font 92

Changing Font Size 95

Changing Font Color 96

Applying Font Styles 100

Applying Font Effects 101

Adjusting Character Spacing 103

Changing the Spacing Between Text Characters 103

Changing Text Case 105

Highlighting Text 106

Copying Character Formatting with the Format Painter 106

Setting AutoFormat as You Type Options 108

Configuring AutoFormat as You Type 108

Clearing Character Formats 109

5   Paragraph Formatting **111**

Understanding Paragraphs 111

Accessing Word's Paragraph-Formatting Tools 112

Aligning Paragraphs 114

Indenting Paragraphs 115

Setting Tab Stops 119

Setting Tab Stops on the Ruler 122

Setting Tab Stops in the Tabs Dialog Box 123

Setting Line and Paragraph Spacing 124

Changing Line Spacing within a Paragraph 124

Changing Paragraph Spacing 127

Adding Borders and Shading to a Paragraph 128

Placing a Border Around a Paragraph 129

Placing Shading Behind a Paragraph 132

Finding and Replacing Paragraph Formatting 134

Using Find and Replace to Change Paragraph Formatting 134

6   Formatting Text with Styles **136**

Understanding Styles 136

    The Advantages of Styles 138

    Styles Versus Quick Styles 139

Mastering Quick Styles 140

    Applying a Quick Style 140

    Changing the Quick Style Set 142

    Removing a Quick Style from the Gallery 143

Using the Styles Pane 144

    Applying a Style from the Styles Pane 144

Using the Apply Styles Pane 146

    Applying a Style from the Apply Styles Pane 147

Clearing Styles and Manual Formatting 148

Creating a New Style 148

    Creating a New Style from an Example 148

    Creating a Quick Style, the Quick Way 151

Modifying an Existing Style 152

    Renaming a Style 152

    Changing a Style's Definition 153

Deleting a Style 156

Part III: Organizing Text into Lists, Tables, and Columns

7   Setting Up Lists **158**

Working with Bulleted Lists 158

    Creating a Quick Bulleted List 160

    Creating a Bulleted List as You Type 160

    Choosing a Different Bullet Character 161

Working with Numbered Lists 164

    Creating a Quick Numbered List 165

    Creating a Numbered List as You Type 166

    Choosing a Different Numbering Format 166

    Resuming or Restarting List Numbering 169

Creating Nested Lists 171

    Creating a Nested List with Bullets Only 171

    Creating a Nested List with Numbers and Bullets 172

Setting Spacing and Indents in a List 173

8   **Creating Tables** **174**

Inserting a Table 174
   Inserting a Table from the Table Menu 175
   Inserting a Table from the Insert Table Dialog Box 177
   Inserting a Quick Table 178

Drawing a Table 180
   Using Your Mouse Pointer to Draw a Table 180

Converting Text to a Table 183
   Converting Tabbed Text into a Table 184

Creating Nested Tables 185
   Inserting a Nested Table 185
   Drawing a Nested Table, Redux 186

Editing a Table 186
   Moving Around in a Table 187
   Adding Text to a Table 187
   Selecting Parts of a Table 188
   Selecting Table Parts with the Mouse 189
   Selecting Table Parts with the Keyboard 191
   Inserting and Deleting Table Parts 191
   Merging and Splitting Cells 195

Changing a Table's Size 197
   Resizing by Dragging 197
   Specifying Precise Table Dimensions 199
   Distributing Rows and Columns 202

Formatting a Table 202
   Using Table Styles 203
   Aligning Text in Cells 203
   Choosing Borders for Cells 204
   Adding Shading 206
   Aligning a Table on the Page 207

Deleting a Table 208

9   **Setting Text in Columns** **210**

Understanding Columns 210

Applying a Preset Column Format 212
   Choosing a Preset Format from the Columns Menu 213
   Choosing a Preset Layout from the Columns Dialog Box 214

Separating Columns with Vertical Lines 216

Creating a Column Layout from Scratch 217

Creating a Custom Column Layout 218

Changing Column Widths 220

Creating Column Breaks..............................220

Converting a Multicolumn Layout to a Single Column 222

Part IV: **Formatting Pages and Documents**

10   **Laying Out a Document's Pages** **224**

Setting Margins 224

Using Preset Margins 226

Creating Custom Margins 226

Inserting Page Breaks 229

Dividing a Document into Sections 231

Understanding Section Breaks 232

Inserting a Section Break 232

Changing a Section Break 233

Removing a Section Break 233

Setting Page Orientation 234

Designating a Paper Size 236

Using a Standard Paper Size 236

Using a Custom Paper Size 236

Numbering the Lines in a Document 238

Numbering Lines the Fast Way 239

Setting Up Line Numbers with Precision 239

Hyphenating a Document 240

Automatic Hyphenation 241

Manual Hyphenation 242

Adding a Watermark to the Page 242

Inserting a Preformatted Watermark 243

Creating a Customized Watermark 244

Removing a Watermark 245

Adding a Colored Background to the Page 245

Placing a Border Around the Page 247

11   **Formatting Documents with Themes and Templates** **249**

Using Themes 249

Applying a Theme 250

Browsing for a Theme 251

Removing a Theme from a Document 252

Modifying a Theme 252
Creating a Custom Theme 258
Deleting a Custom Theme 259

Using Templates 259
What Templates Are 259
Types of Templates 260
Where Templates Are Stored 261
The Normal Template 262
Determining What Template a Document Is Using 263
Applying a Different Template to a Document 263
Modifying a Template 265
Creating a New Template 267

12   Adding Headers and Footers to a Document **269**

Understanding Headers, Footers, and Field Codes 269

Inserting Preformatted Page Numbers 271
Inserting and Formatting Page Numbers 271

Inserting a Preformatted Header or Footer 273
Adding a Preformatted Header to a Document 274

Editing a Header or Footer 276
Getting In and Out of Header and Footer View 276
Moving Between Headers and Footers 276
Editing Text 277
Inserting and Deleting Field Codes 278
Changing the Position of a Header or Footer 279

Creating Different Headers or Footers for Odd
and Even Pages 280

Hiding the Header or Footer on a Document's First Page 281

Removing a Header or Footer from a Document 282

Part V: Taking Your Documents to the Next Level

13   Adding Graphics to Your Documents **284**

Adding a Photo to a Document 284
Adding a Picture to a Document 285

Adding Clip Art to a Document 286
Finding and Inserting a Clip Art Graphic 287

Modifying a Graphic 290
Resizing a Graphic 290
Wrapping Text Around a Graphic 293
Changing a Graphic's Position 296

Cropping a Graphic 298

Adjusting Brightness and Contrast 300

Adding a Picture Style and Effects 302

Resetting a Picture 304

Drawing Shapes in Word 304

Drawing an AutoShape 305

Modifying an AutoShape 307

Adding Text to a Shape 308

Grouping Shapes or Drawn Objects 308

Deleting a Graphic 309

14   Working with Charts and Diagrams **310**

Understanding Charts and Diagrams 310

Chart Basics 310

Diagram Basics 312

Creating a Chart 314

Creating a New Chart 314

Editing Chart Data 316

Modifying a Chart 318

Resizing a Chart 318

Changing a Chart's Text Wrapping Setting 318

Moving a Chart 319

Changing the Chart Type 319

Applying a Different Chart Layout 320

Applying a Chart Style 322

Adding Text Elements to a Chart 323

Inserting a SmartArt Diagram 327

Creating a New Diagram 328

Modifying a Diagram 330

Resizing a Diagram 330

Changing a Diagram's Text Wrapping Setting 331

Moving a Diagram 331

Applying a Different Diagram Layout 331

Applying a SmartArt Style to a Diagram 331

Reversing a Diagram's Direction 332

Adding and Removing Shapes 332

Reorganizing a Diagram 334

15   Using Advanced Text Features **335**

Creating and Formatting Text Boxes 335

Inserting a Text Box 336

Resizing a Text Box 339

Moving a Text Box 340

Formatting a Text Box 341

Formatting Text in a Text Box 342

Linking Text Boxes 343

Using WordArt 345

Inserting WordArt Text 346

Editing WordArt Text 347

Changing the Format of a WordArt Object 347

Addressing Envelopes 351

Addressing an Envelope by Itself 352

Adding an Envelope to a Letter 353

16   Citing Your Sources in a Word Document **355**

Managing Sources 355

Adding a Source 356

Editing a Source 359

Deleting a Source 359

Working with Citations 360

Adding a Citation to a Document 360

Editing a Citation 361

Deleting a Citation 363

Generating a Bibliography 363

Adding a Bibliography to a Document 363

Working with Endnotes and Footnotes 364

Inserting a Footnote 365

Inserting an Endnote 366

Jumping to a Note and Between Notes 367

Deleting a Note 367

Switching from One Type of Note to Another 368

**17   Generating Outlines, Tables of Contents,
and Indexes** **370**

Creating an Outline 370

Working in Outline View 372

Building an Outline 373

Creating a Table of Contents 378

Adding a TOC to a Document 378

Updating a TOC 382

Deleting a TOC 382

Creating an Index 382

    Adding an Index to a Document 383

    Updating an Index 385

    Deleting an Index 385

Part VI: **Using Word Like a Pro**

  18   **Performing Mail Merges** **388**

    Preparing the Main Document 389

        Creating the Main Document for a Mail Merge 389

        Setting Up Merge Fields 390

    Performing a Basic Mail Merge 396

        Previewing a Mail Merge 396

        Creating Merge Documents for Printing 397

  19   **Collaborating with Others** **399**

    Working with Comments 400

        Adding Comments to a Document 400

        Working with a Reviewer's Comments 402

    Tracking Changes 405

        Tracking the Changes You Make to a Document 406

        Accepting and Rejecting a Reviewer's Revisions 406

    Limiting What Other Users Can Do to a Document 408

  20   **Sharing Word Documents Online** **412**

    Sharing a Document Through Email 412

        Attaching a Document to an Email Message 413

        Emailing a Link to a Document 414

    Sharing a Document Through Windows Live and
    Word Web App 417

        Working with SkyDrive 418

        Using Word Web App 426

    Using (or Not Using) Microsoft SharePoint 434

  21   **Adding Components That Work Only on the Screen** **435**

    Working with Hyperlinks 435

        Creating Hyperlinks 436

        Following a Hyperlink 442

        Modifying a Hyperlink 443

        Removing a Hyperlink 443

Using Bookmarks 444

Inserting a Bookmark 444

Jumping to a Bookmark 445

Deleting a Bookmark 449

Working with Cross-References 449

Inserting a Cross-Reference 449

Following a Cross-Reference 451

Deleting a Cross-Reference 451

22   Making Word Your Own **452**

Customizing the Quick Access Toolbar 452

Moving the Quick Access Toolbar 453

Adding Commands to the Quick Access Toolbar 454

Reorganizing the Quick Access Toolbar 458

Removing a Command from the Quick Access Toolbar 458

Restoring the Quick Access Toolbar 459

Customizing the Status Bar 459

Customizing the Ribbon 461

Minimizing the Ribbon 461

Showing and Hiding Tabs 462

Reorganizing the Ribbon 464

Renaming a Tab or Group 465

Creating a Custom Tab 466

Restoring the Ribbon 469

Creating a New Keyboard Shortcut 469

Index **473**

About the Authors

Tim Huddleston is a freelance writer, editor, and publishing consultant with more than 25 years of experience. He provides content development, technical writing, and editorial services for a diverse array of clients, including internationally known educational and trade publishers. Tim specializes in developing practical nonfiction content and has written and developed publications on a broad array of topics for the trade, educational, software, and institutional markets. His work can be found in print, online, and in software and multimedia applications of many kinds. In addition to a successful 15-year career as a freelance writer and editor, Tim has worked on-staff for major publishers such as McGraw-Hill, Macmillan, Que Corp., New Riders Publishing, and *The Indianapolis Star-News*. Tim's background also includes several years as a broadcast journalist. He holds a double B.A. in English and French from Centre College. Tim lives in Charlotte, N.C. with his wife, Tara, their two daughters, Savannah and Lucy, two dogs, a parrot, a collection of fire-bellied toads, and—from time to time—a gecko.

More information can be found at Tim's website, located at www.tim-huddleston.com. You can contact Tim via email at tim@tim-huddleston.com.

Michael Miller has written more than 100 nonfiction how-to books over the past two decades, including Que's *Googlepedia: The Ultimate Google Resource*, *Absolute Beginner's Guide to Computer Basics*, *YouTube for Business*, *Sams Teach Yourself YouTube in 10 Minutes*, and *Sams Teach Yourself Wikipedia in 10 Minutes*. He also authored *The Complete Idiot's Guide to Search Engine Optimization* for Alpha Books. Collectively, his books have sold more than 1 million copies worldwide.

Miller has established a reputation for clearly explaining technical topics to non-technical readers and for offering useful real-world advice about complicated topics. More information can be found at the author's website, located at www.molehillgroup.com. He can be contacted via email at mmiller@molehillgroup.com.

Dedication

To Tara, for her love, her infinite patience, and her ability to keep me going—even when I don't know it's for my own good.

To Savannah, Lucy, and Liz, for filling my life with love and making me feel younger than I really am.

Acknowledgments

Many years ago, I cut my editorial teeth on Using books—nearly all of which have been lost in the mists of time. (Anyone out there remember Using DOS?) But being part of the Que team was a life-shaping experience that exposed me to a cast of unforgettable characters, a world of ever-changing possibilities, and more than a few never-ending friendships. So I must thank my long-time friend and colleague Greg Wiegand for inviting me back into the Que fold and giving me the opportunity to write this book. Greg is a rare find in this industry: He understands that publishing is more about people than about products or technology. I wish him great success and all the happiness in the world.

Senior Acquisitions Editor Katherine Bull deserves all my gratitude, as well, for her understanding and for keeping me afloat when it seemed I would go under. She has encouraged me and lifted my spirits throughout this process, and I thank her with all my heart.

To technical editor Vince Averello, many thanks for his thorough yet gentle review of the manuscript. His keen eye made this book much better than I ever could have made it on my own.

My most sincere appreciation goes to my long-time colleague and fellow drummer Mike Miller, for his skill and patience in creating the media files that accompany this book. All our readers will benefit greatly from Mike's contributions to this package, and we all should be grateful for his involvement.

And a big thanks to everyone on the Que team who lent their talent and skills to this book, including Julie Bess, Lori Lyons, San Dee Phillips, and Sarah Kearns.

We Want to Hear from You!

As the reader of this book, *you* are our most important critic and commentator. We value your opinion and want to know what we're doing right, what we could do better, what areas you'd like to see us publish in, and any other words of wisdom you're willing to pass our way.

As an associate publisher for Que Publishing, I welcome your comments. You can email or write me directly to let me know what you did or didn't like about this book—as well as what we can do to make our books better.

Please note that I cannot help you with technical problems related to the topic of this book. We do have a User Services group, however, where I will forward specific technical questions related to the book.

When you write, please be sure to include this book's title and author as well as your name, email address, and phone number. I will carefully review your comments and share them with the author and editors who worked on the book.

Email: feedback@quepublishing.com

Mail: Greg Wiegand
Associate Publisher
Que Publishing
800 East 96th Street
Indianapolis, IN 46240 USA

Reader Services

Visit our website and register this book at quepublishing.com/register for convenient access to any updates, downloads, or errata that might be available for this book.

Introduction

Welcome to *Using Microsoft Word 2010*! This is a special welcome for two reasons.

First, Word 2010 is a highly anticipated upgrade to the Microsoft Office family of products; many consumers and companies refused to upgrade to the last version of Word (2007) because it was so different from its predecessors. They wanted to -see how the world responded to all those new features before committing to an upgrade. Now they're satisfied and ready to switch to Word 2010.

Second, and just as important, this edition of *Using Microsoft Word* is a departure from past editions. We re-invented *Using Microsoft Word* for people like you: the first-time Word user, the busy person who needs to get things done now, and the task-oriented user who thinks "show me how"—not "give me a lecture on why this works the way it does."

In updating this edition of *Using Microsoft Word*, we focused on productivity and the importance of completing specific tasks instead of developing detailed knowledge of the program's inner workings. So, if you're using this book as your guide to Word, you need to know *how* to add a picture to a document, not a dissertation on the fundamentals of digital photography. You need to access online documents through Word Web App *right now*, without pausing to master the infrastructure of the Internet. In other words, you have work to do, and finishing that work is your priority. And when you're in hurry-up-and-get-it-done mode, jargon, technical details, and lengthy explanations just get in the way. 'Nuff said about that.

So it's time to stop talking, except to say this: We hope you like the new version of Word, and we hope *Using Microsoft Word 2010* and its web-based tools meet all your expectations.

How This Book Is Organized

Each chapter of *Using Microsoft Word 2010* dives right into a specific, related set of tasks. Every section is designed to help you become productive with some aspect of Word in the shortest possible amount of time. The book focuses on tasks that most Word users must complete at least occasionally. Each task is concisely described, and most descriptions are followed by a set of instructions that walk you through the task from beginning to end, without taking any side trips. (When it's practical to explain a task without using numbered steps, we leave them out. That keeps things as brief as possible.)

If Word is totally new to you, the first chapter teaches you basic tasks that are vital to just about any word processing project; by mastering these tasks, you can make the jump from rank beginner to proficient user in no time. When you're comfortable with the basics, skip around and look up the tasks you need to do when you need to do them. You don't have to read the chapters in order; use the material in the manner that suits you. There are no sample files to install, no long-winded examples, nothing to get in your way.

This book is divided into six parts. In some cases, the tasks in one chapter are more difficult than the ones explained in earlier chapters, but that's OK. If you need to know something that's covered in another chapter, a reference will guide you there. Here are the parts of this book in a nutshell:

Part I, "The Basics of Using Word 2010." Here you learn essential skills such as creating a new document, saving and printing documents, entering text, using the Clipboard, building a document from a template, using Building Blocks to create parts of a document, checking your spelling and grammar, and using Word's reference tools.

Part II, "Formatting Characters and Paragraphs." This introduces Word's core formatting tools. You learn how to format individual characters, selected text, and entire paragraphs with Word's easy-to-use formatting tools. You also learn to apply Word's built-in character and paragraph styles, modify styles, and create your own styles.

Part III, "Organizing Text into Lists, Tables, and Columns." Simple text-layout tools such as lists help break up a plain document and make information easier to follow and remember. Tables enable you to arrange a lot of information in a little space and can be customized in any way you can imagine. Columns are handy for creating documents such as newsletters, but have other uses, too. The chapters in Part III not only help you master these layout tools, but also provide ideas for using them in your own documents.

Part IV, "Formatting Pages and Documents." Chapters 10–12 show you the big picture of document formatting, so you can make your pages look neat, uniform, and professional. Page formatting includes tasks such as setting margins, choosing page orientation, dividing a document with breaks and sections, and dressing up your pages with backgrounds or borders. You can format an entire document by applying any of Word's built-in themes or templates, which provide colors, font schemes, and other design elements; you can also modify Word's templates and create your own from scratch. Part IV also shows you how to add headers and footers to a document and how to control their appearance and behavior.

Part V, "Taking Your Documents to the Next Level." Documents can be more than just text, and Part V shows you how to spruce up any kind of document by adding pictures, clip art, geometric shapes, charts, diagrams, and other graphical elements. You also learn to create text boxes and use them to perform cool layout tricks. Part V also shows you how to add special features such as tables of contents, indexes, sources, citations, and reference notes—important features for long documents such as business reports and research papers. (Note that Chapters 15–17 are available online only.)

Part VI, "Using Word Like a Pro." (Part VI is available online only.) The last part of the book introduces you to some of Word's most powerful features—including a few that don't seem to have anything to do with word processing. You learn how to perform a mail merge, collaborate with other Word users to review and mark up shared documents, and store documents on the web and access them through Word Web App. While you're mastering the art of sharing documents electronically, you'll learn how to add features that work only on-screen, such as hyperlinks and bookmarks. Finally, you'll learn how to personalize your copy of Word, so it looks and behaves just the way you want it to.

Using This Book

More than just a book, *Using Microsoft Word 2010* is tightly integrated with online video tutorials, audio insights, and other web-based content, which is designed to provide you with a media-rich, customized learning experience not available through any other book series today. *Using Microsoft Word 2010* is a thorough resource at your fingertips.

This book enables you to customize your own learning experience. The step-by-step instructions in the book give you a solid foundation in using Word, while rich and varied online content, including video tutorials and audio sidebars, provide the following:

Demonstrations of step-by-step tasks covered in the book

Additional tips or information on a topic

Practical advice and suggestions

Direction for more advanced tasks not covered in the book

Here's a quick look at a few structural features designed to help you get the most out of this book:

Chapter objective: At the beginning of each chapter is the objective addressed in that chapter. This enables you to quickly see the information the chapter contains.

Notes: Notes provide additional commentary or explanation that doesn't fit neatly into the surrounding text. Notes give detailed explanations of how something works, alternative ways of performing a task, and other tidbits to get you on your way. You'll find shortcuts, workarounds, and techniques that can help you avoid pitfalls while using Word. And if a task comes with any risks (such as losing data), you'll find a Note giving you a heads-up about it.

Cross-references: Many topics are connected to other topics in various ways. When another section is related to one you are reading, a cross-reference directs you to a specific chapter in the book in which you can find the related information.

LET ME TRY IT Let Me Try It tasks are presented in a step-by-step sequence so you can easily follow along.

SHOW ME Show Me videos walk through tasks you've just got to see—including bonus advanced techniques.

TELL ME MORE Tell Me More audios deliver practical insights straight from the experts.

Special Features

More than just a book, your USING product integrates step-by-step video tutorials and valuable audio sidebars delivered through the **Free Web Edition** that comes with every USING book. For the price of the book, you get online access anywhere with a web connection—no books to carry, content is updated as the technology changes, and the benefit of video and audio learning.

About the USING Web Edition

The Web Edition of every USING book is powered by **Safari Books Online**, enabling you to access the video tutorials and valuable audio sidebars. Plus, you can search the contents of the book, highlight text and attach a note to that text, print your notes and highlights in a custom summary, and cut and paste directly from Safari Books Online.

To register this product and gain access to the **Free Web Edition** and the audio and video files, go to **quepublishing.com/using**.

Bonus Chapters

Chapters 15–22 are part of your Free Web Edition and can be downloaded there.

The Basics of Using Word 2010

1 Creating, Saving, and Printing Documents 7

2 Editing Documents 27

3 Proofing a Document 57

In this chapter, you learn three of the most essential tasks in word processing: creating a document, saving it on a disk, and printing it.

1

Creating, Saving, and Printing Documents

If you're in a hurry to start using Microsoft Word, this chapter is the place to begin. That's because the tasks you'll master in the next few pages form the basis of nearly every project you will do in Word. Creating a document is the first step in any word processing job. Whenever you create a document, you'll probably want to save it on a disk so you can re-open it and work with it again. And when your document is finished, you may need to print it so that you can share it with someone else (or stick it in a file cabinet).

Luckily, these chores are easy and you can master them in no time. Of course, Word lets you create, save, and print documents in lots of different ways. But you don't need to know them all—at least, not yet. To quickly start, we just cover the basics here. You'll learn more advanced options later in this book, where it makes more sense to explain them.

Starting a Document from Scratch

If you were going to write a letter on paper (an idea that sounds crazy to a lot of people these days), you would begin by putting a blank sheet of paper on your desk. When you start Word, it does something similar: It presents you with a new, blank document that looks just like a piece of paper, as shown in Figure 1.1.

If, for whatever reason, a blank document does not appear in the Word window, you can create a new one by pressing Ctrl+N. Actually, you can do this whenever you want to start a new document, no matter what's already open in Word. (You can have multiple documents open at the same time.)

By default, this blank document is already formatted with some standard settings, which make it suitable for many different uses:

- The page size is 8.5" x 11".

- The page's top, bottom, left, and right margins are each 1" wide.

- The document uses a simple 11-point font.

- The lines within each paragraph are a little more than single-spaced, and there's extra space between paragraphs.

Figure 1.1   *A new, blank document in the Microsoft Word window.*

With this blank document on your screen, all you need to do is start typing your text—or *keying*, as we computer geeks call it—and your new document starts taking shape right before your eyes. If you're dashing off a simple letter, memo, or list, this document's default formatting should work just fine. But if not, don't fret; you'll learn all about formatting documents in the next few chapters. For now, let's just stick to the basics.

Starting a Document from a Template

Simply put, a *template* is a special kind of Word document that has been preformatted in some way. The generic blank document that appears when you start Word is actually based on a template, albeit a simple one. Word offers a handful of built-in (local) templates that you can use to create many different kinds of documents, including resumes, business letters, fax cover sheets, and others. Figure 1.2 shows one of Word's local templates for a business letter. If you can't find a local template that suits your needs, you can search for others online.

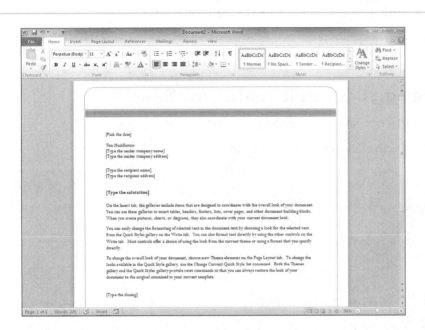

Figure 1.2   *A template for a professionally formatted business letter.*

Every template includes a preset combination of fonts, colors, margins, line and paragraph spacing, and other formatting characteristics such as headers or footers. Many templates contain placeholder text that you can customize or replace. Some templates include graphics, as well. Templates are a huge time-saver because they let you create professional-looking documents without manually formatting text, paragraphs, or pages. Just add your text, and you're done.

The following sections show you how to create a new document from a local template and then search Microsoft's Office.com website for another one. In Chapter 11, "Formatting Documents with Themes and Templates," you'll learn how to modify existing templates and create new ones.

Remember that a template is a different kind of file than a document. When you create a document based on a template, you open and edit a *copy* of the template, not the template itself. The actual template remains unchanged so that you can use it again to create different documents.

Using a Local Template

A *local template* is installed on your computer along with Word. You can create a document from a local template with just a few steps.

 **LET ME TRY IT**

Creating a Document from a Local Template

To start a document from a template, just find one you like and click.

1. On the Ribbon, click the File tab.

> The *Ribbon* was introduced in Word 2007, but it is a new feature for anyone upgrading from version 2003 or earlier. The Ribbon replaces the menu structure found in previous versions of Word and provides an easy way to access common commands and buttons. The Ribbon is divided into tabs, and each tab includes groups of related features.

2. Click New. The File tab displays the available templates (see Figure 1.3).

3. Click Sample Templates. Word displays thumbnail images of available templates.

4. Click the Equity Letter template.

5. In the right pane, make sure the Document option button is selected.

6. Click Create. Word creates a new document based on the template and displays it on your screen.

It's a good idea to spend some time examining Word's templates to see which ones you like best. As you'll see in Chapter 11, you can modify any template so that it looks exactly the way you want, insert your own boilerplate text (such as your company's name), and then save it as your own. The more time you invest in mastering templates, the more time you'll save later in formatting and entering data.

Finding a Template Online

Word's local templates may be the only ones you ever need. If not, you can expand your template collection by visiting the Office.com website and searching for different ones. Finding a template online isn't much different than finding a local template—except that there are hundreds of online templates to choose from.

Local templates appear in the top portion of the window.

File tab

Word displays a miniature image of the selected template here.

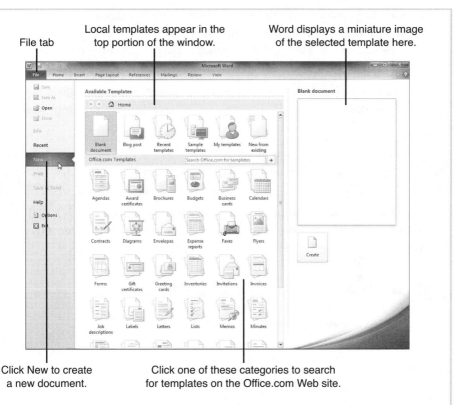

Click New to create a new document.

Click one of these categories to search for templates on the Office.com Web site.

Figure 1.3 *Searching for local templates. Use the top part of the window to find templates stored on your computer.*

 LET ME TRY IT

Creating a Document from an Online Template

You can look for templates online without leaving the Word window. When you download a template from Office.com, Word saves it on your computer so you can access the template locally whenever you want to use it.

1. On the Ribbon, click the File tab.

2. Click New. The Office.com Templates section shows several categories of templates that are available online, as shown earlier in the lower part of Figure 1.3. Each category contains multiple templates.

3. Click Newsletters. Word downloads and displays thumbnail images of newsletter templates currently available from Office.com.

4. Click the Business Newsletter template. A larger image of the template appears in the right pane, along with information about its designer, the file's size, and the rating it has been given by Office.com visitors who have used the template.

5. In the right pane, click Download. Word downloads the template file, creates a new document based on the template, and displays it on your screen.

When Word downloads a template file, it automatically saves the file with Word's other templates. You don't need to select a disk or folder to store the file in.

To reuse a template you've used before, click the File tab, click New, and then click Recent Templates. Word displays thumbnail images of your most recently used templates, both local and online.

 SHOW ME   Media 1.1—Working with Word Templates
Access this video file through your registered Web Edition at
my.safaribooksonline.com/9780132182713/media.

Saving a Document

Soon after you create a document, you should *save* it—that is, tell Word to store the document as a file on a disk. When you save a document, you should give it a logical, plain-English name that will make it easy to identify the file when you need to open it again. For example, if you write an angry letter to your aunt Martha, you might name the file "Angry Letter to Aunt Martha," or some such. You also need to select a location to store the file, such as on your computer's hard disk or a network drive. Word can also save a document in one of several different formats, so you can choose the one that works best for you.

After saving a document for the first time, you can (and should!) resave it frequently as you work on it. Repeatedly saving a document protects you from data loss in case your PC's power goes out or some other problem arises. When you save an existing document, Word simply updates the file to include any changes you made since the last time you saved it.

If the need arises, you can create a different version of a document by saving it with a different name, location, or file type.

 **LET ME TRY IT**

Saving a New Document to a Disk

The first time you save a file, Word displays the Save As dialog box, and you need to take a few steps to tell Word exactly where and how to save it. Updating a saved file is as simple as a mouse click.

1. With an unsaved document open in Word, do one of the following:
   - Click the Save icon on the Quick Access toolbar.
   - Click the File tab and then click Save or Save As.
   - Press Ctrl+S.

   The Save As dialog box appears, as shown in Figure 1.4. By default, the dialog box shows the contents of the My Documents folder.

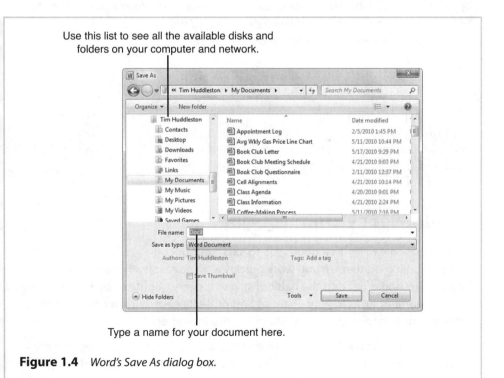

Figure 1.4   *Word's Save As dialog box.*

2. If you want to save the document in the My Documents folder, skip to step 5.

3. To save the document on a different drive or in a different folder, scroll through the list on the left side of the dialog box. The list displays all the drives and folders you can access on your PC or network.

4. Click the drive and folder where you want to store the file.

5. Click in the File Name box and type a name for your document.

6. Click Save. Word saves the document in the location you chose and gives it the name you specified. The document's new name appears in the title bar at the top of the Word window.

    By default, Word saves your document in Word's native *.docx* format—the default file format for Word 2007 and 2010 documents. This format preserves all of Word's features and formatting options. Older versions of Word don't support all these features.

 TELL ME MORE   Media 1.2—Understanding Word's .*docx* Format
Access this audio recording through your registered Web Edition at
my.safaribooksonline.com/9780132182713/media.

The descriptions and illustrations in this book are based on using Word with Microsoft Windows 7. If you use another version of Windows, the steps you take may be slightly different that those described here, and your screen may look somewhat different from the screens shown in this book. But the same kinds of tools will be there, so you can get the same results.

Resaving an Existing Document

As mentioned earlier, it's a good idea to save your documents frequently while you're working on them. If you work quickly and make lots of changes to a document, you should get into the habit of saving it every minute or so. Frequently saving a document locks in your changes and protects your work in case the power goes out or Windows starts misbehaving. (Yes, it happens.)

When you save (resave) a document that has already been saved, Word simply overwrites the current version of the file with a new one. The updated version includes any changes you have made since the last time you saved.

1. With your document open in Word, do one of the following:

    •   Click the Save icon on the Quick Access toolbar.

    •   Click the File tab and then click Save.

    •   Press Ctrl+S.

    That's it—no dialog boxes to get in your way. Just save your work and keep going.

Even if you aren't a very good typist—er, *keyboardist*—you should train yourself to press Ctrl+S at least once every few minutes while you work. Try to make this an automatic habit. You'll keep your work safe without even reaching for the mouse.

Occasionally, Word asks if you want to save your document. For example, if you try to close a file or shut down Word without saving the document, Word prompts you to save it, as shown in Figure 1.5. If you decline to do so, the changes you made since the last time you saved will be lost.

Figure 1.5   *Word sometimes prompts you to save your work.*

   SHOW ME   Media 1.3—**Saving a Word Document**
Access this video file through your registered Web Edition at
my.safaribooksonline.com/9780132182713/media.

 **LET ME TRY IT**

Saving a File with a Different Name, Location, or File Type

You may need to save a file in a different manner than described in the preceding sections. This can be necessary, for example, when you need to

- Create a copy of the document with a different name.
- Share a file with someone who uses a different version of Word or a different word processing program.
- Store a file on a network drive so other users can open it.

All these tasks are done through Word's Save As dialog box.

When you save a file with a different name, type, or location, you're actually creating a copy of your file. (The original version remains unchanged unless you move, rename, or delete it.) However, Word closes the original version; the copy appears on your screen unless you saved the copy in a file format that Word cannot use itself, such as PDF.

1. With your document open in Word, click the File tab.

2. Click Save As. The Save As dialog box appears, as shown in Figure 1.6. The dialog box shows the file's current name, type, and location.

3. To save the document on a different drive or in a different folder, scroll through the list on the left side of the dialog box, and then select the new drive and folder.

4. To give the document a different name, click in the File Name box and type the new name.

5. To save the document in a different file format, click the Save as Type drop-down arrow and choose the desired format from the menu. For example, if you want to save the document in Rich Text Format (a file format that can be used by any word processor), choose that file type from the list.

Select a drive and folder.

Select a different file
format from this list.

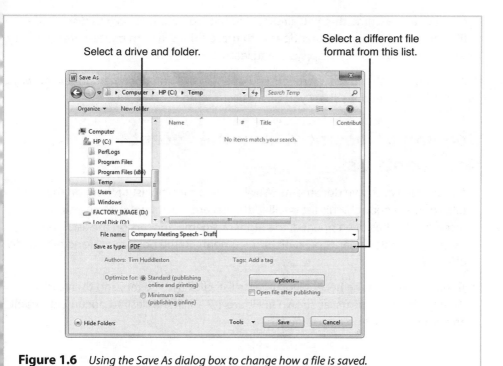

Figure 1.6   *Using the Save As dialog box to change how a file is saved.*

6. Click Save. Word saves the document in the location you chose and gives it
    the name you specified. The document's new name appears in the title bar at
    the top of the Word window and the previous version of the document
    closes.

Opening an Existing Document

To open an existing document, you need to know where it was saved—or how to
search for it. You can save documents on any storage device connected to your
computer. Whether you store your files on your PC's hard disk, a network drive, or a
shared folder on someone else's computer, Word can find and open them.

Of course, this assumes you have the required user rights to open, modify, and do
other things with files stored on a network or someone else's PC. If you don't...well,
that's a topic for another book. Here, we assume you have the rights to do whatever you want, without having to beg some goofy network administrator for permission. (They love to say "no" to ordinary computer users, so avoid them when you

can.) We also assume that you already understand concepts such as disks, folders, files, and what your computer does with these things. If such matters are a mystery to you, check Windows' help system to learn about them.

As with most other tasks, Word lets you open an existing document in several ways. The following sections show you the easiest methods of the lot.

Opening a Document from the Recent Documents List

As you open and save documents, Word keeps a running list of them on the File tab. Logically enough, this list is called the Recent Documents list. The more recently a file has been opened, the higher its name appears on the list. More recently used documents push older documents to the bottom of—and eventually off—the list.

To pick a file from the Recent Documents list, click the File tab, and then click Recent. The list appears, as shown in Figure 1.7. Click the desired document's name, and Word opens it on the Home tab.

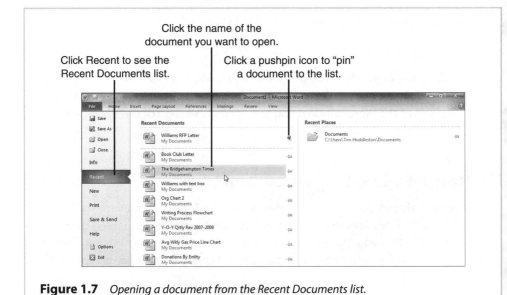

Figure 1.7   *Opening a document from the Recent Documents list.*

To make the Recent Documents list work a bit faster, you can check the Quickly Access This Number of Recent Documents check box. This option tells Word to display a certain number of recently opened documents in the menu on the left side of the File tab. Use the spinner control to set the number of documents to display.

Now you can choose a document from the menu without having to look over at the Recent Documents list. What a timesaver! (Yes, that was sarcasm.)

If you use a document frequently, you can "pin" it to the Recent Documents list so it always appears there. This prevents the document from eventually getting shoved off the list as you open other documents. To pin a document to the list, click the Pushpin icon that appears to the right of the file's name. Click the icon again if you ever want to "unpin" the document from the list.

Opening a Document from the Open Dialog Box

If you haven't opened a certain document lately, it may not show up on the Recent Documents list. But you can open any document through Word's Open dialog box. This dialog box gives you access to all the disks and folders on your computer and network.

 LET ME TRY IT

Using the Open Dialog Box

If you know where a document is stored, you can use the Open dialog box to find and open it.

1. Click the File tab, and then click Open. The Open dialog box appears, as shown in Figure 1.8. By default, the dialog box shows the contents of the My Documents folder.

2. If the document you need is in the My Documents folder, skip to step 4.

3. If the document resides on a different drive or in a different folder, scroll through the list on the left side of the dialog box. The list displays the names of all the drives and folders you can access on your PC or network. Click the drive and folder that contain the desired document.

4. Click the document's name; then click Open.

Instead of clicking a file's name and then clicking Open, you can just double-click the file to open it. Alternatively, you can click the file and press Enter. Then again, you can right-click the file to display a shortcut menu, and click Open. There are other ways to open a file, as well, but let's not get carried away.

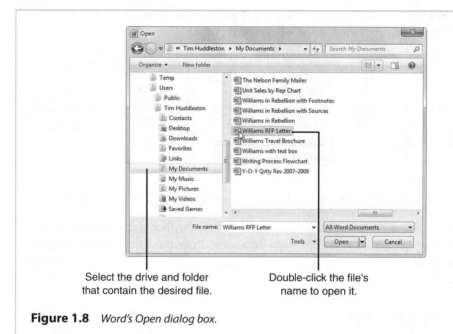

Select the drive and folder   Double-click the file's
that contain the desired file.   name to open it.

Figure 1.8 *Word's Open dialog box.*

By default, the Open dialog box displays all Word documents that reside in the folder you select. You can broaden or narrow your search by clicking the File Type button, which appears to the right of the File Name box. A menu appears, listing the kinds of files you can display in the Open dialog box. So, if you want to find a document that was created in WordPerfect 5.0, for example, click WordPerfect 5.x to see only those documents. Word filters out all the other types of documents in the list to make it easier to find the file you want.

Conversely, if you want the Open dialog box to display every file (even non-Word format files) in the selected folder, click the File Type button; then click All Files. When you choose this option, however, Word may not be able to open every type of file that appears in the Open dialog box.

Searching for a Document in the Open Dialog Box

If you don't remember where a document is stored, the Open dialog box features a search tool that can help you find it.

Using the Open Dialog Box Search Feature

To search a single folder or an entire network for a specific file, you can specify a word or phrase and tell Word to locate the documents that contain it.

1. Click the File tab; then click Open. The Open dialog box appears.

2. In the list of drives and folders, click the name of the drive or folder where you want to start your search. Word will search the specified drive or folder and every folder and subfolder it contains. For example, if you want to search all the drives and folders on your computer, click Computer in the list. If you only want to search a specific drive or folder, click its name.

3. Click in the Search box, and type a word or phrase that will be contained in the document you want to find (as shown in Figure 1.9). Word starts searching as soon as you start typing. If Word finds any documents that contain the word or phrase, it displays their names in the Open dialog box.

4. Double-click the file's name to open it.

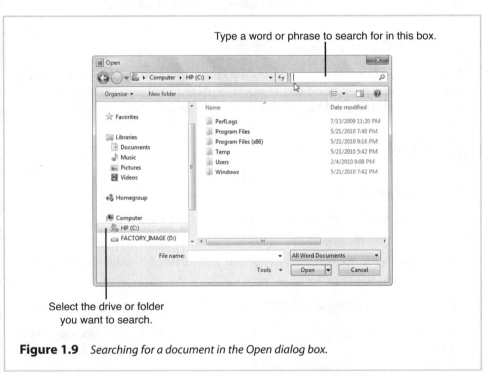

Type a word or phrase to search for in this box.

Select the drive or folder
you want to search.

Figure 1.9 *Searching for a document in the Open dialog box.*

Searching can be a hit-or-miss proposition, especially if you can't remember the name of the file you're looking for. The search feature is not entirely dependable; it may dig up files that don't even contain the word or phrase you specified. Regardless, be patient. (After all, you're dealing with a brainless machine here.) If Word doesn't find the file you need, try searching for a different word or phrase or broadening your search to cover more drives or folders.

Printing a Document

Most documents are meant to be printed at some point in their lives. This is one reason Word has so many formatting features, as you will learn about throughout this book. It can take many hours of effort to get a document to look just right on paper.

The printing process, conversely, is quite easy in Word. That is, as long as a printer is connected to your PC (either directly or via a network) and all the appropriate printer-related software is installed. If not, printing can be difficult or impossible. So we'll assume you have a printer and it's working correctly.

There are two methods of printing a document from Word: the really easy way, and the slightly more difficult way. The following sections show you both.

Quick-Printing a Document

With Word's *Quick Print* feature, no setup is required to print a document. As long as the document looks good on the screen and your printer is working, you can print a copy of the entire document with a single mouse click.

 LET ME TRY IT

One-Step Printing

If you can see the Quick Print button at the top of the Word window, printing is a snap.

1. On the Quick Access toolbar, click Quick Print. Word instantly sends your document to the printer.

2. OK, there is no step 2. But that's the beauty of a one-step *anything*, right?

If the Quick Print button is not visible on the Quick Access toolbar, you can add it to the toolbar. For instructions on this and other customizations to Word, see Chapter 22, "Making Word Your Own (online)."

Printing the (Not-so-Much) Harder Way

Quick-printing isn't always the best option for getting your document onto paper. You may need to print multiple copies, for example, or change other print-related settings before sending the document to the printer. If so, you can set up the perfect print job from the File tab.

LET ME TRY IT

Setting Up a Print Job

The File tab's print options give you complete control over any print job.

1. Click the File tab; then click Print. Word's print controls fill the window, as shown in Figure 1.10.

Print controls appear on this side of the window.   Print Preview pane

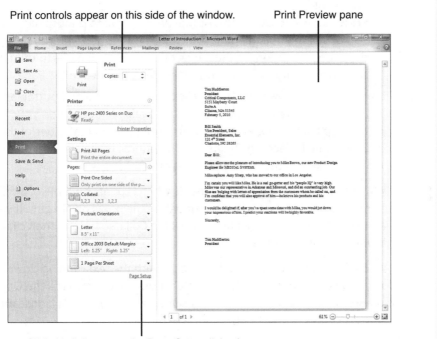

Click this link to open the Page Setup dialog box.

Figure 1.10 *Word's print controls and the Print Preview pane.*

2. To see exactly how the document will look on paper with the current print settings, examine it in the right half of the window. To preview each page, click the Next Page and Previous Page buttons at the bottom of the window.

3. To print multiple copies of the document, click in the Copies box, and type the number of copies you want. (Alternatively, you can click the up or down counter buttons to the right of the box to set the number of copies.)

4. The name of your default printer should appear on the Printer button. To use a different printer, click the button and select a printer from the drop-down list.

5. By default, Word prints the entire document. To print only a portion of the document, click the Pages button and select one of the following options:
   - **Print Selection**—This option prints only the text you have selected before beginning the printing process. If no text is selected, this option is grayed out (unavailable).
   - **Print Current Page**—This option prints the page that contains the insertion point.
   - **Print Custom Range**—This option enables you to print specific pages or sections of the document. If you choose this option, you can designate the pages or sections in the Pages text box. For example, to print only the second and third pages of your document, type 2-3 in the Pages box.

6. To print on both sides of the page, click the Print One Sided button and select the appropriate option. The options available depend on your printer's capabilities. For example, you might print on both sides of the page by manually feeding sheets into the printer. By default, Word prints on only one side of the page with most printers.

7. Word automatically *collates* documents when it prints multiple copies. This means one entire copy is printed out before the next copy begins. If you want your copies to be uncollated, click the Collated button; then click the Uncollated option.

8. Word prints documents in portrait mode (with the text running down the long edge of the page) by default. To change this setting, click the Orientation button; then click the Landscape Orientation option. (In landscape mode, text runs down the short edge of the page.)

9. To select a different paper size, click the Paper Size button, and then click the desired size. The available sizes depend on your printer's capabilities.

10. To change your document's margins, click the Margins button, and choose a different set of margins. If none of the preset options suits your needs, click Custom Margins to open the Page Setup dialog box, as shown in Figure 1.11. Set the margins in the top of the Margins tab; then click OK. (Chapter 10, "Laying Out a Document's Pages," covers margins and other page-setup options in detail.)

Figure 1.11   *The Page Setup dialog box.*

11. Word automatically prints one page of a document per sheet of paper. To print multiple pages on a single sheet, click the Multiple Pages button and select the number of pages you want to appear on each sheet.

12. Click Print.

The Page Setup dialog box provides several other print-control options in addition to those found on the File tab. For example, you can use the dialog box to select a paper tray, apply borders to your pages, change the way headers or footers print, and so on. To open the Page Setup dialog box, click Page Setup at the bottom of the File tab.

SHOW ME   Media 1.4—Printing a Word Document
Access this video file through your registered Web Edition at
my.safaribooksonline.com/9780132182713/media.

Closing a Document

When you finish working on a document, you can either close the file and leave Word running, or close the document and exit Word. Either way, *be sure to save your document before closing it*.

You can close a document and leave Word running by doing one of the following:

- Click File; then click Close.

- On the Windows Taskbar, right-click the document's button, and then click Close Window.

- If more than one document is open, click Word's Close button (at the right end of the title bar). This closes the current document but leaves Word running.

To close all open documents and exit Word, click File and then click Exit.

This chapter introduces Word's text-editing features, which let you create and manage your documents' content—and help you get your message just right.

Editing Documents

You might have noticed that most of this book deals with Word's formatting tools, which make your documents look nice. But even though the lion's share of Word is all about appearances, content is still king. If your text is sloppy or badly organized, no amount of formatting magic can make it more interesting or meaningful.

So, this chapter ignores stuff like fonts and pictures and shows you how to insert, delete, move, and otherwise manage the text that forms the heart and soul of your documents. The following sections also introduce Building Blocks, which can quickly insert predefined text and other objects for you. You'll also learn all about selecting text that's already on the screen—an essential skill for editing and formatting documents.

Adding Text to a Document

The easiest and most obvious way to add text to a document is just to type and watch those characters march across the page like little soldiers. As you type, text appears just behind the *insertion point*—the blinking vertical line that shows your place in the document. The insertion point skitters along from left to right, staying just ahead of each letter or number as you type.

One of the greatest benefits of word processing, though, is that you can put the insertion point wherever you want it and add text right there. You aren't limited to typing in any particular place. So, if you need to add a word to the middle of a sentence—or add a sentence in the middle of a paragraph—just use your mouse or the keyboard's arrow keys to move the insertion point to the right spot, and type away.

We're assuming that you know how to use your mouse and keyboard for tasks such as moving the insertion point and navigating through a document on the screen. If you're new to computing in general or to word processing in particular, though, you'll get the hang of it in no time with a little practice. For example, you can open a template (as explained in Chapter 1, "Creating, Saving, and Printing Documents") and practice jumping around in it, using the scroll bars, moving the insertion point, and inserting text wherever you want.

Understanding Lines and Paragraphs

When you reach the end of a line (that is, when the insertion point hits a spot where it can't go any further, such as the page's right margin), just keep typing. Word automatically moves the insertion point down to a new line—a feature called *text wrapping*. A paragraph of text can contain as many lines as you want.

When you decide it's time to start a new paragraph, press Enter. This tells Word to insert a special character, called a *paragraph return* (or a *hard return*), which indicates the end of a paragraph. The insertion point jumps down again so you can start a new paragraph. Depending on the way your document is formatted, there will probably be more blank space between paragraphs than between the lines within a paragraph.

All this adds up to an important point:

- A *line* ends when your text can't go any further to the right—for example, when you get too close to the margin or an object such as a picture.

- A *paragraph*, on the other hand, is a break that you insert on purpose, when you want to end one paragraph and start another one.

Suppose you want to start a new line, but without creating a new paragraph? You can do this by entering a special character called a *line break* (or a *soft return*). To insert a line break, press Shift+Enter anywhere in the current line of text. Word moves the insertion point to a new, blank line, but keeps you in the same paragraph.

A paragraph can be empty, without any text at all. By pressing Enter one or more times, you can insert empty paragraphs in a document to create space or to mark a place where you want to go back and insert text later.

Viewing Hidden (Nonprinting) Characters

One of the few disadvantages of word processing is that you can lose track of the blank spaces, tabs, and paragraph returns in a document. By default, such characters (called *nonprinting* characters, because they don't appear in a printed document) are hidden on your screen. Other kinds of characters are hidden, as well, such as soft returns and page breaks.

You can see these characters anytime you want, however, by clicking the Show/Hide ¶ button on the Ribbon's Home tab. Figure 2.1 shows how a page of text looks when nonprinting characters are visible. Seeing these characters can be helpful, at least occasionally, but they can clutter up your screen. To hide them, click the Show/Hide ¶ button again.

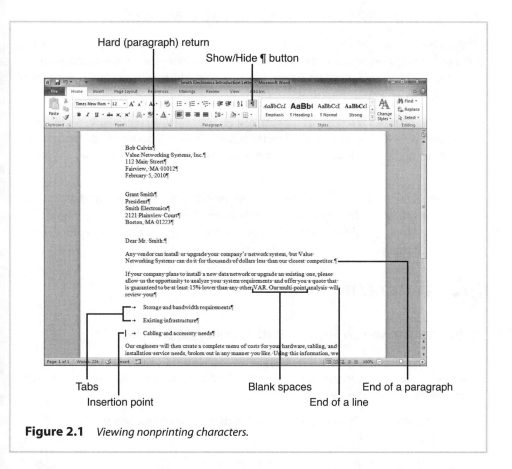

Figure 2.1 *Viewing nonprinting characters.*

Why would you ever want to see these hidden characters? Here are two reasons:

1. Sometimes it's a good idea to examine a document closely before printing it or turning it over to someone else (especially if that other person is an expert Word user). Viewing hidden characters helps you remove excess ones, shrink your file's size just a smidge, and maybe make the document look a little better when you print it.

2. If you see that you're using a lot of blank paragraphs, tabs, and spaces to format your document, you aren't taking advantage of Word's formatting tools. Filling a document with blank hidden characters can give your document an uneven—even sloppy—look. Word's formatting tools give documents a more consistent and professional appearance.

Using Insert Mode and Overtype Mode

By default, Word operates in *Insert Mode*. If you place the insertion point in the middle of a paragraph and start typing, Word simply pushes the existing text to the right to make room for the new text. Hence, Insert Mode lets you insert new characters in between existing ones.

By contrast, Word's *Overtype Mode* lets you replace existing text just by typing new text right over it. If you place the insertion point in the middle of a sentence and start typing, the old characters disappear and are replaced by new ones as you type.

Word lets you switch (or *toggle*, as the geeks like to say) between Insert Mode and Overtype Mode. But first, you need to make sure that Word knows you want to use Overtype Mode. (By default, Word leaves Overtype Mode inactive and works only in Insert Mode.)

 **LET ME TRY IT**

Toggling Between Insert and Overtype Modes

You activate the Insert/Overtype toggle through Word's gigantic Options dialog box. After that, you can use either the keyboard's Insert key or a status bar button to toggle between the two modes:

1. Click the File tab, and then click Options. The Word Options dialog box opens.

2. In the dialog box's left pane, click Advanced. The dialog box displays a set of advanced options for using Word, as shown in Figure 2.2.

Select this check box
to activate Overtype Mode.

Select this check box if you want to use
the Insert key to switch between modes.

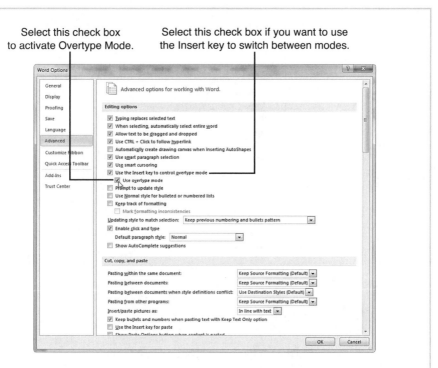

Figure 2.2 *Activating Overtype Mode in the Word Options dialog box.*

3. Click the Use The Insert Key To Control Overtype Mode check box, to place a check mark in it.

4. Click the Use Overtype Mode check box to place a check mark in it.

5. Click OK to close the dialog box.

6. Right-click the status bar at the bottom of the Word window. A menu opens, showing all the options that you can display or activate through the status bar, as shown in Figure 2.3.

7. On the menu, click Overtype.

8. Click outside the menu to close it. Notice that a new *Insert* button appears on the status bar. This indicates that Word is still operating in Insert Mode.

9. To switch to Overtype Mode, click the Insert button on the status bar or press the Insert key on the keyboard.

Either way, Word starts working in Overtype Mode, and the status bar now displays an Overtype button instead of an Insert button.

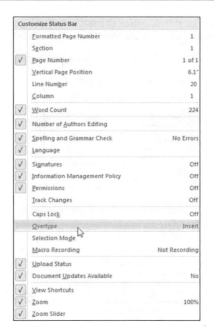

Figure 2.3   *Activating the toggle for Overtype and Insert modes.*

10.   To switch back to Insert Mode, click the Overtype button (or press Insert). The status bar button changes to show the current mode.

Overtype Mode is a holdover from the early days of word processing and grew out of the frustration people felt when they had to deal with typewriters. (Remember those?) A typewriter wouldn't let you just "type over" your mistakes; you had to go back and erase, or even retype the whole page. Overtype Mode gave us some long-overdue relief from that problem. But it created a problem of its own: Now you could accidentally type over your text without meaning to! For this reason, it's usually preferable to work in Insert Mode. If you make a mistake, Word lets you get rid of it in other ways without putting your good text at risk of accidental deletion.

TELL ME MORE   Media 2.1—The Dangers of Overtype Mode
Access this audio recording through your registered Web Edition at
my.safaribooksonline.com/9780132182713/media.

Using Click and Type

You can insert blank spaces, tabs, and paragraphs in a document to move the insertion point wherever you want it to go. This way, for example, if you know you want to have a paragraph about a half-page below the current one, you can just press Enter a few times to go there.

But there's an easier way to put the insertion point anywhere in a document, without inserting all those blank paragraphs and tabs yourself. This feature is called *Click and Type*. With Click and Type, you just point to any spot on the page and double-click; Word puts the insertion point there for you. If any blank paragraphs are needed to fill in the gap, Word inserts them for you. Word left-aligns, center-aligns, or right-aligns the text depending on where you double-click on the page.

 LET ME TRY IT

Extending a Document with Click and Type

Click and Type lets you add text anywhere on the page, even in places that don't have any paragraphs to hold it.

1. Click the Show/Hide ¶ button to display hidden characters on your screen. (This isn't necessary, but makes it easier to see how Click and Type works.)

2. Scroll down to the bottom of your document, past the last paragraph. Make sure there are no empty paragraphs below that point; this part of the page should be totally blank, as shown in Figure 2.4.

3. Click in the last paragraph of the document to place the insertion point there.

4. Move the mouse pointer around in the blank area at the bottom of the page, and notice how the pointer changes shapes. This means Click and Type is active.

5. Double-click in the blank portion of the page. Word inserts empty paragraphs as needed to put the insertion point where you clicked, as shown in Figure 2.5. Word also aligns the insertion point on the page, according to where you clicked.

Document's last paragraph
with the insertion point

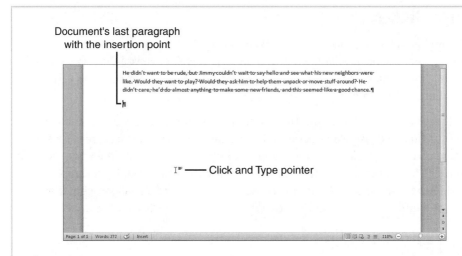

Figure 2.4   *The mouse pointer changes to indicate that Click and Type is active.*

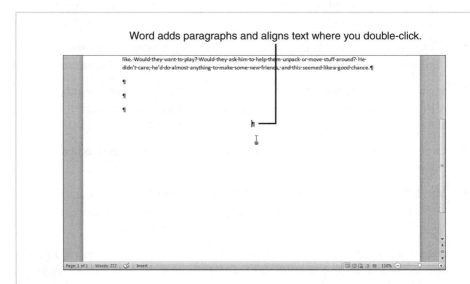

Figure 2.5   *Placing the insertion point in an empty part of the page, with Click and Type.*

Table 2.1 shows what the Click and Type mouse pointers mean.

Table 2.1   Click and Type Mouse Pointers

Pointer	Meaning
I≣	Text left-aligns.
I≣	Text left-aligns with an indented first line.
I≣	Text center-aligns.
I≣	Text right-aligns.

Inserting Nonalphanumeric Characters

A *nonalphanumeric character* is any character that doesn't appear on your key-board. There are two types of nonalphanumeric characters:

- *Symbols* are glyphs, such as the bullet (•), the greater-than/equal-to symbol (≧), and the frowny face (☹). There are hundreds of others, many of which have scientific or linguistic meaning, and some of which are just goofy.

- *Special characters* are typographical elements such as long (em) dashes, non-breaking hyphens, and ellipses.

There was a time when you had to know all sorts of crazy keystroke combinations to add such characters to a document. But now you can just pick one from a menu or dialog box.

 LET ME TRY IT

Adding Symbols and Special Characters

To insert a symbol, do the following:

1. On the Ribbon, click the Insert tab.

2. In the Symbols group at the end of the tab, click the Insert Symbol button. A drop-down palette appears, showing 20 symbols, as shown in Figure 2.6.

Figure 2.6   *The Symbol palette gives you quick access to recently used symbols.*

3. If you see the symbol you want on the palette, click it. Word inserts it at the insertion point's location in your document. If you don't see the symbol you want, skip to step 4.

4. Click More Symbols. The Symbol dialog box appears, as shown in Figure 2.7. By default, the Symbols tab is visible.

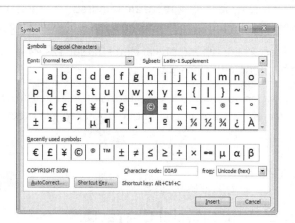

Figure 2.7   *The Symbol dialog box.*

If you need to insert a special typographical character instead of a symbol, click the Special Characters tab in the Symbol dialog box. You can insert these characters in the same manner you insert symbols, as described in the following steps.

5. Scroll through the palette of symbols until you find the one you want. If you don't see the right symbol, click the Font drop-down arrow at the top of the Symbols tab, and select a different font set. (Each font set includes its own unique symbols and some symbols shared by many different font sets.)

6. When you find the symbol you want, click it, and then click Insert. The symbol appears in your document, but the Symbol dialog box stays open. At this point, the dialog box deactivates so you can work in your document.

7. If you need to insert a different symbol, click the dialog box to reactivate it; then repeat steps 5 and 6.

8. When you finish, click Close to close the dialog box.

After you insert a symbol from the Symbol dialog box, Word adds that symbol to the drop-down palette you encountered back in step 2. If you insert lots of symbols, they'll eventually fill the palette. This little trick lets you insert symbols without opening the Symbol dialog box so often.

Deleting Text

When you *delete* text (or anything else, such as a blank paragraph or a picture), you remove it from the document. Word erases the unwanted characters and closes up the space around them, leaving no trace that they ever existed.

If you need to delete only a few characters, it's easiest to use your keyboard:

*   Press Delete once to erase a character that appears to the right of the insertion point. Hold down the key to erase a series of characters.

*   Press Backspace once to erase a character that appears to the left of the insertion point. Hold down the key to erase a series of characters.

Be careful when holding down Delete or Backspace! Before you realize it, Word will be chewing up characters by the dozen, and you'll delete a lot more text than you meant to.

If you need to delete a lot of text, Word offers more efficient ways of doing it. For example, you can select all the unwanted text before pressing Delete. You'll learn how to select text later in this chapter.

Moving Around in a Document

As mentioned already, this book assumes you know how to use your mouse and keyboard to move around in a document. That is, you're a practiced hand at using the scroll bars, the cursor-movement buttons, the Page Up and Page Down keys, and so on. These navigation techniques are common to just about any computer program you'll ever encounter, including web browsers.

In addition to those basic navigation tools, Word offers sophisticated features that enable you to jump from one specific spot to another in a document, without estimating or eyeballing anything while the pages whiz by on the screen. Two of the easiest tools to find and use are the Select Browse Object tool and Word's Go To command.

Browsing a Document

Word's object browsing feature enables you to pick a target—called an *object*—and then jump from one occurrence of that object to the next one. For example, if your document contains lots of tables, you can browse by jumping from one table to the next, skipping over all the other content. You can browse by jumping to each occurrence of a specific word, heading, or other kind of object.

An object is just a specific type of content, and a Word document can hold many kinds of objects. A Word document is basically just a collection of objects.

 LET ME TRY IT

Navigating a Document by Browsing Objects

To browse a document, do the following:

1. Move the insertion point to the location where you want to start browsing.

2. Click the Select Browse Object button (the small button with a circle on it, in the lower-right corner of the Word window, as shown in Figure 2.8). Alternatively, you can press Alt+Ctrl+Home.

   A palette of options flies out from the button, showing the types of objects you can browse, as shown in Figure 2.9.

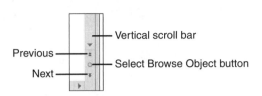

Figure 2.8   *Word's browsing tools appear below the vertical scroll bar.*

Figure 2.9   *You can browse for these types of objects in a Word document.*

3. On the palette, click the type of object you want to browse. If such an object exists in the document, Word moves the insertion point to it.

4. Continue browsing by doing either of the following:

   - To jump to the next occurrence of the same object, click the Next button (the double arrow below the Select Browse Object button). Alternatively, press Ctrl+Page Down.

   - To jump to the previous occurrence of the object, click the Previous button (the double arrow above the Select Browse Object button). Alternatively, press Ctrl+Page Up.

Table 2.2 shows what each icon in the Select Browse Object palette means.

Table 2.2 Browsable Objects in Word

This Icon...	Lets You Browse By...
→	Using the Go To tab of the Find and Replace dialog box
🔍	Using the Find tab of the Find and Replace dialog box
✎	Edits (if Word's Track Changes feature is active)
☰	Heading
🖼	Graphic

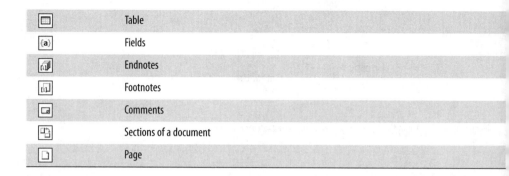

▦	Table
(a)	Fields
📖	Endnotes
📖	Footnotes
🗩	Comments
🗗	Sections of a document
🗋	Page

Using the Go To Command

Word's Go To command does exactly what its name implies: It lets you go to a specific place in a document. You may use Go To most often to jump to a specific page, but you can use it to jump to other places and objects in a document, as well.

 LET ME TRY IT

Moving Through a Document with Go To

To use the Go To command, do the following:

1. On the Home tab, click the Find button's drop-down arrow. A drop-down menu opens from the button.

2. Click Go To. The Find and Replace dialog box opens with the Go To tab visible, as shown in Figure 2.10.

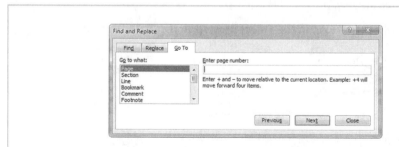

Figure 2.10   *The Go To tab of the Find and Replace dialog box.*

3. In the Go to What list, click the kind of object you want to go to. (For example, to go to a specific page, click Page.)

4. Use the box on the right side of the Go To tab to enter or select information that describes where you want to go. (For example, type a page number to jump to that page.)

5. Click Next.

6. Click Close to close the dialog box.

SHOW ME   Media 2.2—Browsing a Word Document
Access this video file through your registered Web Edition at
my.safaribooksonline.com/9780132182713/media.

Selecting Text

In Word, as in many programs, you often must *select* text before you can perform an action with it. For example, if you want to apply a different font to a heading, copy a sentence, or move a paragraph to a different place in the document, you have to select the text first.

Selecting is a timesaver, too. For example, if you want to delete a large passage of text—such as a paragraph—you can select the whole thing and press Delete once to erase it. This process is a lot faster than holding down the Delete key and erasing the passage one character at a time.

You can select as much or as little text as you need—from a single character to an entire document. When text is selected, Word highlights it on the screen by placing a blue background behind it, as shown in Figure 2.11. The highlighting lets you know Word is ready to perform whatever tasks you want with the text.

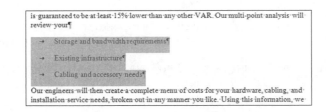

Figure 2.11   *Selected text appears highlighted in a document.*

The most common way to select text is by dragging the mouse pointer over it. That is, place the mouse pointer at the beginning of the text, hold down the left mouse button, and drag the mouse pointer across the text. Word highlights the text as you drag.

> Different types of objects can be selected in different ways. To select a picture, for example, just click it once. You'll learn how to select different objects in later chapters, as each type of object is introduced. Here we just focus on selecting text.

Aside from simply dragging the mouse pointer, there are lots of different techniques for selecting text, as shown in Tables 2.3–2.5. Most experienced Word users know several methods and use the one that seems most appropriate for the situation.

Table 2.3　Selecting Text with the Mouse

Selection	Action
Character	Drag the mouse pointer across the character.
Word	Double-click the word.
Line	Move the mouse pointer into the left margin at the beginning of the line. When the pointer becomes a right-tilting arrow, click once.
Paragraph	Move the mouse pointer into the left margin next to the paragraph; when the pointer becomes a right-tilting arrow, double-click. You can also triple-click anywhere inside the paragraph.
Document	Move the mouse pointer into the left margin; when the pointer becomes a right-tilting arrow, triple-click.

Table 2.4　Selecting Text with the Keyboard

Selection	Action	Note
Character	Shift+arrow key	Use the right arrow to select a character to the right of the insertion point; use the left arrow to select a character to the left.
Word	Ctrl+Shift+arrow key	Use the right arrow to select a word to the right of the insertion point; use the left arrow to select a word to the left.
Line from beginning to end	Shift+End	Place the insertion point at the beginning of the line to select the entire line; otherwise, Word selects the text from the insertion point to the end of the line.
Line from end to beginning	Shift+Home	Place the insertion point at the end of the line to select the entire line; otherwise, Word selects the text from the insertion point to the beginning of the line.

Paragraph from beginning to end	Ctrl+Shift+down arrow	Place the insertion point at the beginning of the paragraph to select the entire thing; otherwise, Word selects the text from the insertion point to the end of the paragraph.
Paragraph from end to beginning	Ctrl+Shift+up arrow	Place the insertion point at the end of the paragraph to select the entire thing; otherwise, Word selects the text from the insertion point to the beginning of the paragraph.
From the insertion point to the end of the document	Ctrl+Shift+End	
From the insertion point to the beginning of the document	Ctrl+Shift+Home	
Entire document	Ctrl+A	This key combination selects the entire document, no matter where the insertion point is located.

Table 2.5   Selecting Text with Keyboard-Mouse Combinations

Selection	Action
Sentence	Press Ctrl and click anywhere in the sentence (Ctrl+click).
Rectangular block of text	Press Alt and drag across the text. The block of text can stretch across multiple paragraphs.
Any amount of contiguous text	Click at the beginning of the selection to place the insertion point there. Move the mouse pointer to the end of the text to be selected; then click while pressing Shift (Shift+click).
Any amount of non-contiguous text	Select the first piece of text using any method you prefer. Move the mouse pointer to the beginning of the next piece of text you want to select; press Ctrl and drag across the text. Repeat to select as many individual pieces of text as you need.

When you finish working with the selected text (that is, unless you delete or replace it), you need to *deselect* it before doing anything else. To deselect text, click anywhere in the document or press an arrow key.

You can replace selected text simply by typing new text over it. But always be careful when working with selected text! If you select a paragraph and then accidentally press the spacebar, for example, Word replaces the selection with a blank space. Luckily, you can use the Undo command to reverse such mistakes and get your text back. The Undo command is discussed later in this chapter.

Copying and Moving Text

After you type some text into a document, you can use it again and again without retyping it. That is, you can make a copy of the text and insert the copy in another place, or you can move text from one spot to another.

For example, you can select a passage of text, copy it by using Word's Copy command, and then insert the copy somewhere else in the document by using the Paste command. You can paste copied text back into the document as many times as you want; you can even paste it into a different document. When you use the Copy command, Word leaves the original text in its place. An exact duplicate of the text is put in a special storage area called the *Clipboard*. Once an object is on the Clipboard, it stays there until you remove it or shut down Windows.

You can also use the Cut command to remove a piece of text from the document and place it on the Clipboard. As long as the text is on the Clipboard, you can insert it into back into the document (or a different one) by using the Paste command.

The Cut, Copy, and Paste commands are all located in the Clipboard group of the Home tab, as shown in Figure 2.12.

Figure 2.12   *The Clipboard group contains the Cut, Copy, and Paste commands.*

Remember that text is just one type of object in Word. You can use the Cut, Copy, and Paste commands (and the Clipboard) to copy and move all sorts of objects, including pictures, tables, and others.

Alternatively, instead of using all these commands, you can copy or move text by dragging and dropping it with your mouse.

LET ME TRY IT

Copying and Pasting Text

Copying text and pasting the copy back into a document is a simple four-step process.

1. Select the text you want to copy.

2. On the Home tab, click the Copy button (or press Ctrl+C).

3. Move the insertion point to the location where you want to paste the copied text, whether it's in the same document or a different one.

4. On the Home tab, click the Paste button (or press Ctrl+V).

The original piece of text remains in place, and Word inserts the copy at the insertion point. The copied text also remains on the Clipboard.

 **LET ME TRY IT**

Moving Text

Moving text is just like copying, with one slight difference. That is, you start by cutting the text out of the document.

1. Select the text you want to move.

2. On the Home tab, click the Cut button (or press Ctrl+X).

3. Move the insertion point to the location where you want to paste the text, whether it's in the same document or a different one.

4. On the Home tab, click the Paste button (or press Ctrl+V).

The text is removed from its original location, and Word inserts it at the insertion point. The cut text also remains on the Clipboard.

Working Directly with the Clipboard

The Cut, Copy, and Paste commands work just fine as described in the preceding examples, but there are two small drawbacks (if you want to call them that). First, you can't see the Clipboard's actual contents. Second, you paste only the most recently cut or copied text from the Clipboard. This is all fine, but it doesn't give you access to the full power of the Clipboard—which can actually hold up to 24 cut or copied objects.

By opening the Clipboard task pane, you can see everything it contains, even objects that have been cut or copied in other Office applications. (That's because the Clipboard is a shared feature; any Office application has access to it.) When the Clipboard is visible, you can paste any object it contains into any open document in any Office application.

Remember that we're talking about the Office Clipboard here—not the Windows Clipboard, which is a slightly different (and smaller) animal. The Office Clipboard, with its 24-object capacity, is available only to Microsoft Office applications. The Windows Clipboard, conversely, is available to any Windows application but stores only one object.

 LET ME TRY IT

Pasting Text Directly from the Clipboard

You can benefit from the following steps only if your Clipboard contains more than one cut or copied object. If it contains only one item, just use the Cut, Copy, and Paste commands as described earlier.

1. Cut or copy several different pieces of text, just to make sure that your Clipboard is well populated.

2. On the Home tab, at the lower-right corner of the Clipboard group, click the Clipboard task pane opener (the little button with the diagonal arrow, as shown in Figure 2.13). The Clipboard task pane appears.

3. In your document, place the insertion point where you want to paste some text.

4. Click one of the text objects in the Clipboard task pane. Word pastes the text at the insertion point's location.

5. To close the Clipboard, click the Close button in the upper-right corner of the task pane.

Clipboard pane opener

Figure 2.13   *The Clipboard task pane.*

If you want to remove an item from the Clipboard, point to it in the task pane. A drop-down arrow appears to the right of the item. Click the drop-down arrow; then click Delete. To remove everything from the Clipboard, click the Clear All button at the top of the task pane.

Using Paste Options

In the preceding examples, the pasted text was identical to the original version—whether you copied or cut it. By default, pasted text maintains the same formatting characteristics it had when it was placed on the Clipboard. You can change this by selecting one of Word's Paste Options when you paste the text into its new location. You can access these options by clicking the Paste button's drop-down arrow on the Home tab (see Figure 2.14), or by clicking the Paste Options button that appears next to freshly pasted text in the document (see Figure 2.15).

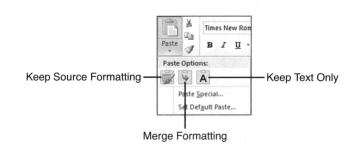

Keep Source Formatting ———   ——— Keep Text Only

Merge Formatting

Figure 2.14   *The Paste Options are available from the Paste button's drop-down menu.*

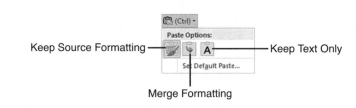

Keep Source Formatting ———   ——— Keep Text Only

Merge Formatting

Figure 2.15   *The Paste Options button appears next to pasted text.*

Word offers three Paste Options, as follows:

- **Keep Source Formatting:** This option (the default) maintains the text's original formatting, so it looks just the way it did when you cut or copied it. This applies even if the text came from a different document.

- **Merge Formatting:** This option removes the text's original formatting and updates it to match the formatting of its new surroundings.

- **Keep Text Only:** This option removes the text's original formatting but does not apply any new formatting. The pasted text is unformatted.

The Paste Options drop-down menu (on the Home tab) also displays the Paste Special command. This command opens the Paste Special dialog box—and with it, a whole new set of ways to muddle up an otherwise simple procedure. We won't get into the Paste Special brouhaha here because we're only dealing with text. If you're pasting pictures, content from a web page, or some other type of object, however, the Paste Special command can be handy indeed.

Using Drag-and-Drop

The Cut, Copy, and Paste commands give you a lot of control, which is especially helpful if you're working with many different objects or multiple documents. But if you just need to copy or move a little bit of text a short distance, all you need is your mouse. This procedure is called *drag-and-drop* (or *dragging-and-dropping*), because you simply drag the text to its new location and drop it there.

Here's how:

- To move text to a different spot, select the text; then point to it. When the mouse pointer changes to an arrow, click the left mouse button and hold it down. Drag the selected text to its new location and drop it there by releasing the mouse button.

- To copy text from one place to another, select it and point to it. When the mouse pointer changes to an arrow, drag the selected text while holding down the Ctrl key. You'll notice that a little plus sign (+) appears next to the pointer as you drag; this means you're dragging a copy of the selected text. To drop the copied text in its new spot, release the Ctrl key and the mouse button at the same time.

Like the Cut, Copy, and Paste commands, dragging-and-dropping works with all kinds of objects, including pictures, tables, and others.

 SHOW ME   Media 2.3—Dragging and Dropping Text in a Word Document
Access this video file through your registered Web Edition at
my.safaribooksonline.com/9780132182713/media.

Undoing, Redoing, and Repeating an Action

Everybody makes mistakes. But one of the nice things about making a mistake on a computer is that you can actually *undo* it. That's right—you can use Word's Undo command to make a mistake go away, just like it never happened. (Try that in real life!) Here's how to undo an erroneous action:

1. Make a mistake. Any mistake. For example, accidentally delete some text.

2. On the Quick Access toolbar, click the Undo button (or press Ctrl+Z) as shown in Figure 2.16. Voilà! Your mistake is undone.

Figure 2.16   *The Undo and Redo buttons on the Quick Access toolbar.*

Of course, being human, you might accidentally undo something you actually meant to do. Fortunately, computer scientists (being humans themselves) foresaw this possibility and built a Redo command into Word. The Redo command lets you undo something you just undid! Here's how to redo an undo that you shouldn't have undone:

1. Use the Undo command to undo your last action.

2. On the Quick Access toolbar, click the Redo button (or press Ctrl+Y). Your last Undo command is reversed.

> The Redo button does not always appear on the Quick Access toolbar. It appears only when you've just used the Undo command, because Word assumes that you may want to redo whatever you just undid. When the Redo button isn't available, Word displays the Repeat button in its place.

Occasionally, you might do something really good—something worth repeating. Maybe you'll type a hard-to-spell word just right, for once. Whatever really good action you take, you can instantly repeat it by using Word's Repeat command. Here's how:

1. Do something you like.

2. On the Quick Access toolbar, click the Repeat button (or press Ctrl+Y). Word performs the action again for you.

Working with Building Blocks

Writing would be quite monotonous if you actually had to type everything yourself. Luckily, Word offers a set of tools, called *building blocks*, which can automate some of your text-entry chores. A building block can be a preformatted bit of text, a picture, a part of a document such as a cover sheet, or something else. You can create your own building blocks, but Word already has dozens of blocks built in and ready to be added to any document.

You can access building blocks through the Quick Parts gallery (on the Insert tab), as shown in Figure 2.17. The gallery gives you access to the following types of quick parts:

- **AutoText:** An *AutoText* entry is a piece of text that Word can insert into a document for you. You can create your own AutoText entries and add them to the AutoText gallery.

- **Document Properties:** A *document property* is a special text box you can add to a document. Each box stores a unique type of information about the document, such as the author's name, keywords, the document's current status, and so on. These properties stay with the document. Only a fixed number of document property building blocks are available.

- **Fields:** A *field* is a small object that stores code. The code tells Word to display a specific type of information at the field's location in a document. Fields can display the current date, page number, title, and many other types of information. Word features dozens of built-in fields. You can modify many of Word's fields through the Field dialog box, which appears when you click Fields in the Quick Parts gallery.

Figure 2.17   *The Quick Parts gallery.*

The *Building Blocks Organizer* is also available through the Quick Parts gallery. This organizer lists all the building blocks available in Word, as shown in Figure 2.18. The list includes all of Word's built-in quick parts, your AutoText entries, and predesigned elements such as title pages, headers, footers, text boxes, and more. You can choose a building block from the organizer to add to a document, or you can add, edit, and delete building blocks.

Inserting a Building Block

Inserting a building block can be as simple as choosing it from the Quick Parts gallery. If you don't find the building block you want, you may need to look in the Building Blocks Organizer for it.

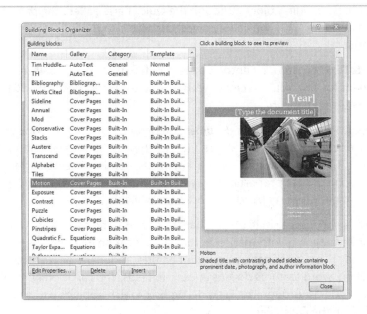

Figure 2.18 *The Building Blocks Organizer.*

 LET ME TRY IT

Inserting a Building Block from the Quick Parts Gallery

Depending on how a building block was created and saved, it may appear directly on the Quick Parts gallery. If not, it may be available as an AutoText entry, a document property, or a field.

1. In your document, place the insertion point where you want to insert the building block.

2. On the Insert tab, click Quick Parts.

3. If the item does not appear on the Quick Parts gallery, do one of the following:

   - Click AutoText to see if the item is an AutoText entry. If so, click the entry to add it to your document.
   - Click Document Property to see the list of available properties. If the item you want is in this list, click it to add it to the document.
   - If you need to insert a field into your document, click Field to open the Field dialog box. This dialog box lists all the available fields in Word and

can show you each field's built-in codes, as well. You can select options for many different fields to customize the kind of information they display in your documents.

 LET ME TRY IT

Inserting a Building Block from the Building Blocks Organizer

The Building Blocks Organizer lists all the available building blocks.

1. On the Insert tab, click Quick Parts.

2. Click Building Blocks Organizer.

3. Scroll through the building blocks listed in the organizer. When you find a block that looks like the one you want, click its name to view it in the preview pane.

4. When you find the right building block, click its name, and then click the Insert button to add it to your document.

 SHOW ME   Media 2.4—Inserting Building Blocks in a Word Document
Access this video file through your registered Web Edition at
my.safaribooksonline.com/9780132182713/media.

Creating a New Building Block

You can create all sorts of building blocks, such as return addresses, logos, personalized cover pages, pictures, and more. Any object that can be contained in a Word document can be saved as a building block.

 LET ME TRY IT

Creating a Building Block

No matter what type of building block you create, you have the same options for naming and storing it.

1. In a document, select the content you want to save as a building block.

2. On the Insert tab, click Quick Parts.

3. At the bottom of the Quick Parts gallery, click Save Selection to Quick Part Gallery. The Create New Building Block dialog box opens, as shown in Figure 2.19.

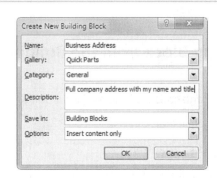

Figure 2.19   *The Create New Building Block dialog box.*

4. Click in the Name box, and give the new building block a brief, descriptive name that will help you remember its contents or purpose.

5. Click the Gallery drop-down arrow and pick the gallery where you want to place the new block. By default, Word adds new building blocks to the Quick Parts gallery.

Placing a building block right on the Quick Parts gallery gives you fast access to it, but the gallery will fill up quickly if you create a lot of blocks. So, when you create new building blocks, consider putting them in the most appropriate place. For example, if you create a building block for a mailing address, place it in the AutoText gallery.

6. Skip the Category drop-down list unless you want to create new categories for your building blocks. This is necessary only if you create lots of blocks and need a more detailed method of categorizing them than Word's default method.

7. Click in the Description box and type a short description for your new building block. This step is optional, but may be helpful; your description will appear with the block in the Building Blocks Organizer.

8. Click the Save in drop-down arrow and select the template in which you want to save the new building block. By default, Word stores building

blocks in the Building Blocks template, making them available to every document, no matter what template a document is based on. If you select the Normal option, your new building block will be available only to documents based on Word's Normal template.

9. Click the Options drop-down arrow and choose how you want the building block to be inserted into your documents. You have three options:

   - **Insert content only:** The building block will be placed at the insertion point's location in the document.
   - **Insert content as its own paragraph:** The building block will be placed in a separate paragraph.
   - **Insert content as its own page:** The building block will be placed in the document as a separate page.

10. Click OK.

Inserting a Blank Page

You may find yourself deep into a document and realize that you need to insert a whole new page in the middle of it. If so, no problem. To insert a blank page, just do this:

1. Place the insertion point where you want the blank page to go. This will usually be between two paragraphs, but may be between a paragraph and a table, or between two other objects.

2. In the Pages group of the Insert tab, click the Blank Page button. An entire blank page appears at the insertion point's location.

Inserting One Word Document into Another

Some documents' contents are so useful, you may want to copy them into other documents in their entirety. For example, suppose you have created a short questionnaire that you want to insert into letters to the members of your book club. You can insert the entire questionnaire into the letter, without doing any copying or pasting. You don't even have to open the questionnaire. Here's what to do:

1. In the current document, place the insertion point where you want to insert the second document's contents.

2. In the Text group of the Insert tab, click the Object button's drop-down arrow.

3. In the drop-down menu, click Text from File. The Insert File dialog box opens, as shown in Figure 2.20.

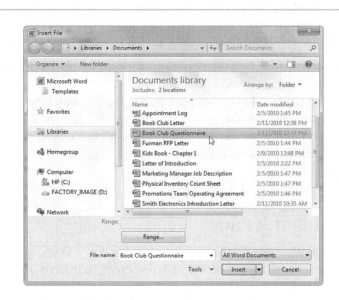

Figure 2.20   *Choosing a file to insert into the current document.*

4. Use the dialog box to find and select a file, just as you would use Word's Open dialog box. (The Open dialog box is discussed in Chapter 1.)

5. Click Insert. Word inserts the selected document's contents into the current document.

This chapter introduces Word's powerful proofing tools, which can find errors in your documents and help improve the readability of your text.

3

Proofing a Document

The word "proofing" can mean a lot of different things. For example, proofing a document means reading it carefully to check for mistakes. Proofing can also mean looking for opportunities to improve the quality of your writing—revising sentences, making stronger word choices, and editing text to make it as meaningful as possible to your audience. Proofing is an important part of the writing process; the more energy you spend on it, the better your documents will be.

Word offers several sets of tools that can help with proofing chores, especially in the areas of spelling and grammar. Word can also help you find words and phrases that you want to change, in one spot or throughout a document. And you can launch Word's research tools to gather information on just about any subject, to look up definitions, and to find synonyms.

Viewing a Document's Statistics

Ever wonder how many words you've written so far? Word makes it easy to check statistics like word count, character count (including blank spaces), the number of lines in a document, and so on. The Word Count feature is a lifesaver if you need to make sure a document meets a specific length requirement, as is often the case when writing reports, term papers, and articles.

 **LET ME TRY IT**

Finding Document Statistics

Here's how to get a quick view of the statistics in any open document:

1. On the Ribbon, click the Review tab.
2. In the Proofing group, click the Word Count button. The Word Count dialog box appears, as shown in Figure 3.1.

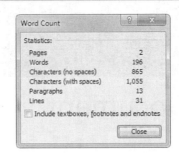

Figure 3.1   *Checking a document's statistics.*

3. If your document contains text boxes, footnotes, or endnotes and you want to include them in the statistics, click the Include Textboxes, Footnotes, and Endnotes check box. Word updates the statistics in the dialog box.

4. Click Close.

TELL ME MORE   Media 3.1—The Truth About Word's Proofreading Power

Access this audio recording through your registered Web Edition at
my.safaribooksonline.com/9780132182713/media.

Evaluating a Document's Readability

It might be hard to believe, but Word can "grade" a document's readability. This isn't the same as having other people read your document and give you their opinions of it, but it's close enough to be helpful. Word examines your text and applies different formulas to determine how easy it is to read.

Without getting into details (because they're confusing and boring), Word grades readability based on two scales and displays the results in the Readability Statistics dialog box, as shown in Figure 3.2.

The *Flesch Reading Ease* scale tells you how easy a document is to read, based on a score of 0–100; the higher the score, the better. The *Flesch-Kincaid Grade Level*

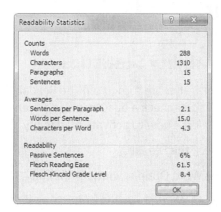

Figure 3.2 *Evaluating a document's readability.*

determines what level of education is required to read a document; for example, if this score is 5, your audience needs a fifth-grade education to comprehend the document.

The Readability Statistics dialog box also reveals the percentage of passive sentences (Boo! Hiss!) in the document. The higher this percentage, the worse your writing...that is, according to the lords of grammar.

You can write sentences in either *active voice* or *passive voice*. The following examples show the difference:

Active: "Aliens have invaded the city."

Passive: "The city has been invaded by aliens."

In this example, the two sentences pretty clearly mean the same thing. In some cases, however, passive voice can reduce the clarity of your writing. This does not mean passive sentences are wrong. To the contrary, the passive voice has its place in writing. But if Word (or an English teacher) points out a passive sentence, examine it carefully. The sentence may be clearer if you rewrite it in active voice.

LET ME TRY IT

Activating Readability Statistics

By default, readability statistics are turned off. The Readability Statistics dialog box appears only when you spell-check a document, and then only if you tell Word to display these statistics. Here's how to activate readability statistics:

1. On the Ribbon, click the File tab.

2. Click Options. The Word Options window appears.

3. Click Proofing to see Word's proofing options, as shown in Figure 3.3.

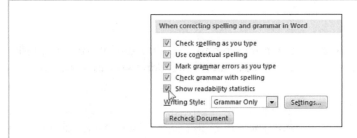

Figure 3.3 *Activating readability statistics.*

4. Click the Show Readability Statistics check box.

5. Click OK.

Checking Your Spelling and Grammar

If spelling and grammar weren't your favorite subjects in school, you can still get by with a little help from your computer. Word's built-in spelling and grammar checkers can help you catch potential errors and fix them before anyone else sees your document. When it finds a potential mistake, Word displays options for correcting it (that is, if Word knows of any options, which isn't always the case).

Word automatically checks spelling and grammar on-the-fly and warns you of potential mistakes as you type. If these warnings are a nuisance, you can turn them off and check an entire document when you're ready.

The key word here is "potential." Although Word has an impressive spelling dictionary and a big ol' database of grammatical rules, it still can't spot every mistake you make. And often enough, Word will erroneously flag a word or sentence that is actually correct. For example, if your document contains a word that isn't included in Word's spelling dictionary, Word can't recognize that term...and flags it as a misspelling, even if you spelled it correctly. Conversely, if you use the wrong word but spell it correctly, the spelling checker may ignore it.

The message here is that when Word flags a word, phrase, or sentence as an error, you should examine it carefully before deciding what to do.

Finding and Fixing Errors While You Type

By default, Word is set to check spelling and grammar in real time, as you type. If you leave this setting unchanged, Word "flags" potential errors whenever they pop up, as follows:

- If a word is misspelled, Word places a wavy red line underneath it. This means the word doesn't exist in Word's spelling dictionary.

- If a word is misused, Word places a wavy blue line underneath it. Word sometimes misses the boat on this one, but the flag may truly mean you've chosen the wrong word.

- If a sentence contains a grammatical error—whether it involves a word, a phrase, or the entire sentence—Word places a wavy green line underneath it.

Figure 3.4 shows an example of each kind of error, with Word's wavy warnings in place. The following sections briefly show you what to do when these errors appear on your screen.

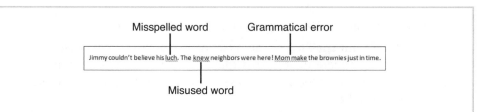

Figure 3.4 *Word's flags for a misspelled word, a misused word, and a grammatical error.*

LET ME TRY IT

Fixing a Spelling Error as You Type

If a wavy red line appears under a word while you're typing, here's what to do:

1. Right-click the misspelled word. A shortcut menu opens, as shown in Figure 3.5.

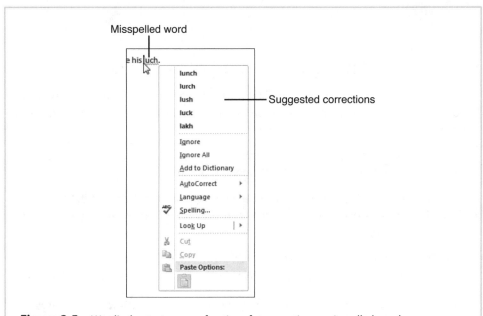

Figure 3.5   *Word's shortcut menu of options for correcting a misspelled word.*

2. Choose the appropriate option from the shortcut menu:

   - **A different spelling:** If Word's dictionary contains potentially correct spelling options for the word, they appear at the top of the shortcut menu. If one of the alternatives is correct, click it and Word inserts it in place of the flagged word.
   - **Ignore:** Word overlooks this occurrence of the word and removes the flag but will flag any other occurrences of the misspelling elsewhere in the document.
   - **Ignore All:** Word overlooks (and unflags) the word throughout the document.

- **Add to Dictionary:** This option adds the word—as it is spelled—to the spelling dictionary.
- **AutoCorrect:** This option displays a submenu containing the same spelling options that appear at the top of the shortcut menu. If you choose one of these alternative spellings, Word inserts it in place of the misspelled word and automatically creates an AutoCorrect entry for this specific misspelling. (AutoCorrect is discussed later in this chapter.)
- **Language:** Word lets you pick another language for checking the spelling. We won't go there right now...or later.
- **Spelling:** This option opens the Spelling dialog box, which is discussed later in this chapter.

3. Resume typing. If Word encounters another potential spelling mistake, another wavy red underline will appear.

Use caution before adding a word to the spelling dictionary, especially if it's an unusual word, a specialized term, or if you are purposely using an "alternative" spelling just for the current document. When you add a word to the dictionary, Word won't flag it as a misspelling again.

 LET ME TRY IT

Fixing a Misused Word as You Type

If a wavy blue line appears under a word while you're typing, here's what to do:

1. Right-click the word to open a shortcut menu. This menu is similar to the one that appears for a misspelled word. Do one of the following:
   - At the top of the shortcut menu, look for a list of words that might correctly replace the flagged word. If one of these words is correct, click it.
   - If you want to leave the word in place, click Ignore.
   - If Word has flagged the same error multiple times and you want to leave them all unchanged, click Ignore All.
   - If you want to check the word using a different language, click Language.
   - To open the Spelling dialog box, click Spelling.

2. Resume typing. If Word spots another misused word, another wavy blue underline will appear.

 **LET ME TRY IT**

Fixing a Grammatical Error as You Type

If a wavy green line appears under a word, phrase, or sentence while you're typing, here's what to do:

1. Right-click the error. A shortcut menu opens, as shown in Figure 3.6.

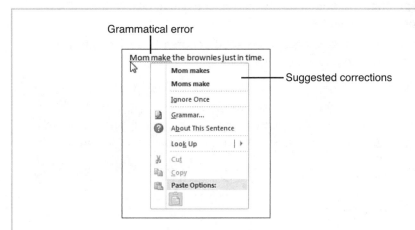

Figure 3.6 *Word's shortcut menu of options for correcting a grammatical error.*

2. Choose the appropriate option from the shortcut menu:
   - **A different wording:** If Word can offer one or more potentially correct wordings, they appear at the top of the shortcut menu. If one of these options is correct, click it and Word inserts it in place of the flagged text.
   - **Ignore Once:** This option tells Word to overlook this occurrence of the text in question. Word removes the error flag but will flag any other occurrences of the error elsewhere in the document.
   - **Grammar:** This option opens the Grammar dialog box, which is discussed later in this chapter.
   - **About This Sentence:** This option opens a Help window that explains the error, at least as Word sees it. If the text actually contains a grammatical problem, the information in this window may help you fix it.
3. Resume typing. If Word finds another potential grammar error, another wavy green underline will appear.

Don't be intimidated by Word's grammar-checker. It has been known to make its share of mistakes, and you'll probably wind up using the *Ignore Once* option a great deal. If you aren't sure about a rule of grammar and Word doesn't provide helpful information, find a good grammar resource and look it up there.

Changing Options for Checking Spelling and Grammar as You Type

If Word's wavy lines get on your nerves (or if you're completely confident in your own spelling and grammatical skills), you can disable them. You can set these options for all documents, or just for a currently open one.

 LET ME TRY IT

Changing Word's On-the-Fly Proofing Options

You can turn on some on-the-fly proofing options while turning others off. For example, if you like seeing spelling errors, you can leave them active and turn off grammar-related warnings. Here's how:

1. On the Ribbon, click the File tab.

2. Click Options. The Word Options window appears.

3. Click Proofing to see Word's proofing options.

4. To set the spelling- and grammar-checking options for all documents, scroll to the When Correcting Spelling and Grammar in Word section of the window, as shown in Figure 3.7. Check and uncheck the options to suit your preferences.

5. To show or hide spelling or grammar errors in a currently open document, scroll to the Exceptions For section of the window and do the following:
   • Click the Exceptions For drop-down arrow; then select a currently open document.
   • To show or hide spelling errors in the selected document, check or clear the Hide Spelling Errors in This Document Only check box.
   • To show or hide grammar errors in the selected document, check or clear the Hide Grammar Errors in This Document Only check box.
   These options apply only to the selected document, not to any others.

6. Click OK.

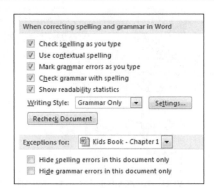

Figure 3.7   *Changing options for checking spelling and grammar as you type.*

Checking Spelling and Grammar in an Entire Document

Whether you disable the on-the-fly options as described in the preceding section or just ignore Word's error flags as they appear on your screen, you can check an entire document for mistakes and deal with them all in one fell swoop.

You can check all or part of a document by using the Spelling and Grammar dialog box. When this dialog box is active, Word skims through the document, points out any errors it finds, and offers suggestions for correcting each mistake in turn.

 **LET ME TRY IT**

Checking an Entire Document

You'll know that you need to run a spelling or grammar check if Word displays error flags in your document, but it's especially important to check your spelling and grammar if you have turned error flags off. To check an entire document, take these steps:

1. Place the insertion point where you want to start checking for errors. The beginning of the document is usually the best place to start.

2. Click the Review tab.

3. Click the Spelling & Grammar button. The Spelling and Grammar dialog box appears, as shown in Figure 3.8.

4. If you want to check spelling but not grammar, clear the Check Grammar check box before proceeding.

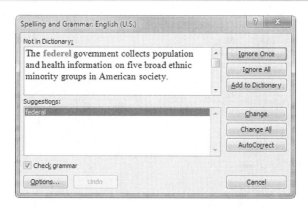

Figure 3.8   *The Spelling and Grammar dialog box displays errors and offers options for fixing them.*

5. When Word finds a misspelled word (that is, a word that does not exist in the spelling dictionary), it appears in red in the Not in Dictionary box.

6. Choose the appropriate option in the dialog box:

    -   **A different spelling:** If Word's dictionary contains potentially correct spelling options for the word, they appear in the Suggestions box. If one of these options is correct, click it and click the Change button. Word inserts it in place of the flagged word. (To replace every occurrence of the word throughout the document, click the Change All button instead.)

    -   **Ignore Once:** Word overlooks this occurrence of the word and removes its flag but will flag any other occurrences of the misspelling elsewhere in the document.

    -   **Ignore All:** Word overlooks (and unflags) the word throughout the document.

    -   **Add to Dictionary:** This option tells Word to add the word—as it is spelled—to the spelling dictionary.

    -   **AutoCorrect:** If you choose an alternative spelling from the Suggestions box and click the AutoCorrect button, Word inserts it in place of the misspelled word and automatically creates an AutoCorrect entry for this specific misspelling. (AutoCorrect is discussed later in this chapter.)

    After you choose an option, Word resumes searching the document for errors. Repeat step 6 for each misspelled word.

7. If Word encounters a grammatical error, it appears in green at the top of the dialog box, as shown in Figure 3.9. The box's name changes to indicate which grammatical rule the error violates.

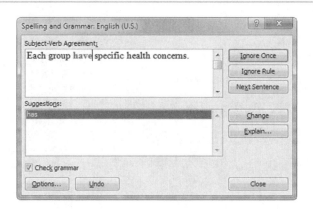

Figure 3.9 *A grammatical error in the Spelling and Grammar dialog box.*

8. Choose the appropriate option in the dialog box:
   - **A different wording:** If Word can provide a potentially correct wording, it appears in the Suggestions box. If the option is correct, click it and click the Change button.
   - **Ignore Once:** Word overlooks this occurrence of the error and removes its flag but will flag any other occurrences of the error elsewhere in the document.
   - **Ignore Rule:** This option tells Word to overlook the rule of grammar that was used to flag this error. Word unflags any other occurrences of the same error in the document.
   - **Next Sentence:** Word skips the current error and moves to the next one.
   - **Explain:** This option opens a help window that provides information about the error.

   After you choose an option, Word resumes searching the document for errors. Repeat step 8 for each grammatical error.

9. Click Close to close the Spelling and Grammar dialog box and stop checking the document. Another dialog box may appear, notifying you that the check is complete; click OK to close it. Otherwise, when Word finishes checking, the dialog box closes automatically. If you have activated readability statistics (as described earlier in this chapter), the Readability Statistics dialog box appears.

In some cases, Word won't have a suggestion for fixing an error. For example, if it finds a sentence fragment, Word will simply suggest that you "consider revising" the text. To make a change, click outside the Spelling and Grammar dialog box, click in the sentence, and make your change. Then click the dialog box to reactivate it, and click the Resume button to continue checking the document.

 SHOW ME   Media 3.2—Working with Word's Spelling Checker
Access this video file through your registered Web Edition at
my.safaribooksonline.com/9780132182713/media.

Finding and Replacing Text

One of the most common mistakes in writing is to use one word when you actually meant to use another. For example, you might use "Tim" throughout a document when you should be referring to "Tom." Or you might repeatedly mistype a word— such as typing "**fine**" instead of "**find**." Word's spelling or grammar checker may not always pick up such mistakes.

But in these situations, you don't have to read the entire document to find your mistake(s). Word can locate any piece of text in a document and can also replace it with any other text you specify. You can replace a single instance of the text or every occurrence in the document.

Finding Text

The Find command lets you search for a character, word, phrase, number, or other text string. You can also select options that refine text searches to yield more accurate results.

The following sections show you how to find text by using Word's Navigation task pane, which opens when you issue the Find command. You can also find text (and formats and special characters) by using the Find and Replace dialog box, which is discussed later in this chapter.

LET ME TRY IT

Searching for a Specific Piece of Text

Suppose that you want to find a specific word in a document. Here's how:

1. On the Home tab, click the Find button. (Alternatively, press Ctrl+F.) The Navigation task pane opens.

2. Click in the Search Document box; then type the word you want to find. Word searches the document and lists every occurrence of the word in the task pane, as shown in Figure 3.10. The task pane shows you how many matches were found and displays each one in a series of boxes.

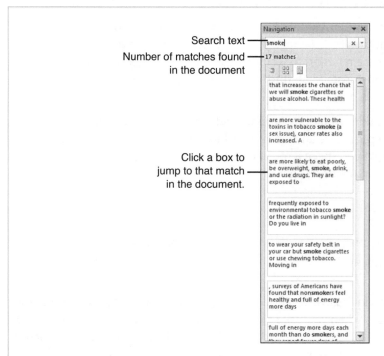

Figure 3.10   *Searching for a word in the Navigation task pane.*

3. To jump to a specific match in the document, click the appropriate box in the task pane. Alternatively, you can click the Previous Search Result and Next Search Result arrows to jump from one occurrence of the word to another.

4. To clear this search and look for a different piece of text, click the button marked with an X at the right end of the Search Document box; then repeat steps 2 and 3.

5. To close the Navigation task pane, click the Close button (marked with an X) in the pane's upper-right corner.

Word can search for other objects besides text. In the Navigation task pane, click the drop-down arrow at the right end of the Search Document box. From the drop-down menu, click either Graphics, Tables, Equations, Footnotes/Endnotes, or Comments to search for one of these kinds of objects. If Word finds any instances of the selected object, they are listed in the task pane just as described in the preceding steps.

 LET ME TRY IT

Refining a Text Search

Using Word's Find Options, you can set more specific criteria for finding text. For example, you can search for words that match the case of the text you type in the Search Document box or words with a certain prefix. Here's how to access the Find Options:

1. Click the drop-down arrow at the right end of the Search Document box.

2. From the drop-down menu, click Options, as shown in Figure 3.11. The Find Options dialog box opens, as shown in Figure 3.12.

Figure 3.11 *The Find Options drop-down menu in the Navigation task pane.*

Type your search text here.

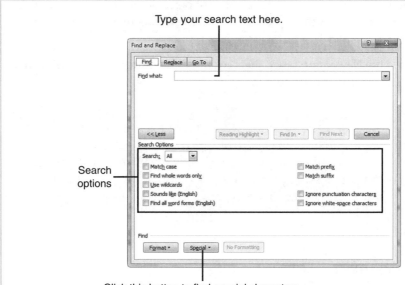

Search options

Click this button to find special characters.

Figure 3.12   *Setting options for conducting a text search. Here, only the default options are selected.*

3. In the Find Options dialog box, clear or select the check boxes that will give you the most accurate results for the current search.

4. If you want to make your selections the default settings, click the Set as Default button.

5. Click OK and continue your search as described in the preceding section.

Finding Text with the Find and Replace Dialog Box

The Navigation task pane is new to Word 2010. If you have used a previous version of Word, you may prefer to use the old, familiar Find and Replace dialog box rather than the Navigation task pane. If you're new to Word, you may prefer the Find and Replace dialog box because it puts all your options in one place and allows you to search for items the Navigation pane can't, such as special characters and formats.

 **LET ME TRY IT**

Searching for Text on the Find Tab

You may recall seeing the Find and Replace dialog box in Chapter 2, "Editing Documents," when you learned about the Go To command. You can use the dialog box's Find tab to search for text. Here's how:

1. On the Home tab, click the Replace button. (Alternatively, press Ctrl+H.) The Find and Replace dialog box opens.

2. Click the Find tab.

3. Click the More button. The dialog box expands to display more options, as shown in Figure 3.13. (Notice that the More button now says Less; you can click it to hide these additional search options.)

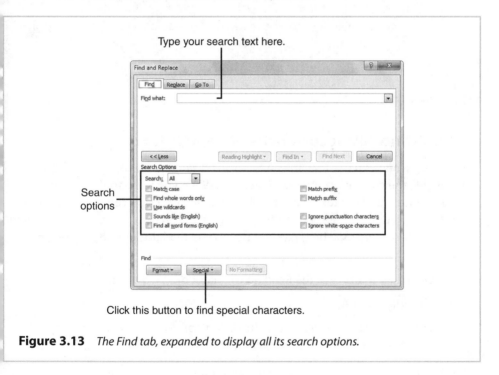

Figure 3.13   *The Find tab, expanded to display all its search options.*

4. Click the Find What box and type the text string you want to find.

5. Click the Search drop-down arrow, and choose the direction you want to search in, starting from the insertion point's current location.

6. In the Search Options section, select any of the options that will improve the accuracy of your search.

7. Click the Find In drop-down arrow and select the part of the document to search. By default, Word searches the main body of the document, but you can search the document's headers, footers, and text boxes, if applicable.

8. Click Find Next to locate the first occurrence of the text after the insertion point. Word finds the text and highlights it. You can click this button repeatedly to move from one instance of the text to the next.

9. Click Cancel to close the dialog box when you finish with your search.

You can continue searching for other instances of the text after closing the Find and Replace dialog box. To do this, click the Previous Find/Go To and Next Find/Go To buttons to jump to the preceding or following occurrence of your search text, respectively. These are the double-arrow buttons in the lower-right corner of the Word window, above and below the Select Browse Object button. Alternatively, you can press either Ctrl+Page Up or Ctrl+Page Down.

 LET ME TRY IT

Highlighting All Occurrences of Search Text

Normally, when you use the Find and Replace dialog box to search for text, Word highlights the current occurrence of the text. When you jump to the next (or previous) occurrence of the text, Word highlights it. However, you can tell Word to highlight *every* instance of the text in the document; that way, you can close the dialog box and view every matching piece of text as you read through the document. Here's how:

1. On the Find tab, click the Reading Highlight drop-down arrow.

2. Click Highlight All.

3. Click the Close button to close the dialog box. Now you can see every instance of the search text highlighted in the document.

To clear the highlighting, take the following steps:

1. Re-open the Find and Replace dialog box.

2. On the Find tab, click the Reading Highlight drop-down arrow.

3. Click Clear Highlighting.

4. Click the Close button to close the dialog box to return to your document.

LET ME TRY IT

Searching for Special Characters

In addition to text, Word can search for special characters in a document. These include some of the nonprinting characters (tabs, page breaks, and so on) described in Chapter 2, along with certain typographical characters such as long (em) dashes. Here's how to search a document for special characters:

1. Open the Find and Replace dialog box; then click the Find tab.

2. Click the More button to display the Search Options section of the dialog box.

3. Click the Special drop-down arrow to view a list of special characters, as shown in Figure 3.14.

Figure 3.14 *Searching for a special character in the Find tab.*

4. Click the type of character you want to find. You can repeat this step to tell Word to search for a series of characters.

You can also type characters or words among the special characters to pinpoint your search. For example, you might select Tab Character from the Special list and then type the word **The** immediately after it in the Find What box. This tells Word to find instances of tab stops followed by **The** and makes for faster searching than searching for either tabs or **The** alone.

5. Click Find Next to locate the first occurrence of the character after the insertion point. Word finds and highlights the character. You can click this button repeatedly to move from one instance of the character to the next.

6. Click Cancel to close the dialog box when you finish searching.

Some special-character search options may be more trouble than they're worth, unless you're desperate to find something. For example, if you choose Any Character, Word finds and highlights every single character in the document, one at a time. This makes for incredibly slow searching. If you need to find something tiny, try searching for it in some sort of context.

As mentioned earlier, you can use the Find and Replace dialog box to search for (and replace) formatting. Chapter 5, "Paragraph Formatting," covers this feature in detail.

Replacing Text

Word's Replace feature is just an extension of the Find feature. That's why they share the same dialog box. Notice that the Replace tab looks just like the Find tab but has an extra box where you can type your replacement text.

 **LET ME TRY IT**

Finding and Replacing Text in a Document

After you master the art of finding text, replacing text involves just a few more easy steps. Here's a quick example that proves the point:

1. Open the Find and Replace dialog box; then click the Replace tab.

2. Click in the Find What box and specify the text (or special character) you want to find and replace.

3. In the Search Options section of the dialog box, select any options that might increase the accuracy of your search.

4. Click in the Replace With box and specify the text (or special character) you want to use as the replacement.

   Your dialog box should resemble the one shown in Figure 3.15.

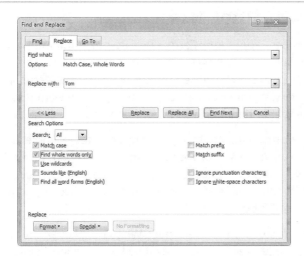

Figure 3.15   *Specifying options for replacing a word in a document.*

5. Click the Find Next button to find the first instance of the search text. (If you want to skip any instance of the text without replacing it, click the Find Next button again to go to the next instance.)

6. Click the Replace button to replace that instance of the search text with the new text. Word then jumps to the next instance of the text.

7. Keep clicking either Replace or Find Next to replace or skip each subsequent occurrence of the text until you reach the end of the document.

   Alternatively, you can click the Replace All button to find and replace every occurrence of the text in your document at the same time.

8. When you finish, click the Close button.

Be careful when using the Replace All feature. If you don't set your search options just right, Word may replace text you don't mean to change. For example, if you want to replace one whole word with another whole word, be sure to check the Find Whole Words Only check box. Otherwise, Word will replace every occurrence of the search text, even if it is part of another word. So, if you want to change the name "Tom" to "Tim," Word may change "Tomorrow" to "Timorrow" and do similar kinds of damage throughout your document.

Working with AutoCorrect

As its name implies, Word's AutoCorrect feature can automatically correct errors in a document as soon as you type them. For example, if you type **siad**, Word can instantly change it to **said** because AutoCorrect works hand-in-hand with Word's spelling dictionary. When AutoCorrect runs the way you want it to, it can drastically reduce the number of minor errors in your documents.

That said, AutoCorrect can also be a pain. Suppose, for example, that you frequently use the characters *(c)* in your documents—perhaps for professional reasons. If so, you may get annoyed if Word always changes those characters to the © symbol. This is an example of a "correction" that isn't exactly correct, and AutoCorrect makes it by default.

Luckily, you aren't stuck with AutoCorrect. When it makes an on-the-fly correction you don't like, you can reject the change and keep moving. You can customize AutoCorrect by adding your own common misspellings and typing errors to its list, and by removing items from the list if you don't want them to be changed. If you find that AutoCorrect is just a headache, you can disable it completely.

If you're new to Word, it's a good idea to watch AutoCorrect in action for a while before changing or disabling it. It's configured to catch and fix many of the most common typographical errors. AutoCorrect also corrects certain oversights, such as capitalizing the names of days when you forget to.

Rejecting a Change Made by AutoCorrect

Suppose you're typing a list, and for stylistic reasons you don't want to capitalize the first letter of each sentence in the list. (Hey, writers do stranger things than this on purpose.) After you type the first word of a sentence and press the spacebar, however, AutoCorrect flies into action and capitalizes the word's first letter. Here's how to reject the change and restore the word to its noncapitalized state:

1. Hover the mouse pointer over the word that AutoCorrect changed. A small blue rectangle appears under the word's first letter.

2. Point to the blue rectangle. The rectangle changes to the AutoCorrect Options button, as shown in Figure 3.16.

3. Click the button's drop-down arrow to open a menu of options.

4. Do one of the following:

    *   Click the Undo option to undo this instance of the change. Word will make the same type of change in the future.

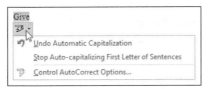

Figure 3.16   *Using the AutoCorrect Options button to reject a change.*

- Click the Stop option to stop Word from making this change again. This creates an *exception* in AutoCorrect, which prevents Word from treating your original action as an error.
- Click Control AutoCorrect Options to open the AutoCorrect dialog box. (We'll explore this dialog box in the next section, "Changing AutoCorrect Settings.")

Word accepts your change, and you can resume typing.

To simply undo an AutoCorrect change without using the options button, press Ctrl+Z to issue the Undo command. However, you must use Undo immediately after the AutoCorrect change appears; otherwise, you'll undo any other action you took since the automatic correction was made.

Changing AutoCorrect Settings

When you open the AutoCorrect dialog box, you see that you can control many of the feature's actions. Study the AutoCorrect options to determine which ones you like and don't like; then turn them on or off accordingly. You can also add and delete specific exceptions to some of AutoCorrect's rules, which is handy if you want to force Word to accept certain spellings or capitalizations.

 LET ME TRY IT

Changing AutoCorrect's Capitalization Settings

By default, AutoCorrect automatically capitalizes words under several different circumstances. If you don't like any of these capitalization settings, here's how to change them:

1. Click the File tab.

2. Click Options to open the Word Options window.

3. Click Proofing to view Word's proofing options.

4. Click the AutoCorrect Options button. The AutoCorrect dialog box opens with the AutoCorrect tab visible, as shown in Figure 3.17.

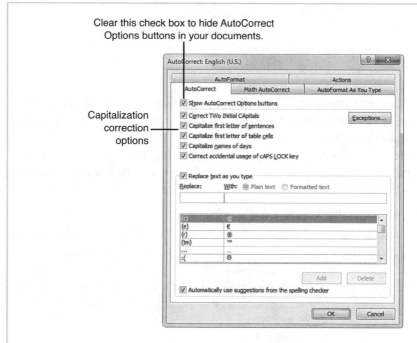

Clear this check box to hide AutoCorrect
Options buttons in your documents.

Capitalization
correction
options

Figure 3.17   *The AutoCorrect dialog box, with the default settings shown.*

5. Clear the Show AutoCorrect Options Buttons check box if you want Word to stop displaying these buttons in your documents.

6. Clear any of the next five check boxes to deactivate a capitalization setting. For example, if you prefer that Word never automatically capitalize the first letter of your sentences, clear the Capitalize First Letter of Sentences check box.

7. Click OK.

 **LET ME TRY IT**

Creating Exceptions to AutoCorrect's Rules

AutoCorrect is flexible about enforcing its rules for capitalization and spelling. In fact, Word has dozens of predefined exceptions to these rules. You can create your own exceptions or delete existing ones. Here's how:

1. Open the AutoCorrect dialog box.

2. Click the Exceptions button to open the AutoCorrect Exceptions dialog box, as shown in Figure 3.18. This dialog box lets you create specific exceptions for Word's automatic capitalization rules. Here's how the dialog box's three tabs work:

    - The First Letter tab lists commonly used abbreviations that end with a period, such as "approx." and "etc." Because you typically would not capitalize a word immediately following one of these abbreviations, Word does not do so automatically.
    - The INitial CAps tab lists abbreviations or words whose first two letters are typically capitalized, such as "IDs." When Word encounters a word or abbreviation included in this list, AutoCorrect does not change the capitalization.
    - The Other Corrections tab provides a blank list where you can create your own exceptions. Typically, you would use this tab to tell Word to accept spellings that it would ordinarily correct. For example, if you want Word to accept the British spelling "behaviour" instead of changing it to the American "behavior," you can add the British spelling to this list.

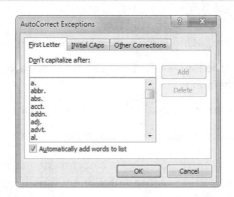

Figure 3.18 *The AutoCorrect Exceptions dialog box.*

3. To add your own abbreviation or word to any of the lists of exceptions, type it in the Don't Capitalize After box or the Don't Correct box; then click Add.

4. To remove an entry from the list, click it, and then click the Delete button.

5. Click OK twice to close both dialog boxes.

Adding and Deleting AutoCorrect Entries

If you frequently misspell a word and Word doesn't automatically correct it for you, your particular misspelling might not be covered by AutoCorrect. If that's the case, you can create a new AutoCorrect entry to correct the misspelling for you. You can also delete existing AutoCorrect entries.

 LET ME TRY IT

Creating a New AutoCorrect Entry

Suppose you often type **diapslay** when you mean to type **display**. Word flags the misspelled word with a wavy red underline but does not correct it automatically. Here's how to create a new AutoCorrect entry for this misspelling:

1. Open the AutoCorrect dialog box, and click the AutoCorrect tab if necessary.

2. Click in the Replace box to place the insertion point there.

3. Type your misspelling (such as **diapslay**).

4. Click in the With box.

5. Type the correct spelling (such as **display**), as shown in Figure 3.19.

6. Make sure that the Replace Text as You Type check box is checked. (It should be, by default.)

7. Click the Add button to add your new entry to the list.

8. Click the OK button to close the dialog box.

To make sure your new entry works, open a document, purposely type the misspelled word, and press the spacebar. AutoCorrect should replace the misspelled word with the correct spelling.

AutoCorrect doesn't make a correction until you "complete" the entry. That is, Word waits for you to press the spacebar, Enter, some other key that causes the insertion point to move to a new word, paragraph, table cell, and so on. At that point, AutoCorrect kicks into gear and makes its change.

 SHOW ME   Media 3.3—Creating an AutoCorrect Entry
Access this video file through your registered Web Edition at
my.safaribooksonline.com/9780132182713/media.

Type the correct spelling here.

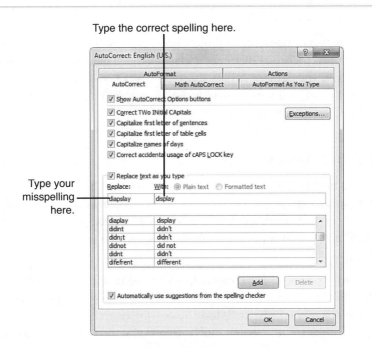

Type your
misspelling
here.

Figure 3.19   *Creating a new AutoCorrect entry to replace a misspelled word.*

 LET ME TRY IT

Deleting an AutoCorrect Entry

If you decide you don't need a specific AutoCorrect entry, you can remove it from
the list of automatic corrections. Word might still flag the text as a misspelling but
should no longer apply the AutoCorrect change. Here's how to delete an entry:

1.   Open the AutoCorrect dialog box, and click the AutoCorrect tab if
     necessary.

2.   Scroll through the list of errors and corrections to find the entry you want
     to delete.

3.   Click the entry to select it.

4.   Click the Delete button.

5.   Click the OK button to close the dialog box.

Disabling AutoCorrect

If you just can't stand dealing with the whole AutoCorrect thing, turn it off. To do this, open the AutoCorrect dialog box, clear all the check boxes on the AutoCorrect tab—especially the Replace Text as You Type check box—then click OK. Word won't replace anything else you type, ever again. To enable AutoCorrect again, just go back and recheck those check boxes.

Using Word's Research Tools

There was a time when most of us kept a few reference books on hand—a dictionary, a thesaurus, maybe even a complete encyclopedia. But if you have Word and an Internet connection, you can look up definitions and synonyms or even do in-depth topical research without ever looking away from your screen. Isn't that a thrilling prospect?

Just as Word's spelling checker can help you make sure all your words are spelled correctly, Word's research tools can take your language to a higher level. These features can help you make better word choices, for example, or write more accurately about your subject. The research tools are available through the Research task pane. (Note that you need an Internet connection for most of the research tools to work because they find their content online.)

Finding Definitions and Synonyms

If you want to be sure you're using a word correctly, you need to know its meaning. Word makes it easy to look up definitions by giving you access to Microsoft's Encarta Dictionary. Similarly, the Research task pane provides links to English-, French-, and Spanish-language thesauruses (or thesauri, if you prefer), where you can find synonyms for nearly any word.

 LET ME TRY IT

Looking Up a Definition

Before you look up a definition, make sure the word is typed completely and spelled correctly. Then take the following steps:

1. Click the word. (You don't have to select the entire word.)
2. Click the Review tab.

3. Click the Research button. The Research task pane opens, as shown in Figure 3.20.

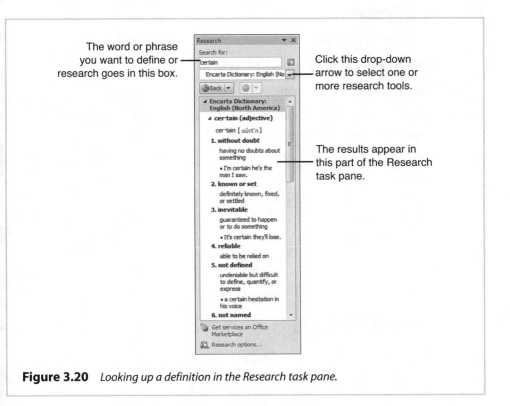

The word or phrase you want to define or research goes in this box.

Click this drop-down arrow to select one or more research tools.

The results appear in this part of the Research task pane.

Figure 3.20   *Looking up a definition in the Research task pane.*

4. Your word should already appear in the Search For box. If not, type it into the box.

5. Click the drop-down arrow at the end of the box below the Search For box. A menu appears and displays a selection of available reference books.

6. Click Encarta Dictionary. The word's definition and other information appear in the task pane.

7. To look up the definition for a different word, select the word currently in the Search For box and type a new word over it; then press Enter.

8. When you finish, click the Close button in the task pane's upper-right corner to close it.

LET ME TRY IT

Finding a Synonym

Here's how to find synonyms for a word using the Research task pane:

1. Click the word. (You don't have to select the entire word.)

2. Open the Research task pane.

3. Your word should already appear in the Search For box, as shown in Figure 3.21. If not, type it into the box.

Figure 3.21   *Looking up synonyms in the Research task pane.*

4. Click the drop-down arrow at the end of the box below the Search For box. A menu appears and displays a selection of available reference books.

5. Click Thesaurus: English (U.S.). One or more synonyms for the word appear in the task pane. Antonyms may appear, as well.

6. To replace the original word with a synonym, point to the synonym; a drop-down arrow appears. Click the drop-down arrow, and then click Insert.

7. To look up synonyms for a different word, select the word currently in the Search For box and type a new word over it; then press Enter.

8. When you are finished, click the Close button in the task pane's upper-right corner to close it.

> A faster way to find synonyms is to right-click a word to open a shortcut menu. On the shortcut menu, point to Synonyms; a list of synonyms pops out. Click a synonym to insert it in place of your original word.

Looking Up Information in the Research Pane

The Research pane gives you access to a few selected online resources. These sources are websites that can look up information on just about any topic imaginable. The general-purpose research sites are Bing, Factiva iWorks™, and HighBeam™ Research. These sites can pull together hundreds of thousands of articles, encyclopedia entries, newspaper reports, and information from many other online sources.

The Research pane also gives you access to business and financial research through MSN Money Stock Quotes and Thomson Gale Company Profiles. Both of these sites are authoritative sources for up-to-the-minute corporate and financial information.

> Don't be surprised if the Research pane overwhelms you with results. A search on the term "stent," for example, yielded 1.2 million results! (Your results may vary.) It can be difficult or impossible to winnow through all these entries in the Research pane, which is relatively small in comparison to a full-screen web browser. If Word gives you more resources than you can reasonably handle, open your web browser and use your favorite search techniques to do your research.

Here's a simple example to introduce you to Word's research tools:

1. Open the Research task pane.

2. Click in the Search For box and type a word, phrase, company name, or other item you want to find information about.

3. In the box below, click the drop-down arrow, and click the name of the research site you want to use. (You can click the All Research Sites option, but this is just about guaranteed to yield more results than you'll want to see.) The results appear in the task pane, as shown in Figure 3.22.

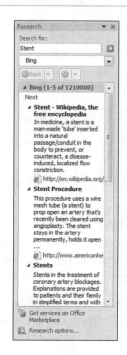

Figure 3.22   *Research results for the term "stent," as provided by Bing.*

4. Scroll through the results. When you find one that looks interesting or relevant, click the hyperlink that appears below it. Word opens your default web browser, which displays the linked web page.

 SHOW ME   Media 3.4—Using Word's Research Pane
Access this video file through your registered Web Edition at
my.safaribooksonline.com/9780132182713/media.

II

Formatting Characters and Paragraphs

4 Character Formatting **90**

5 Paragraph Formatting **111**

6 Formatting Text with Styles **136**

This chapter shows you how to change the appearance of individual characters to enhance your documents' readability and add emphasis to specific words or phrases.

4

Character Formatting

In word processing, the term "formatting" means changing the appearance of some part of a document, whether it's a single character, a paragraph, or a page. You can format individual characters and words to make them bold or italic, for instance, or to apply special effects to them. Character formatting is the most basic type of formatting in Word, but it may be the most important. Consistent formatting makes your documents easier to read and helps you place emphasis on key words or phrases so that they stand apart from the rest of your text.

Word features a small arsenal of character-formatting tools. These tools are easy to use and give you great flexibility in setting the appearance of the individual letters and numbers in a document. Word even has a tool that enables you to copy the formatting of selected text and "paint" it onto other characters, and a feature that automatically formats certain characters as you type them.

Accessing Word's Character-Formatting Tools

Most of the character-formatting tools you need reside in the Font group of the Ribbon's Home tab. Throughout this text, we give preferential treatment to the Ribbon's tools and keyboard shortcuts because you can access them quickly.

But Word offers two other ways to access these tools: The mini toolbar and the Font dialog box.

The Mini Toolbar

The *mini toolbar* is a small palette of formatting tools that pops up whenever you select text or an object in a document. It contains several of the text-formatting tools described in this chapter and a few others. Figure 4.1 shows the mini toolbar.

When you select text in a document, the mini toolbar appears faintly near the selected text. Point to the toolbar to bring it into full view and make its tools available for use. As long as the mouse pointer rests on the toolbar, it remains available.

Figure 4.1 *The mini toolbar appears when you select text.*

To use a tool on the mini toolbar, just click it as you would click the same tool on the Ribbon. To get rid of the mini toolbar without using it, move the mouse pointer away or press Esc.

The Font Dialog Box

The Ribbon and the mini toolbar are handy when you want to make a single formatting change. But if you need to make a bunch of formatting changes at the same time, it may make more sense to use the Font dialog box, as shown in Figure 4.2.

Figure 4.2 *The Font dialog box provides nearly all of Word's character-formatting tools in one place.*

To open the Font dialog box, do one of the following:

- Click the Font dialog box launcher in the lower-right corner of the Font group.

- Press Ctrl+D.

- Right-click any piece of selected text to open a shortcut menu; then click Font.

 SHOW ME   Media 4.1—Character Formatting in Word
Access this video file through your registered Web Edition at
my.safaribooksonline.com/9780132182713/media.

The instructions in this book generally follow the "select-then-act" method of formatting. That is, you select some existing text or an object first and then perform an action on it. We follow this method because people typically create their text before formatting it. However, you can set character formats before typing any text. To do this, place the insertion point where you want to type, make your formatting choices, and then start typing. The new text will appear already formatted, and the formatting will carry to the next paragraph when you press Enter.

Changing the Font, Size, and Color of Text

A *font* is a complete set of typographic characters of the same design. The term "font" means basically the same thing as "typeface." Word has dozens of built-in fonts, some of which are highly professional and some of which are highly goofy. Regardless, you can apply any font to any character in a document. Figure 4.3 shows some examples of commonly used fonts that come with Word 2010.

Selecting a Different Font

When you start a new document from scratch (using the Blank Document template, as described in Chapter 1, "Creating, Saving, and Printing Documents"), Word automatically uses the Calibri font for your text. Calibri is a clean, easy-to-read font that is appropriate for many kinds of documents. It's wise to use this kind of font when creating documents you want to be taken seriously, such as business reports or academic papers.

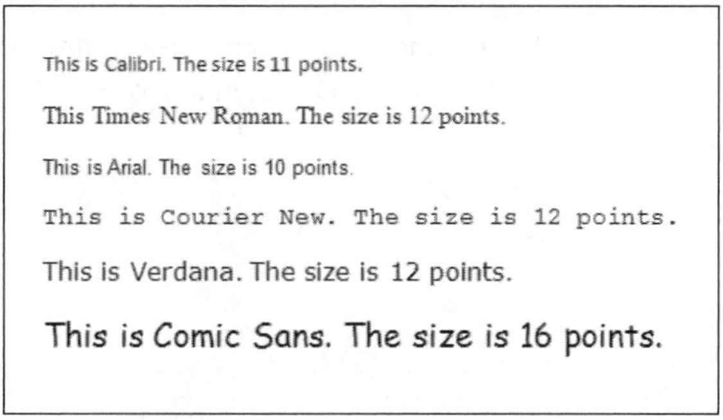

This is Calibri. The size is 11 points.

This Times New Roman. The size is 12 points.

This is Arial. The size is 10 points.

This is Courier New. The size is 12 points.

This is Verdana. The size is 12 points.

This is Comic Sans. The size is 16 points.

Figure 4.3   *A few examples of popular fonts built into Word 2010.*

Word's templates use a variety of fonts to create different moods or effects. Many templates use Times New Roman as their basic font, for example, because it is professional-looking and is easy on the eyes. Times New Roman has been around for a long time, is very widely used, and is known to look good in print. Conversely, more modern fonts such as Verdana are popular because they look good on the screen and give documents a clean, contemporary look.

When choosing fonts for your documents, take a tip from the pros: Think about your readers and their expectations. If you're creating a resume, for example, prospective employers will definitely expect to see consistency and professionalism in your formatting choices. If you're writing a letter to a young relative, a silly font might make it more fun to read.

 **LET ME TRY IT**

Applying a Different Font to Your Text

Even though Word automatically uses a given font, you can apply a different one whenever you like. You can apply a new font to a single character, a word, a paragraph, or a whole document. Here's how:

1.   Select the text that will get the new font. You can select any amount of text.

If you select a blank paragraph, any text you type into that paragraph will be formatted with the new font. This is true for all the character-formatting choices described in this chapter.

2. On the Ribbon, click the Home tab, if necessary.

3. In the Font group, click the Font drop-down arrow. (Alternatively, press Ctrl+Shift+F.) The Font list appears, as shown in Figure 4.4.

Figure 4.4 *Selecting a font from the Font list.*

4. Scroll through the list to find the font you want to use.

5. Point to a font. If Live Preview is enabled, the selected text changes to show how it will look if you choose this font.

6. Click the desired font. The Font list closes and Word applies the new font to the selected text.

7. Deselect the text by clicking anywhere outside it.

Live Preview is a feature that lets you see how text and objects will appear before you actually apply a formatting change. By default, Live Preview is enabled. To disable or re-enable this feature, go to the File tab and click Options. On the General page of the Word Options dialog box, check or clear the Enable Live Preview check box. Click OK.

Although there are thousands of different fonts out there, most text fonts fall into two basic categories: serif and sans serif. A *serif* font has short, decorative lines (called serifs) at the starting and/or ending points of its strokes. A *sans serif* font has no such lines. Times New Roman is an example of a serif font; Calibri is a sans serif font.

Generally, a font from one category is used for headings, whereas a font from the other category is used for body text. Many professional designers suggest using a serif font for headings and a sans serif font for body text, but this is not a hard-and-fast rule. Word's templates use complementary fonts for different parts of a document; this is a good reason to start any document from a template.

Changing Font Size

In word processing, a character's size is measured in points. A *point* equals 1/72 inch, so if a character is 6 points in size, it is 6/72-inch (1/12-inch) tall. This measure actually applies to the printed page—not to text as it appears on your screen. This is because characters' sizes can change drastically when you zoom in or out of a document on the screen.

And speaking of drastic, Word lets you set text sizes that range from really tiny (1 point) to enormous (1638 points). For most documents, such as letters and reports, body text of 8–12 points is usually appropriate and easy to read. The size you choose, however, also depends on the font you are using. For example, 10-point Arial actually looks bigger than 10-point Times New Roman.

 LET ME TRY IT

Applying a Different Font Size

Everything we said in the previous section (about choosing a new font) applies here. That is, you can apply a different font size to any amount of text, and so on.

1. Select the text you want to resize.

2. In the Font group, click the Font Size drop-down arrow. (Alternatively, press Ctrl+Shift+P.) The Font Size list appears, as shown in Figure 4.5.

3. Scroll through the list and point to a size. If Live Preview is enabled, the selected text changes to show how it will look if you choose this font size.

4. Click the desired font size. The Font Size list closes and Word resizes the selected text.

5. Deselect the text by clicking anywhere outside it.

Figure 4.5   *Selecting a font size from the Font Size list.*

The Font Size list shows sizes only in given increments. The increments may range from a single point at the low end to 72 or more points at the high end. If none of the sizes in the list suits you, simply click in the Font Size box to select the current size; then type an exact size in its place. You can enter any value from 1 to 1638. The value can include a half-point, such as 10.5 points.

Instead of using the Font Size list, you can change the text's size incrementally by clicking either the Grow Font or Shrink Font buttons in the Font group. These buttons appear to the right of the Font Size list.

Changing Font Color

You can make text virtually any color you want. Your color choices can make a document as serene as an autumn forest or as vibrant as a hot-air balloon festival. When you pick a font color, Word offers a palette of complementary colors based on the document's current theme. (Themes are covered in detail in Chapter 11, "Formatting Documents with Themes and Templates.") By sticking with thematically related colors, you can be sure that your color choices will match one another and your document will be attractive. But you aren't limited to using only the theme's colors; you can select any of the millions of colors available through the Colors dialog box.

Color selection has been elevated to an art form, and we could spend many pages discussing it. But unless you're a designer, that would be boring and unnecessary. So we'll keep it simple here. Basically, you can use the Font Color palette to apply any of five color options to your text:

- **Automatic:** This is the font color that Word applies automatically to achieve the best contrast between the text and the document's current background. If the background is light, the Automatic color is dark—but not necessarily black. If the document's theme calls for a dark background, the Automatic color will be light.

- **Theme Colors:** This is a set of coordinating colors used by the document's current theme. Each theme includes a palette of coordinating colors. If you select a different theme, these colors change accordingly so that they are always coordinated. You can apply a pure theme color or a lighter or darker shade of it.

- **Standard Colors:** A standard color is fixed; that is, it never changes in the document, even if you apply a different theme.

- **More Colors:** If you choose this option in the Font Color palette, Word displays the Colors dialog box so that you can pick a specific color. These colors are fixed.

- **Gradient:** This is a special effect that "fills" text or an object with different shades of a color that change from darker to lighter as they fill the object. For example, you can choose a gradient that applies a dark blue color at one edge of a paragraph and changes to light blue at the other edge. Gradients are best used with larger fonts, where the effect is most visible.

The Font Color button is located in the Font group of the Home tab, as shown in Figure 4.6. It is also available on the mini toolbar. In the Font dialog box, click the Font color drop-down arrow to open the palette.

If you change a font's color and decide you don't like it, you can always go back to the Automatic color. The Automatic color may be the best choice anyway, unless you really want to make a piece of text "pop."

 LET ME TRY IT

Selecting a Text Color from the Font Color Palette

The easiest way to recolor your text is to pick one of the preset options in the Font Color palette. Here's how:

1. Select the text you want to recolor.

2. In the Font group, click the Font Color drop-down arrow. The Font Color palette appears, as shown in Figure 4.6.

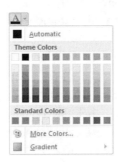

Figure 4.6   *Choosing a color from the Font Color palette.*

3.   Point to a color in the Theme Colors or Standard Colors sections of the palette. If Live Preview is enabled, the selected text changes to show how it will look if you choose this color.

4.   Click the desired color. The Font Color palette closes, and Word recolors the selected text.

5.   Deselect the text by clicking anywhere outside it.

 LET ME TRY IT

Specifying a Font Color in the Colors Dialog Box

If you have a specific color in mind for a piece of text, you can pick it from the Colors dialog box. Here's how:

1.   Select the text you want to recolor.

2.   In the Font group, click the Font Color drop-down arrow.

3.   Click More Colors. The Colors dialog box opens with the Standard tab visible, as shown in Figure 4.7.

4.   On the Standard tab, click any color in the large group of colored hexagons or the small group of grayscale hexagons. You can preview your selection in the New/Current pane in the lower-right corner of the dialog box, so you can compare it to the font's current color.

5.   If you like your color selection, click OK to apply it to your text. If not, go to step 6.

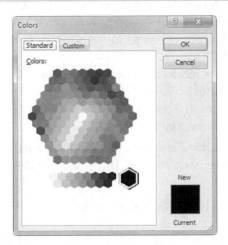

Figure 4.7   *The Standard tab of the Colors dialog box.*

6. Click the Custom tab. As shown in Figure 4.8, this tab enables you to spec-
    ify an exact color.

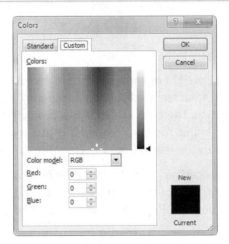

Figure 4.8   *The Custom tab of the Colors dialog box.*

7. Do one of the following:
    *   Click in an area of the Colors palette. A group of related colors appears in
        the vertical bar to the right of the palette. Click a color on the bar to pre-
        view it in the New/Current pane.

- Click the Color model drop-down arrow; then click RGB. Use the counter tools to set specific values for the level of red, green, and blue in the color you want. The color changes in the New/Current pane as you change the individual RGB values.
- Click the Color model drop-down arrow; then click HSL. Use the counter tools to set specific values for the hue, saturation, and luminosity of the color you want. The color changes in the New/Current pane as you change the individual HSL values.

8. When you are satisfied with the color you have selected by using one of the preceding methods, click OK. The dialog box closes and Word recolors the selected text.

9. Deselect the text by clicking anywhere outside it.

Not all printers can produce the variety of colors available in the Custom tab of the Colors dialog box. For this reason, it's a good idea to test-print your document before distributing it to others. Test-print the document on the actual printer you intend to use, on the same type of paper you plan to use for the final document. Test-printing might reveal that your printed results don't match what you see on the screen. If this happens, try using only standard colors.

Applying Font Styles

A *font style* changes the weight or angle of text. For example, the **bold** (or bold-face) font style makes characters thicker and heavier-looking, so they jump out from the surrounding text. The *italic* font style tilts characters slightly to the right, so they appear to be leaning. You can combine the two styles to create ***bold-italic*** text, which really catches the reader's attention as long as it isn't used too often.

Technically speaking, underlining is not a font style because it doesn't change the actual thickness or angularity of characters. When you underline text, you simply put one or more lines under it. Regardless, we'll group underlining with bold and italic for simplicity's sake.

Here's how to quickly apply these font styles:

1. Select the text to be styled.

2. Do one of the following:

   - To make the text bold, click the **Bold** button or press Ctrl+B.
   - To make the text italic, click the *Italic* button or press Ctrl+I.

- To underline the text, click the <u>Underline</u> button or press Ctrl+U.

You can combine any or all these styles.

The Bold, Italic, and Underline buttons all work as toggles, meaning they turn the style on and off. To remove any of these font styles, select the text and click the Bold, Italic, or Underline button.

The Bold, Italic, and Underline buttons are located in the Font group of the Home tab, as shown in Figure 4.9. They are also available on the mini toolbar. In the Font dialog box, you can select any of these styles from the Font style list.

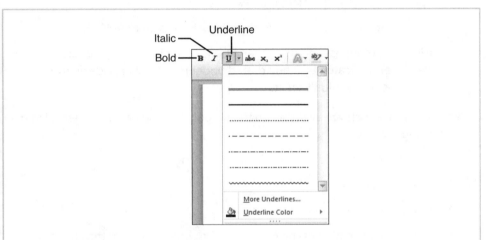

Figure 4.9   *Font style buttons in the Font group. The Underline button's drop-down list is expanded to show different underlining styles.*

By default, underlining places a single, thin line below the text. However, Word offers several underlining styles, including double underlines, dotted and dashed underlines, and others. To pick one of the different styles, click the drop-down arrow next to the Underline button; then click the desired style.

Applying Font Effects

Font effects are text styles with specific purposes. Word provides seven simple font effects, which are used as follows:

- Strikethrough is usually used to indicate text that should or will be deleted from the document. Here is an ~~example~~.

- Double strikethrough typically has the same use as strikethrough, but may be used for greater emphasis or to indicate that more than one person has suggested passages for deletion. Here is an ~~example~~.

- Superscript makes text small and raises it to the same height as the current font's ascenders. Here is an ^{example}.

- Subscript makes text small and lowers it to the same level as the current font's descenders. Here is an $_{example}$.

- Small caps are often used for headings or emphasis. When small caps are used, uppercase letters appear as full-size capitals but lowercase letters appear a little smaller. Here is an EXAMPLE.

- All caps are most often used for headings. Here is an EXAMPLE.

- Hidden text appears on the screen but does not print. On your screen, hidden text is indicated by a fine dotted underline. (We'd provide an example here, but you wouldn't see it.)

A few of these effects are available on the Ribbon, but you can find them all in the Font dialog box.

To apply one or more font effects, take the following steps:

1. Select some text.

2. Open the Font dialog box.

3. In the Effects section of the Font tab, check one or more of the check boxes, as shown in Figure 4.10.

4. Click OK to close the dialog box.

You can combine some of the font effects, but the following effects cannot be applied to the same text:

- Strikethrough and double strikethrough

- Superscript and subscript

- Small caps and all caps

Figure 4.10 *Selecting font effects in the Font dialog box.*

Adjusting Character Spacing

One way to fine-tune your text for better readability is to change the amount of space between characters. In some cases, you may want Word to insert more space between characters; in other cases, less space may be more appropriate.

By default, Word uses normal character spacing, meaning that the same amount of space is inserted between all characters of the same font family. Character spacing is based on the font, its size, and other attributes. For this reason, it's wise to adjust spacing only for characters of the same font and size; the spacing may not look the same when applied to characters of a different font or size.

 **LET ME TRY IT**

Changing the Spacing Between Text Characters

If you're tinkering with character spacing for the first time, it's best to experiment before settling on a given setting. To get the most accurate on-screen view of your spacing, hide nonprinting characters and set your zoom level to 100%. Be sure to print your document to see how the new spacing looks on paper.

1. Select the text whose spacing you want to change.

2. Open the Font dialog box.

3. Click the Advanced tab. The character spacing options appear at the top of this tab, as shown in Figure 4.11.

Figure 4.11 *Setting character spacing options.*

4. Click the Spacing drop-down arrow; then click one of the following options:

   - **Normal:** This is the default setting. Word does not expand or condense the character spacing when this setting is active.
   - **Expanded:** This setting increases the amount of space between characters. You will set the exact amount of space in the next step.
   - **Condensed:** This setting reduces the amount of space between characters. You will set the exact amount of space in the next step.

5. If you chose either Expanded or Condensed in the previous step, use the By spinner tool to set the precise amount of spacing. By default, Word expands or condenses character spacing by 1 point. Clicking the arrows increases or decreases the spacing in 1/10-point increments.

6. Click OK.

In addition to setting character spacing, you can turn on Word's kerning feature in the Font dialog box' Advanced tab. *Kerning* tightens up the spacing between adjacent characters based on their shapes. For example, kerning may squeeze the letters Aw closer together because their shapes allow for this without bumping into one another. Kerning works best with larger fonts, so if you turn on kerning, set it to affect fonts of 10 points or larger. When used with small fonts, kerning can cause some letters to look jumbled together.

Changing Text Case

The easiest way to set the case of one or more characters is by using the Shift or Caps Lock keys as you type. Sometimes, however, you may need to capitalize the first letter of every word in a sentence, or even all the characters in a sentence. This is often the case when creating headings.

Word's Change Case tool offers five options for setting the case of selected text, as shown in Figure 4.12:

- **Sentence case:** Word capitalizes only the first character of the selected text.

- **lowercase:** Word changes all selected text to lowercase letters.

- **UPPERCASE:** Word changes all selected text to uppercase letters.

- **Capitalize Each Word:** Word capitalizes the first letter of each selected word.

- **tOGGLE cASE:** Word switches the case of each selected character.

To change the case of existing text, select it, click the Change Case tool's drop-down arrow, and then select the appropriate option from the list. Unlike most character-formatting tools, the Change Case tool does not have any effect on text before it is typed; you must select existing text before using the tool to change its case.

Figure 4.12   *The Change Case tool's options.*

Highlighting Text

Word's Text Highlight Color tool works just like an old-fashioned highlighting pen—but without the odor. The tool lets you highlight text by placing a colored background behind it, the same way you can highlight text on paper by dragging a highlighting pen across it.

Here's how to highlight text:

1. Select the text you want to highlight.

2. In the Font group, click the Text Highlight Color button's drop-down arrow. A palette of colors appears, as shown in Figure 4.13.

Figure 4.13 *Selecting a text highlighting color.*

3. Click a color. (The default color is yellow.) Word highlights the selected text with that color.

You can also turn the mouse pointer into a highlighter, so you can highlight text as you read without using the Text Highlight Color tool over and over. To activate highlighting, click the Text Highlight Color tool without selecting any text first. The mouse pointer changes shape to look like a highlighting pen. While the pointer has this shape, you can highlight any text just by dragging over it. To turn off highlighting, press Esc.

To remove the background color from highlighted text, select the text, click the Text Highlight Color tool's drop-down arrow, and then click No Color.

Copying Character Formatting with the Format Painter

Suppose you want to apply the same formatting to all the headings in your document. Luckily, you don't have to format each heading individually. Simply format the first heading so it looks exactly the way you want; then copy the formatting to other headings by using Word's Format Painter. The Format Painter can copy formatting from a single character, a word, or a paragraph.

Here's how to use the Format Painter:

1. Format the initial piece of text the way you want it; then select that text.

2. In the Clipboard group of the Home tab, click the Format Painter button. (Alternatively, press Ctrl+Shift+C.) The mouse pointer changes to display a small paintbrush, as shown in Figure 4.14.

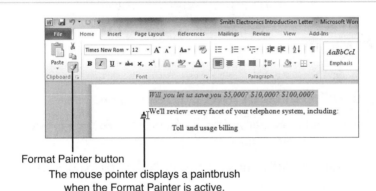

Format Painter button

The mouse pointer displays a paintbrush when the Format Painter is active.

Figure 4.14 *Using the Format Painter.*

3. Drag across another piece of text to "paint" the copied formatting onto it. When you release the mouse button, Word stops painting.

To paint formatting onto multiple pieces of nonadjacent text, double-click the Format Painter button. Double-clicking leaves the tool active indefinitely; Word will continue painting the copied formatting over every piece of text you select. To deactivate painting, click the Format Painter button again or press Esc.

SHOW ME   Media 4.2—Using Word's Format Painter

Access this video file through your registered Web Edition at
my.safaribooksonline.com/9780132182713/media.

Setting AutoFormat as You Type Options

After you spend a little time creating documents in Word, you'll notice that it does a few things seemingly on its own. For example, if you type two hyphens in the middle of sentence, Word changes them to a long dash—called an *em dash* in typographic terms. Or when you surround a sentence with quotation marks, Word automatically makes them "smart," or curly.

This automatic formatting is controlled by a feature called (oddly enough) AutoFormat as You Type. It works by replacing some of the plain characters that you type with specially formatted ones. Word can automatically make 14 such formatting changes, and, by default, all but two of them are enabled.

 **LET ME TRY IT**

Configuring AutoFormat as You Type

You can enable and disable any of Word's AutoFormat As You Type options to best suit your preferences. Here's how:

1. On the File tab, click Options. The Word Options dialog box opens.

2. Click Proofing.

3. Click the AutoCorrect Options button. The AutoCorrect Options dialog box appears.

4. Click the AutoFormat As You Type tab, as shown in Figure 4.15.

5. Enable or disable any option by checking or clearing its check box.

6. Click OK twice.

Even if you find the AutoFormat feature annoying, think twice before disabling any of its options. AutoFormat makes short work of tasks such as setting up fractions and superscripting the letters that follow an ordinal number (such as changing 1st to 1st). It also takes care of little chores that you can easily forget to do while you're busy writing (such as inserting real em dashes).

 SHOW ME   Media 4.3—Setting AutoFormat as You Type Options in Word

Access this video file through your registered Web Edition at
my.safaribooksonline.com/9780132182713/media.

Figure 4.15 *Setting AutoFormat as You Type options.*

Clearing Character Formats

You can spend a lot of time formatting text, only to dislike the results. When this happens, you can easily start over again by clearing the formatting from the text. To remove formatting, just select some formatted text and do one of the following:

- Click the Clear Formatting button, as shown in Figure 4.16.

- Press Ctrl+Spacebar.

Word strips all formatting from the text, except for highlighting. Highlighting must be turned off separately, as described earlier in this chapter.

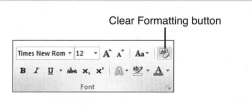

Figure 4.16 *The Clear Formatting button.*

TELL ME MORE   Media 4.4—Formatting: Is More Always Better?

Access this audio recording through your registered Web Edition at
my.safaribooksonline.com/9780132182713/media.

Paragraphs are the true building blocks of any document. Clean, consistent paragraph formatting ultimately determines your document's readability.

5

Paragraph Formatting

As you learned in Chapter 2, "Editing Documents," (unless you haven't read that chapter yet, which is fine), a *paragraph* is any amount of text followed by a paragraph return. A *paragraph return* (also called a *hard return* or a *paragraph mark*) is a special character that looks like this: ¶

Paragraphs are the real building blocks of any document; if you don't divide your text into paragraphs, it will just be a bunch of lines. By organizing your text into paragraphs, you make your message more sensible and easier to navigate. Just like well-written paragraphs, well-designed paragraphs encourage readers to take your documents seriously.

This chapter introduces Word's formatting tools for paragraphs. You learn how to align, indent, and space paragraphs, and how to add decorative touches such as borders and shading. We also show you how to change paragraph formats by using the Find and Replace tool.

Understanding Paragraphs

Despite the definition we gave earlier, a paragraph is really more than a bunch of text followed by a character that looks like a backward P. That paragraph return, you see, not only marks the end of the paragraph, but stores all the information about the paragraph's formatting. This is important because the majority of document formatting is done at the paragraph level, although you can still format individual characters, entire pages, and everything in between.

The easiest way to format paragraphs is by using Word's *styles*; these are preset formats that you can apply to a selected character or a paragraph with just a mouse click. Chapter 6, "Formatting Text with Styles," covers styles in detail. Here, however, we focus on manually formatting paragraphs. When you understand manual formatting, you can create and modify styles with ease.

So, remember: When you format an entire paragraph in any way, the formatting is stored with the paragraph return. If the insertion point is anywhere in that paragraph and you press Enter to create a new paragraph, Word automatically applies the current paragraph's formatting to the new one, as shown in Figure 5.1. This enables you to create text that is consistent in appearance from one paragraph to the next.

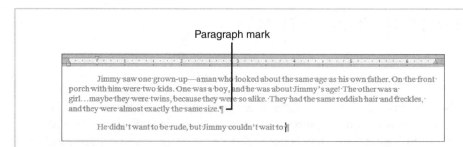

Paragraph mark

Figure 5.1   *When you press Enter, the current paragraph's formatting carries over to the new one.*

This "formatting-carries-to-the-next-paragraph" rule doesn't always apply when you use styles, as you will see in Chapter 6. A style can be defined so that, when you press Enter, the new paragraph takes a different style. For example, you can set up a heading style so that when you press Enter, the new paragraph is styled as body text. But we'll get to those details later.

If you include the paragraph return when you cut or copy a paragraph, the paragraph retains its formatting when you paste it somewhere else. If you want to paste a paragraph without its formatting, select only its text (and not its paragraph return) before cutting or copying it.

When working with entire paragraphs, it's easier to keep track of the hard returns' locations when nonprinting characters are visible, as shown in Figure 5.1. If you can't see these characters on your screen, click the Show/Hide ¶ button (located in the Paragraph group of the Home tab).

Accessing Word's Paragraph-Formatting Tools

Most of the paragraph-formatting tools you need reside in the Paragraph group of the Ribbon's Home tab. We give preferential treatment to the Ribbon's tools and keyboard shortcuts because you can access them quickly, but you can find nearly all Word's paragraph-formatting tools in the Paragraph dialog box, as shown in Figure 5.2.

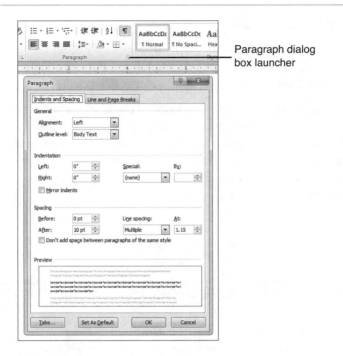

Paragraph dialog
box launcher

Figure 5.2   *The Paragraph dialog box provides nearly all of Word's paragraph-formatting tools in one place.*

To open the Paragraph dialog box, do one of the following:

- Click the Paragraph dialog box launcher in the lower-right corner of the Paragraph group, on either the Home tab or the Page Layout tab.

- Right-click anywhere in a document to open a shortcut menu; then click Paragraph.

Paragraph-formatting tools are actually sprinkled throughout Word. For example, you'll find such tools on the Page Layout tab, the Styles dialog box, and elsewhere. As we introduce different tools, we'll point out their locations.

To format a single paragraph, click anywhere in the paragraph and then make your formatting choices. To format multiple paragraphs, select them all before applying the formats.

Aligning Paragraphs

Alignment refers to the way a paragraph is positioned horizontally in a given space. This is usually the space between a page's margins but can also be the space within a table's cell, text box, or in any other object that can hold text.

To align a paragraph, click it; then click one of the four alignment buttons in the Paragraph group. You can horizontally align a paragraph in one of four ways, as shown in Figure 5.3. The figure also shows Word's rulers, which appear across the top of the document window and along its left side in Print Layout view. The horizontal ruler shows the locations of the document's right and left margins, tabs, and some other alignment settings.

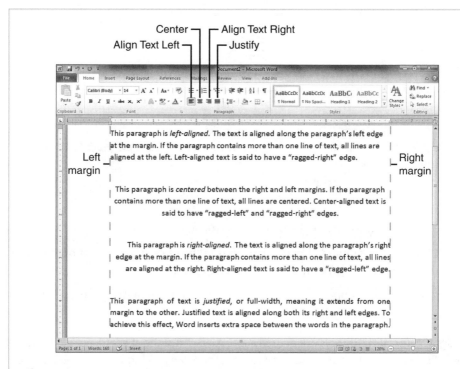

Figure 5.3   *Four different paragraph alignments and the Alignment tools.*

Word's rulers are valuable formatting aids because they show the location of text and objects in relation to the page's printed size. By default, Word assumes your documents will be printed on standard 8.5"-by-11" paper. The rulers show the page's dimensions, in one-eighth-inch increments, starting from the top and left margins. The white portions of the ruler indicate the space between the margins; the gray portions indicate the space outside the margins.

By default, the rulers aren't visible on your screen. To turn them on, click the View tab; then select the Ruler check box. When you work in Print Layout view, both rulers are visible. Only the horizontal ruler is visible in Web Layout view and Draft view; neither ruler is visible in Full Screen Reading view and Outline view.

Table 5.1 describes each type of paragraph alignment and shows you which tool to use to get that alignment.

Table 5.1   Paragraph Alignments

Alignment	Description	Button	Keyboard Shortcut
Left	Aligns the paragraph flush along the text's left edge.		Ctrl+L
Center	Aligns the paragraph along an imaginary center line between the text's right and left edges.		Ctrl+E
Right	Aligns the paragraph flush along the text's right edge.		Ctrl+R
Justified	Extends the paragraph all the way from the left margin to the right margin. Word inserts extra spaces as needed to extend each line of a justified paragraph.		Ctrl+J

You can also use the Paragraph dialog box to align a paragraph. To do this, open the Paragraph dialog box, click the Alignment drop-down arrow, click the desired alignment option, and then click OK.

SHOW ME   Media 5.1—Aligning Paragraphs in Word
*Access this video file through your registered Web Edition at **my.safaribooksonline.com/ 9780132182713/media**.*

ndenting Paragraphs

When you *indent* a paragraph, you insert blank space between it and a margin. For example, you can indent the entire left edge of a paragraph by one-half inch. Either or both edges of a paragraph can be indented. You can also indent only the first line of a paragraph to create a formal appearance.

A special type of indentation, called a *hanging indent*, indents all but the first line of a paragraph. Hanging indents are used with bulleted and numbered lists, but you can use a hanging indent without an introductory character.

A paragraph (or its first line) can also be "outdented," meaning that it extends past the right or left margin. Outdenting is often used to stylize headings in a document but is not generally used with body text.

Figure 5.4 shows several examples of indented paragraphs. In the figure, look at the ruler to see where the document's right and left margins are.

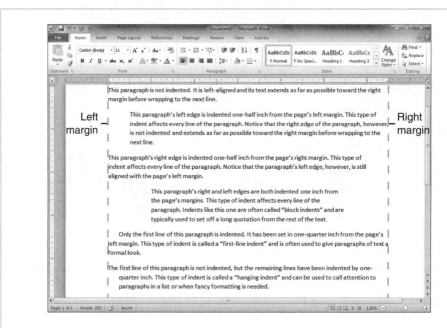

Figure 5.4 *Paragraph indents.*

The following sections describe some of the ways you can create indents.

 **LET ME TRY IT**

Indenting from the Ribbon

The Paragraph group includes two buttons that let you quickly set the left indent of an entire paragraph (see Figure 5.5):

- Click the Increase Indent button to increase the current paragraph's indentation from the left margin.

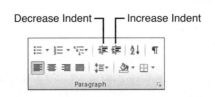

Figure 5.5 *The Increase and Decrease Indent buttons.*

- Click the Decrease Indent button to reduce the current paragraph's indentation from the left margin. (This button will not "outdent" the paragraph past the left margin.)

Both buttons change the paragraph's indentation in one-half-inch increments.

The Increase Indent and Decrease Indent buttons change only the paragraph's indentation from the left margin. To change the indentation on the right side, use one of the methods described in the following sections.

 LET ME TRY IT

Setting Indents on the Ruler

Word's horizontal ruler displays four *indent markers*, as shown in Figure 5.6. You can set the indents for any paragraph by dragging one or more of the markers to different positions on the ruler. Table 5.2 tells you how to use each of these markers.

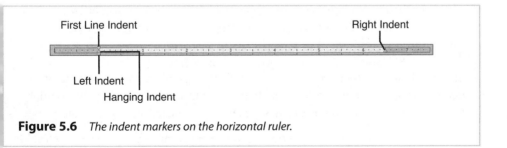

Figure 5.6 *The indent markers on the horizontal ruler.*

Table 5.2   Using Paragraph Indent Markers

Marker	Name	Description
	First Line Indent	Drag this marker to indent the paragraph's first line in relation to the left margin.
	Hanging Indent	Drag this marker to indent all lines except the first line in relation to the left margin.
	Left Indent	Drag this marker to indent the entire paragraph in relation to the left margin. When you move this marker, the first-line and hanging indent markers move with it.
	Right Indent	Drag this marker to indent the entire paragraph in relation to the right margin.

You can drag any of the indent markers outside the margins to create an "outdent."

 LET ME TRY IT

Specifying Indents in the Paragraph Dialog Box

The Paragraph dialog box enables you to set specific values for every indent, with greater precision than is possible with the tools on the ruler or ribbon. Here's how:

1. Select one or more paragraphs; then open the Paragraph dialog box.

2. Do one of the following:
   - To set a left or right indent for an entire paragraph, use either the Left or Right spinner control to set a value. Click the up button to increase the indent's width; click the down button to decrease it.
   - To indent the paragraph's first line, click the Special drop-down arrow (as shown in Figure 5.7); then click First line. Use the By spinner control to set a value for the indent.
   - To create a hanging indent, click the Special drop-down arrow; then click Hanging. Use the By spinner control to set a value for the indent.

3. Click OK.

In the Indentation section of the dialog box, the spinner buttons increase or decrease the indent in one-tenth-inch increments. Instead of using the spinner buttons, you can click in any of the spinner control boxes and type a value.

Right and left indent values can be negative. For example, you can specify a value of **-0.5"** to extend a paragraph one-half inch beyond the right or left margin. (This is the previously mentioned "outdent.") However, you cannot specify a negative value for a first-line or hanging indent in the Paragraph dialog box; instead, drag

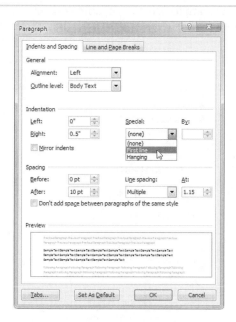

Figure 5.7   *Setting an indent in the Paragraph dialog box.*

either the First Line Indent or Hanging Indent marker on the horizontal ruler, as described in the preceding section.

Left and Right indent controls, like those found in the Paragraph dialog box, are also located in the Paragraph group of the Page Layout tab.

SHOW ME   Media 5.2—Indenting Paragraphs in Word
Access this video file through your registered Web Edition at
my.safaribooksonline.com/9780132182713/media.

Setting Tab Stops

A *tab stop* is a special character that tells Word where to place the insertion point when you press the Tab key. Word moves the insertion point to that position and backfills the void with white space—the tab itself—as shown in Figure 5.8. Tabs and tab stops are another holdover from the days of typewriters, and are most often used to vertically align text and numbers into tables or columns. (Of course, it's easier and more accurate to use Word's table and column tools for this purpose, but tabs are fine for short lists where accurate positioning isn't a big deal.)

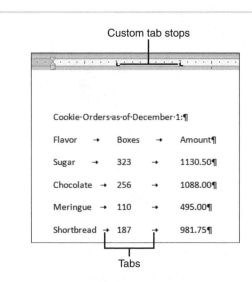

Custom tab stops

Cookie·Orders·as·of·December·1:¶

Flavor	→	Boxes	→	Amount¶
Sugar	→	323	→	1130.50¶
Chocolate	→	256	→	1088.00¶
Meringue	→	110	→	495.00¶
Shortbread	→	187	→	981.75¶

Tabs

Figure 5.8   *Tabs and two custom tab stops in a document, with nonprinting characters displayed.*

Custom tab stops (tab stops you create) appear on the horizontal ruler, as shown in Figure 5.8. When nonprinting characters are visible on your screen, tabs appear as right-pointing arrows in your document.

By default, Word automatically places a tab stop at every half-inch mark on the horizontal ruler. These default tab stops don't appear on the ruler, but they're always there unless you override them by setting custom tab stops. When you create a custom tab stop, Word ignores any default tab stops to the left of it. By creating custom tab stops, you avoid the need to insert multiple tabs to get to the desired point in a line. Figure 5.8 shows two custom tab stops. Figure 5.9 shows the same list using the default tab stops; more tabs are needed to create the same spacing when the default stops are used because they are separated by only one-half inch of space.

You can align text with four kinds of tab stops; text aligns on each type of stop in a different way. The fifth type lets you insert vertical bars between columns of text that are aligned with tabs. As Table 5.3 shows, each type of tab stop is identified by a unique indicator, which appears on the ruler. Figure 5.10 shows several paragraphs of text aligned with all five types of tab stops.

There are two ways to set tab stops: on the horizontal ruler (the easy way) and through the Tabs dialog box (the less-than-easy way).

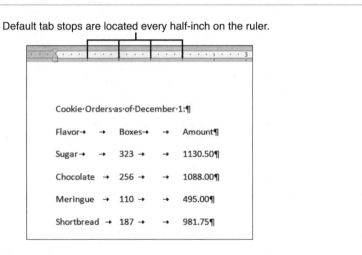

Default tab stops are located every half-inch on the ruler.

Figure 5.9   *The same list, using default tab stops.*

Table 5.3   Tab Stops

Indicator	Name	Description
L	Left	Text is left-aligned from this stop, extending to the right from the stop's position.
⊥	Center	Text is center-aligned on this stop, extending equally to the right and left from the stop's position.
⅃	Right	Text is right-aligned from this stop, extending to the left from the stop's position.
⊥	Decimal	This stop is used to align numeric data that includes decimal points. Text is vertically aligned on the decimal points at the stop's position.
│	Bar	This type of stop places a vertical bar at the stop's position and is used to create a separator between columns of tabbed information.

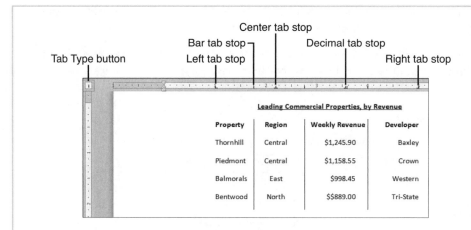

Figure 5.10   *A list aligned with all five types of tab stops.*

 LET ME TRY IT

Setting Tab Stops on the Ruler

You can use the ruler to set tab stops with just a few clicks. You start by choosing the type of tab you want and then adding it to the ruler. Here's how:

1. Select one or more paragraphs.

2. Click the Tab Type button (at the far left end of the horizontal ruler) one or more times, until it displays the type of tab stop you want to create.

3. Click anywhere on the ruler to place the selected tab type at that position.

4. Click somewhere else on the ruler to place another tab of the same type in a different position. As long as the desired type of tab appears on the Tab Type button, you can continue adding that type of tab to the ruler.

Repeat steps 2–4 until all the desired tab stops have been added to the paragraph.

The Tab Type button displays all five types of tabs shown in Table 5.3 but also displays the First Line Indent and Left Indent markers so that you can set them on the ruler. Ignore those markers when setting tabs.

You can adjust a tab stop's position by dragging it to the right or left on the ruler.

To remove a tab stop, click it, and then drag it off the ruler.

LET ME TRY IT

Setting Tab Stops in the Tabs Dialog Box

Setting tab stops on the ruler is easy because it's visual, and that's fine if you can get by with eyeballing your tab stops' locations. But if you need precision—for example, if your first tab stop *must be* 1.43" from the left margin—then the Tabs dialog box is the place to go.

To open the Tabs dialog box, open the Paragraph dialog box; then click the Tabs button. The Tabs dialog box appears, as shown in Figure 5.11. If the selected paragraph already has one or more tab stops, the dialog box lists their positions.

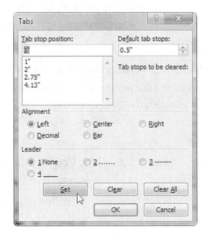

Figure 5.11   *Setting tab stops in the Tabs dialog box.*

To create a new tab stop, do the following:

1. Click in the Tab stop position box and type the new tab's location in inches from the left margin. For example, to place the new stop at the 6" mark on the ruler, type **6"** in the Tab stop position box.

2. In the Alignment section, select the type of tab you want to create.

3. Click Set.

4. Repeat steps 1–3 for each new tab stop you want to create; then click OK.

You can add leader lines to your tabs, if you like. A leader line is a series of dots or dashes that appears in the blank space where a tab is located. Leader lines are typically used in lists such as tables of contents or indexes but not in many other situations. Leader lines can make a long list or table look cluttered, so be careful not to overuse them.

You can also use the Tabs dialog box to edit the tab settings of the selected paragraph(s). Here's how:

- To clear a tab stop, click it in the Tab Stop Position list; then click Clear. Repeat this procedure for each stop you want to remove, and then click OK to close the dialog box.

- To clear all tab stops, click Clear All, and then click OK.

- To change an existing tab stop's type, click it in the Tab Stop Position list, select a new type in the Alignment section, and then click Set. Repeat this procedure for each stop you want to change; then click OK.

SHOW ME Media 5.3—Using Word's Ruler to Set Tab Stops
Access this video file through your registered Web Edition at
my.safaribooksonline.com/9780132182713/media.

TELL ME MORE Media 5.4—Tabs Versus Spaces in Word Processing
Access this audio recording through your registered Web Edition at
my.safaribooksonline.com/9780132182713/media.

Setting Line and Paragraph Spacing

Line spacing refers to the amount of space between lines within a paragraph. *Paragraph spacing* refers to the amount of space between paragraphs in a document. Line and paragraph spacing is measured in points, the same way fonts are measured. You can set different line and paragraph spacing wherever you want, but it's wise to keep spacing consistent throughout your document.

Changing Line Spacing within a Paragraph

You can set line spacing by specifying an amount of space in points or by choosing a multiplier. Either way, the space is based on points. For example, if you're using a 12-point font, single-spaced text has 12 points of space between the lines. If you want to double-space the lines, you can specify a setting of 24 points or a multiplier of 2.

The quickest way to set line spacing is by using the Line and Paragraph Spacing tool on the ribbon, but you can also use the Paragraph dialog box.

 LET ME TRY IT

Using the Line and Paragraph Spacing Tool

The Line and Paragraph Spacing tool lets you set line spacing by picking a multiplier. Here's how.

1. Select one or more paragraphs of text.

2. In the Paragraph group, click the Line and Paragraph Spacing tool's drop-down arrow. A list of preset multipliers appears, as shown in Figure 5.12.

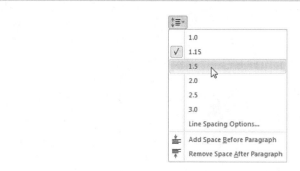

Figure 5.12   *Setting line spacing with the Line and Paragraph Spacing tool.*

3. Click a multiplier. The list closes and Word resets the line spacing in the selected paragraphs.

By default, line spacing is set at a multiplier of 1.15 for documents created with the Normal (blank document) template. So, if you start a document from scratch and use a 12-point font, your line spacing will automatically be set at 13.8 points.

 **LET ME TRY IT**

Setting Line Spacing in the Paragraph Dialog Box

The Paragraph dialog box lets you use a multiplier to set line spacing but also lets you set spacing at a specific point value.

1. Select one or more paragraphs of text.

2. Open the Paragraph dialog box.

3. Click the Line spacing drop-down arrow, as shown in Figure 5.13. A list appears and displays the following six options:

   - **Single:** Lines will be single-spaced. This is the same as choosing 1 from the Line and Paragraph Spacing drop-down list.
   - **1.5 lines:** This option inserts an extra one-half line of blank space between lines. If you're using 12-point type, for example, this option gives you a line spacing of 18 points.

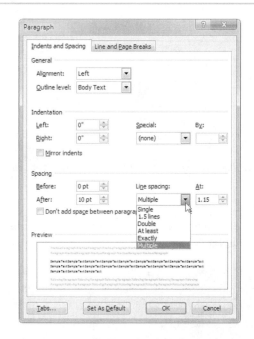

Figure 5.13   *Setting line spacing in the Paragraph dialog box.*

- **Double:** Lines will be double-spaced, with twice as much space between lines than single-spacing. This is the same as choosing 2 from the Line and Paragraph Spacing drop-down list.
- **At least:** This option lets you set a minimum amount of space to go between lines. If you select this option, use the At spinner control to specify the minimum line spacing, in points.
- **Exactly:** This option enables you to set an exact amount of spacing to go between lines. Use the At spinner control to specify the amount of spacing, in points.
- **Multiple:** This option enables you to specify any multiple of single spacing. If you want to quadruple-space the lines in a paragraph, for example, choose this option and set the At spinner control to 4.

4. Click OK.

Changing Paragraph Spacing

Paragraph spacing works just like line spacing, only simpler because you don't have to deal with multipliers or do any math in your head. You can set paragraph spacing by using the Line and Paragraph Spacing tool, or by using the Paragraph dialog box.

 LET ME TRY IT

Setting Paragraph Spacing with the Line and Paragraph Spacing Tool

The Line and Paragraph Spacing tool gives you only two choices for changing paragraph spacing.

1. Select one or more paragraphs of text.

2. In Paragraph group, click the Line and Paragraph Spacing tool's drop-down arrow.

3. Do one of the following:

- Click Add Space Before Paragraph to insert 12 points of blank space above the selected paragraph.
- Click Remove Space After Paragraph to remove 12 points of blank space below the selected paragraph.

LET ME TRY IT

Setting Paragraph Spacing in the Paragraph Dialog Box

The Paragraph dialog box lets you use a multiplier to set line spacing but also lets you set spacing at a specific point value.

1. Select one or more paragraphs of text.

2. Open the Paragraph dialog box.

3. Use the Before and/or After spinner controls to set the amount of spacing around the paragraph, in points.

4. To avoid adding extra space around adjacent paragraphs that use the same style, select the Don't Add Space Between Paragraphs of the Same Style check box. This option is helpful if you select multiple paragraphs that are formatted with different styles, but some of the adjacent paragraphs have the same style. This option leaves the style-based spacing between those paragraphs unchanged. (Styles are discussed to the point of pain in Chapter 6.)

5. Click OK.

Before and After spacing controls, like those found in the Paragraph dialog box, are also located in the Paragraph group of the Page Layout tab.

Remember that paragraph spacing adds up. If you put 12 points of spacing before your paragraphs and 12 points of spacing after, that gives you 24 points of blank space between paragraphs. For this reason, it may be a good idea only to insert spacing before or after paragraphs (but not both) if you are setting the spacing yourself.

Adding Borders and Shading to a Paragraph

Decorative elements can make a paragraph stand out from the rest of a document. If you're creating a newsletter, for example, you might put a border around a short article or a list of events, and even place some shading behind it. Figure 5.14 shows an example of this kind of formatting. Used judiciously, borders and shading can add shape to a document and give it greater eye appeal. Decorative touches can also guide the reader to an important element of a document.

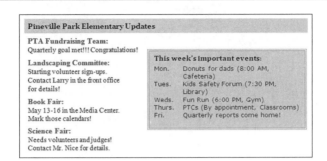

Figure 5.14   *Borders and shading can draw the eye to key parts of a document.*

Placing a Border Around a Paragraph

The easiest way to surround a paragraph with a simple border is to use the Border tool. To create more elaborate borders, use the Borders and Shading dialog box.

 LET ME TRY IT

Using the Border Tool

The Border tool, which is located in the Paragraph group, enables you to apply a basic straight-line border to any or all sides of a paragraph.

1. Select one or more paragraphs of text.

2. Click the Border tool's drop-down arrow. A list of border options appears, as shown in Figure 5.15.

3. Click any of the available options to place a thin border along any side of the paragraph or to surround the paragraph completely. As long as the paragraph is selected, you can re-open the list and select different options until you get the look you want.

4. Deselect the paragraph by clicking anywhere outside it.

To place a horizontal line in your document, move the insertion point to a blank paragraph, click the Border tool's drop-down arrow, and then click Horizontal Line. This option inserts a gray horizontal line that stretches from the left margin to the right margin. If a paragraph is selected when you choose this option, Word replaces the selected text with the horizontal line.

Figure 5.15 *Using the Border tool to place a border around a paragraph.*

  LET ME TRY IT

Creating Borders with the Borders and Shading Dialog Box

Borders and Shading enables you to select different border styles, weights, and colors. You can set borders for paragraphs, pages, tables, and other parts of a document.

1. Select one or more paragraphs of text.

2. Click the Border tool's drop-down arrow.

3. Click Borders and Shading. The Borders and Shading dialog box opens, as shown in Figure 5.16.

4. Click the Borders tab, if necessary.

5. In the Setting section, click one of the following options:
    - **None:** Leaves the selected paragraph without any border (default).
    - **Box:** Places a plain, straight-line border around the paragraph.
    - **Shadow:** Places a "shadow box" border around the paragraph. This type of border has special trim on two sides, creating the impression that the box is floating and casting a shadow down onto the page beneath it.
    - **3-D:** Creates the impression that the border is raised or embossed, resulting in a three-dimensional effect.
    - **Custom:** Enables you to create different borders for any or all sides of the paragraph.

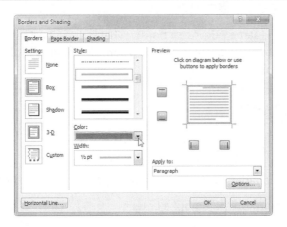

Figure 5.16   *Adding a border to a paragraph, through the Borders and Shading dialog box.*

6. Scroll through the Style list and select the type of border you want.

7. Click the Color drop-down arrow and choose a color for the border. This color palette is similar to the one used for fonts (as described in Chapter 4, "Character Formatting"); it contains theme-based and standard colors, and lets you open the Colors dialog box to choose an exact color.

8. Click the Width drop-down arrow and choose a width for the border. Border widths are measured in points.

9. In the Preview area, click one of the four buttons to remove the border from the corresponding side of the paragraph, if desired.

10. Click the Apply to drop-down arrow; then click Paragraph, if necessary. (If you selected a paragraph before opening the dialog box, this option should already be chosen for you.)

11. Click OK to close the dialog box and apply the border.

12. Deselect the paragraph by clicking anywhere outside it.

The Borders and Shading dialog box's Options button enables you to set the amount of space between the border and your text. You can specify a different amount of space (measured in points) for each side of the paragraph.

Placing Shading Behind a Paragraph

Shading serves the same purpose a border: That is, it calls attention to a paragraph. You can apply shading to a paragraph by using the Shading tool or the Borders and Shading dialog box.

 LET ME TRY IT

Using the Shading Tool

The Shading tool enables you to apply shading of any color behind a paragraph.

1. Select one or more paragraphs of text.

2. In the Paragraph group, click the Shading tool's drop-down arrow. A color palette appears, as shown in Figure 5.17. This color palette is similar to the one used for fonts (as described in Chapter 4); it contains theme-based and standard colors, and enables you to open the Colors dialog box to choose an exact color.

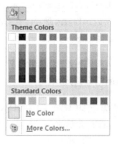

Figure 5.17   *Using the Shading tool to place shading behind a paragraph.*

3. Point to a color in the Theme Colors or Standard Colors sections of the palette. If Live Preview is enabled, the selected text changes to show how it will look if you apply shading of this color.

4. Click the desired color. The Shading palette closes and Word places the shading behind the selected paragraph.

5. Deselect the paragraph by clicking anywhere outside it.

LET ME TRY IT

Adding Shading with the Borders and Shading Dialog Box

The Borders and Shading dialog box provides the same color choices as the Shading tool but also gives you the option of applying a patterned background to the paragraph.

1. Select one or more paragraphs of text.

2. Click the Border tool's drop-down arrow.

3. Click Borders and Shading. The Borders and Shading dialog box opens.

4. Click the Shading tab, as shown in Figure 5.18; then do one of the following:

   - To apply simple colored shading to the paragraph, click the Fill drop-down arrow and make a color choice.
   - To apply a patterned background to the paragraph, click the Style drop-down arrow and select an effect. (You can select a density for shading or apply a pattern, such as hash marks or dots, to the shading.) Then click the Color drop-down arrow and pick a color.

5. Click the Apply to drop-down arrow, and then click Paragraph, if necessary. (If you selected a paragraph before opening the dialog box, this option should already be chosen for you.)

6. Click OK to close the dialog box and apply the shading.

7. Deselect the paragraph by clicking anywhere outside it.

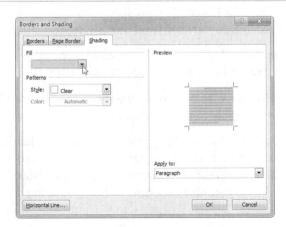

Figure 5.18   *Adding shading to a paragraph through the Borders and Shading dialog box.*

Finding and Replacing Paragraph Formatting

Chapter 3, "Proofing a Document," showed you how to use the Find and Replace dialog box to search a document for a piece of text and then automatically replace it with different text. You can also use the Find and Replace dialog box to look for paragraphs that are formatted a certain way and apply different formatting to those paragraphs.

 **LET ME TRY IT**

Using Find and Replace to Change Paragraph Formatting

In the Find and Replace dialog box, the Format button lets you search for many different kinds of formatting. This gives you an easy way to find paragraphs that are formatted with a given line spacing, for example, and change them to a different spacing.

1. On the Home tab, click the Replace button. (Alternatively, press Ctrl+H.) The Find and Replace dialog box opens.

2. Click the Replace tab.

3. Click in the Find What box.

4. Click the More button. The dialog box expands to display more options.

5. Click the Format button to open a list of the types of formatting Word can search for in the document, as shown in Figure 5.19.

6. Click Paragraph. The Find Paragraph dialog box opens; it is identical to the Paragraph dialog box you have used throughout this chapter.

7. In the Paragraph dialog box, select any formats you want to search for, and then click OK to return to the Find and Replace dialog box.

8. Click in the Replace With box; then repeat steps 5–7 to specify the formatting you want to apply to the paragraphs.

9. Click Find Next to locate the first occurrence of the formatting after the insertion point. Word finds a paragraph with the specified formatting and highlights it. (You can click this button repeatedly to move from one instance of the formatting to the next without replacing it.)

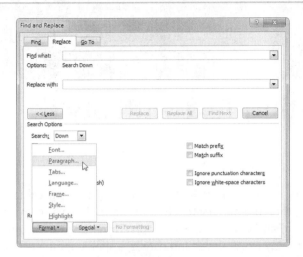

Figure 5.19 *Selecting a formatting option in the Find and Replace dialog box.*

10. Click the Replace button to replace that instance of the formatting with the new format. Word then jumps to the next instance of the formatting.

11. Keep clicking either Replace or Find Next to replace or skip each subsequent occurrence of the formatting until you reach the end of the document.

12. Alternatively, you can click the Replace All button to find and replace every occurrence of the formatting in your document at the same time.

13. When you finish, click the Close button.

This chapter shows you how to work with styles in Word. Styles take most of the work out of formatting your text, and ensure that your documents have a consistent, professional look.

Formatting Text with Styles

When you're cranking out short, informal documents and great-looking formatting isn't a big deal, then the manual text formatting tools covered in Chapter 4, "Character Formatting," and Chapter 5, "Paragraph Formatting," are probably all you need. For most day-to-day word processing chores, a simple template and a little bold or italic can give you nice-looking results without a lot of hassles.

But when formatting truly matters, you need more powerful tools. This is where Word's styles can make the difference between an ordinary document and a polished, professional-looking one. Despite their power, styles are easy to use, when you understand how they work. And if you already know how to manually format characters and paragraphs, you're well on your way to mastering styles.

This chapter shows you how to use styles to format parts of a document with ease. You learn how to create, rename, modify, and delete styles.

Understanding Styles

A *style* is a set of formats that has been saved and given a name. For example, Word automatically applies a style named Normal to your paragraphs when you create a new document based on the Blank Document template (as described in Chapter 1, "Creating, Saving, and Printing Documents"). By default, this version of the Normal style applies the 11-point Calibri font to your text, left-aligns your paragraphs, inserts 1.15 lines' worth of space between the lines of a paragraph, and inserts 10 points of space after each paragraph.

It may not be obvious, but Word applies a style to every paragraph, even if you don't. If you change a paragraph's formatting and then undo those changes, Word reapplies the paragraph's default style.

Although the Normal style is automatically used for body text, Word also features heading styles (named Heading 1, Heading 2, and so on) that you can use to make a document's headings stand out. The Heading 1 style, for example, applies the 14-point Cambria font, makes the text bold and changes its color to dark blue, and inserts 24 points of space after the paragraph. When you press Enter at the end of the heading, Word automatically applies the Normal style to the new paragraph, assuming you want to add body text after the heading.

Other kinds of styles have very specific uses. For example, some styles are designed to format entries in an index or a table of contents. Some styles let you format complex lists and tables, whereas others can format eye-catching quotations or references.

As you work with templates, you'll notice that different templates use different styles...or at least different-looking styles. The Normal style used in one of Word's sales letter templates, for example, might look different from the Normal style used in the Blank Document template.

Table 6.1 describes the five types of styles available in Word. Figure 6.1 shows a few paragraphs that have been formatted with some of Word's built-in styles.

Table 6.1   Types of Styles in Word

Style	Description
Paragraph	Formats an entire paragraph and everything in it. Paragraph styles can include paragraph-specific formats (indents, tabs, line spacing, and so on) and character-specific ones (font type and size, character spacing, and so on).
Character	Formats characters only. Character styles can include any kind of character-specific formats, but not paragraph-specific ones.
Linked	Formats paragraphs and/or characters, depending on whether you apply the style to an entire paragraph or just part of it.
Table	Formats one or more cells in a table. A table format can include paragraph and character formats and table-specific formats, such as cell shading, row height, and much more.
List	Formats items in a list. A list can be numbered or bulleted, or simply indented in a way that makes it stand apart from normal body text.

Word includes dozens and dozens of ready-to-use styles, but you can create new ones to suit your specific formatting needs. You can also modify existing styles so that they contain exactly the formats you want.

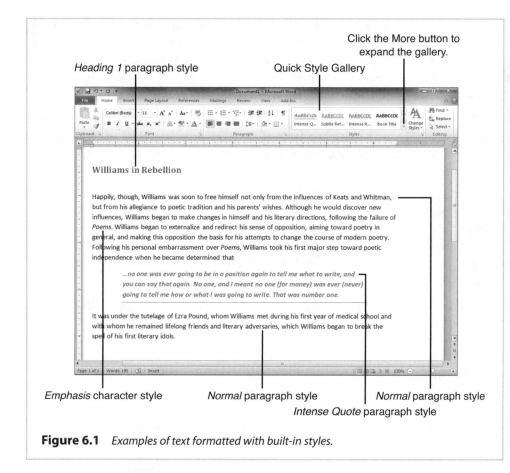

Figure 6.1 *Examples of text formatted with built-in styles.*

The Advantages of Styles

If you haven't worked with styles before, you may be wondering why they're worth all this fuss. In a nutshell, styles offer several advantages over manual formatting:

- When you apply a style, the formatting is applied with a single mouse-click. You don't need to set the font, spacing, effects, and other attributes. You need to make these formatting choices when you create a style, but after it has been created, you can quickly apply the style .

- Styles ensure consistency in your formatting. When you format with styles, you can be sure all your headings are identically formatted, for example. Consistency is critical to professional-looking documents.

- Styles are easy to update. Suppose you change your mind about the way your headings should look; for example, you want them to be red instead of blue. If you formatted the headings with a style, you can make the change to the style itself, and Word automatically updates all the headings. This frees you from manually reformatting all the headings.

There are other advantages to using styles. But if you aren't convinced by now, feel free to jump to another chapter...and keep formatting everything the hard way.

In the interest of full disclosure, we must advise you that it's easy to go overboard with styles. They're so easy to create and modify, you may one day find that you've created hundreds of styles and can't remember what most of them are for. Luckily, styles are also easy to delete, as you'll see later in this chapter. Still, to avoid confusion and duplication of effort, create only the styles you need and give them meaningful names that remind you of their purpose.

Styles Versus Quick Styles

As you'll see throughout this chapter, Word offers lots of different ways to apply styles. One of these methods is called *Quick Styles*, and they get their name from the way you apply them—by picking one from a gallery on the Ribbon. In other words, a Quick Style is just a style (like any other style) that can be applied quickly.

So, remember this as you read on: All Quick Styles are styles, but not all styles are Quick Styles. The styles in the Quick Style Gallery are a selection of commonly used styles. Not all of Word's styles appear in the gallery. If they did, the gallery would be too big to deal with, especially if you added your own styles to it.

Confused? Don't be. This will all become clear as we go along. In fact, let's go ahead and take a detailed look at Quick Styles in the next section.

 TELL ME MORE   Media 6.1—Using Word's Styles to Get Professional-Looking Documents in Less Time
Access this audio recording through your registered Web Edition at **my.safaribooksonline.com/9780132182713/media**.

 SHOW ME   Media 6.2—Seeing Word's Styles in Action
Access this video file through your registered Web Edition at **my.safaribooksonline.com/9780132182713/media**.

Mastering Quick Styles

As mentioned already, a Quick Style is just a style that is available through a gallery on the Ribbon's Home tab. The Quick Style Gallery displays thumbnail previews of all the available Quick Styles. Quick Styles make applying a style as easy as clicking an icon.

Applying a Quick Style

The joy of Quick Styles is in their speed. They let you format text in no time, with no fuss. If you use nothing but Word's built-in Quick Styles, you will get neat, professional-looking documents without any nail biting or hair pulling. Just remember to be consistent in the way you apply the styles, and you can't go wrong.

 LET ME TRY IT

Formatting Text with Quick Styles

The ribbon displays only a portion of the Quick Style Gallery. You can expand the gallery to see all the styles. The following steps show you how to expand the gallery, apply a paragraph style, and apply a character style.

1. To format a paragraph as a heading, click anywhere in the paragraph to place the insertion point in it. (You don't need to select the entire paragraph when applying a paragraph style.)

2. In the lower-right corner of the Quick Style Gallery, click the More button to expand the gallery and view all the available Quick Styles, as shown in Figure 6.2.

3. Point to a Heading style. If Live Preview is enabled, Word displays the paragraph as it will look if you select this style. You can point at other styles to see how they will look.

4. Click the desired Heading style.

5. To format a portion of a paragraph, select the desired text (but not the paragraph return), expand the Quick Style Gallery, and then pick a character style. Figure 6.3, for example, shows the Emphasis style being applied to a selected word, making the word italic.

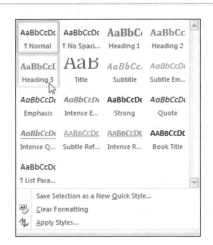

Figure 6.2   *Applying a paragraph style (Heading 3) to an entire paragraph.*

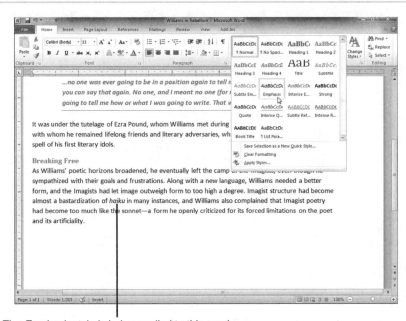

The *Emphasis* style is being applied to this word.

Figure 6.3   *Applying a character style (Emphasis) to a selected word.*

You may wonder why you should use the Emphasis style to make a word italic, when you can just use the Italic tool on the Ribbon. That's a good question, and it has a good answer. Just go back to the section titled "The Advantages of Styles" and review the third advantage in the list.

Changing the Quick Style Set

If you don't like the styles in the Quick Style Gallery, or if you need some variety, you can replace the default set of styles with a new set. Word features several Quick Style sets, and each one provides a different definition for each style. Changing sets frees you from choosing a different template for your document, and from creating or modifying styles.

Here's how to select a new Quick Style set:

1. Click the Change Styles icon; then click Style Set, as shown in Figure 6.4.

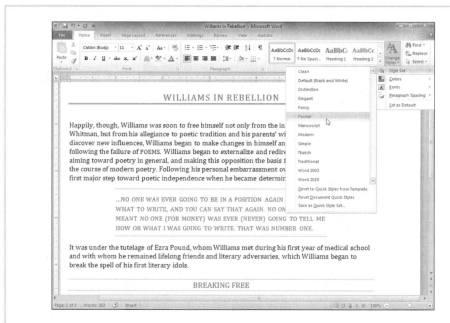

Figure 6.4 *Selecting a different set of Quick Styles.*

2. Point to any of the style sets in the menu. If Live Preview is active, the entire document changes to show you how it will look with each different set.

3. Click the desired style set. This set of Quick Styles becomes available in the Quick Style Gallery.

If you really like the style set you've chosen, you can make it your default set. To do this, click the Change Styles icon; then click Set as Default.

If you want to go back to the style set that was in use when you started the document, click the Change Styles icon, click Style Set, and then click Reset to Quick Styles from Template.

Removing a Quick Style from the Gallery

If the Quick Style Gallery includes a style that you never use, you can remove it from the gallery. Here's how:

1. Expand the Quick Style Gallery.

2. Point to the style you want to remove.

3. Right-click the style to open a shortcut menu.

4. Click Remove from Quick Style Gallery, as shown in Figure 6.5.

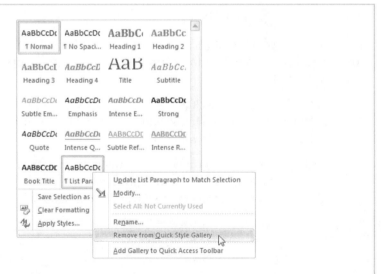

Figure 6.5   *Removing a style from the Quick Style Gallery.*

Removing a style from the Quick Style Gallery does not delete the style. The style still exists and is available through the Styles pane and the Apply Styles pane, which you will read about next. If you want to delete a style completely, look ahead to the section titled "Deleting a Style."

Using the Styles Pane

Unlike the Quick Styles Gallery, the *Styles pane* can display all of Word's available styles or a subset of them, such as the styles used in your current document.

You can open and close the Styles pane whenever you like, or you can leave it open all the time. The pane can display a simple unformatted list of styles (the default) or it can show you a preview of each style. The Styles pane shows which style has been applied to the current paragraph. Applying a style is as simple as choosing the one you want from the list.

 **LET ME TRY IT**

Applying a Style from the Styles Pane

Depending on your monitor's size and resolution, the Styles pane can take up a lot of space on your screen. For this reason, you might prefer to open the pane only when you need it.

1. In the Styles group, click the Dialog Box Launcher. The Styles pane opens, as shown in Figure 6.6. In the figure, the pane is shown "docked" to the right edge of the Word window.

2. Click the Show Preview check box at the bottom of the pane. The pane now displays each style as it will appear when applied to text. (If you prefer to work without the preview, clear this check box.)

Whether or not you use the Styles pane in preview mode, the pane indicates which styles are paragraph styles (¶), character styles (a), or linked styles (¶a).

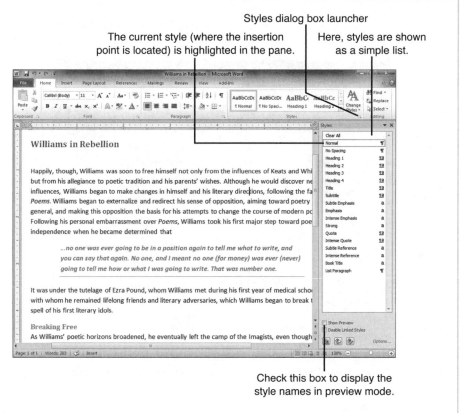

Styles dialog box launcher

The current style (where the insertion point is located) is highlighted in the pane.

Here, styles are shown as a simple list.

Check this box to display the style names in preview mode.

Figure 6.6 *The Styles pane, docked to the right edge of the Word window.*

3. To "undock" the Styles pane (that is, to tear it loose from the edge of the window and place it where you want on the screen), point to the pane's title bar and drag it toward the center of the screen, as shown in Figure 6.7.

4. To see a complete description of a style, rest the pointer on the style's name.

5. To apply a style, do one of the following:

   - To format a paragraph, click anywhere in the paragraph; then click the desired paragraph or linked style in the Styles pane.
   - To format a character, word, or any part of a paragraph, select the text; then click a character or linked style in the Styles pane.

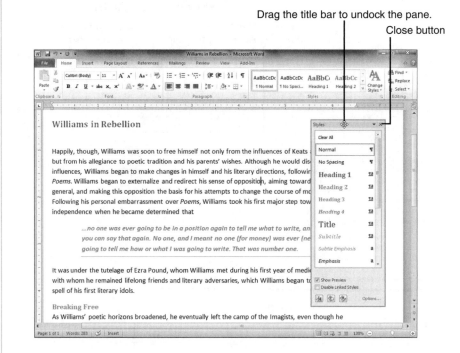

Figure 6.7   *The undocked Styles pane, displaying the styles in preview mode.*

6. To close the Styles pane, click the Close button at the right end of the pane's title bar.

By default, the Styles pane displays only "recommended" styles. To see other styles, click Options at the bottom of the Styles pane. In the Style Pane Options dialog box, click the Select Styles To Show drop-down arrow; then select a different set of styles to view. If you click All Styles, the Styles pane displays all the available styles in Word. (The *In use* option shows only the styles that are currently applied in the document; the *In current document* option shows all the styles that have ever been used in the document.) Click OK after making your selection.

Using the Apply Styles Pane

The *Apply Styles pane* is a miniature version of the Styles pane and is most useful if you know your styles and their names. That's because the Apply Styles pane does not show the styles in a fancy preview format. Further, the Apply Styles pane shows *all* of Word's available styles—not just the ones currently being used in the document.

 LET ME TRY IT

Applying a Style from the Apply Styles Pane

The Apply Styles pane features an editable drop-down menu. You can select a style by typing its name in the menu's text box or by opening the menu and clicking the style.

1. Expand the Quick Style Gallery.

2. At the bottom of the gallery, click Apply Styles. The Apply Styles pane appears, as shown in Figure 6.8.

Figure 6.8   *The Apply Styles pane.*

3. Select the paragraph or characters you want to format.

4. Click in the Style Name box to select the current style's name; then do one of the following:
   - Begin typing the name of the desired style. If the AutoComplete Style Names check box is checked, Word tries to complete the style's name for you, based on the first few letters you type.
   - Click the drop-down arrow to open a menu of Word's styles; then find and click the desired style.

5. Click Reapply. (This button's name changes to *Apply* if you choose a style that has not been applied to the selected text before.)

The Apply Styles pane can be docked, undocked, moved, and closed in the same manner as the Styles pane, described in the preceding section.

If you decide that you like the Styles pane better than the Apply Styles pane, click the Styles button in the lower-right corner of the Apply Styles pane. Word opens the Styles pane. (But the Apply Styles pane remains open, as well, so you need to close it.)

Clearing Styles and Manual Formatting

You can clear (remove) styles and manual formats from your text. This capability is handy when you're guilty of formatting overkill or can't remember everything you've done and need to start over again.

Start by selecting the text whose formatting you want to clear; then do one of the following:

- Open the Styles pane and click Clear All.

- Expand the Quick Styles Gallery and click Clear Formatting.

Either way, Word removes applied styles and manual formats from the text and then applies the Normal style.

If you want to clear manual formatting but leave styles in place, select the text and press Ctrl+Spacebar.

Creating a New Style

Even though Word offers many built-in styles, they might not meet all your formatting requirements. If you find that you're constantly adding manual formats to text even after applying a style, you probably need to create a new style that includes all the formatting.

Word lets you create new styles in two ways—by modeling the new style on existing text or by creating a new style definition from scratch. But because time and page count are of the essence (and because creating a new style definition is a long, difficult process), we'll just show you the first method.

 **LET ME TRY IT**

Creating a New Style from an Example

To create a style by example, you start by formatting some existing text (the example) so that it looks just the way you want. Then you create the style. You can customize the style in several ways, and even add it to your Quick Style Gallery. Here's how:

1. Type some text into a Word document, and apply all the formatting options you want. You can apply an existing paragraph style and character styles as needed or use the manual formatting options described in Chapters 4 and 5.

2. Double-check your formatting; then check it again. Remember formats such as line and paragraph spacing, character spacing, effects, and others.

3. Do one of the following:
   - To create a new character style, select some of the formatted text, but don't select the paragraph return.
   - To create a new paragraph style, select the entire paragraph, including the paragraph return, as shown in Figure 6.9.

4. Open the Styles pane.

5. Click the New Style button, in the bottom-left corner of the Styles pane. The Create New Style from Formatting dialog box opens, as shown in Figure 6.9.

6. In the Name box, type a name for the new style.

I really have to nag you about naming your styles wisely. Otherwise, you may wind up forgetting their purpose, having trouble telling them apart, or wondering why you created them in the first place. Avoid cryptic names such as "ESH" because they may become meaningless after a while. Try naming styles according to their function, such as "Chapter Title" or "Signature." If a style already exists with your chosen name, go ahead and use the name but add a number after it, as in "Signature 2."

7. If you don't want to make any other changes, just click the OK button to save the style and you're done. To further customize the style, continue with the next step.

8. Click the Style type drop-down arrow, if necessary, and select the type of style you want to create. In Figure 6.9, Word displays Paragraph as the style type because the entire sample paragraph was selected. You have the option of creating a character, linked, table, or list style.

9. Click the Style for Following Paragraph drop-down arrow, and select a style. In the future, when you create a paragraph based on your new style and press Enter, the next paragraph will take the style you specify here. If you aren't sure which style to go with, choose Normal; it's the safest bet.

Formatted text (the example) is selected.

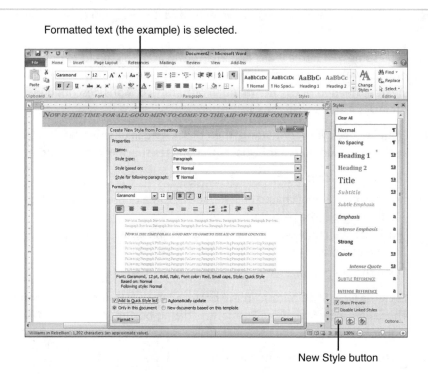

New Style button

Figure 6.9 *Creating a new paragraph style by example.*

10. Check or clear the Add to Quick Style List check box, according to your preference. If the box is checked, the new style appears in the Quick Style Gallery and the Styles and Apply Styles panes.

11. Do *not* check the Automatically Update check box unless you want to get in trouble. See the following Note to find out why.

12. If you want to use the new style in other documents, click the New Documents Based on This Template option button. Otherwise, the style will be available only in the current document.

13. Click OK. The dialog box closes and the new style appears in the Styles pane.

The Automatically Update option might sound like a timesaver, but it's really more of a troublemaker. Suppose you choose this option when creating a new style and then you apply the style to several paragraphs in a document. Then you go back and manually change the formatting of one of those paragraphs. Because the Automatically Update option is active, Word applies your manual changes not only to that paragraph, but also to the style itself...and to any other text to which the style has been applied. If you forget that you activated the Automatically Update option, you may be surprised later when you find that all paragraphs of a certain style now look different than they should, and you'll have a mess to clean up.

 LET ME TRY IT

Creating a Quick Style, the Quick Way

If you know that you want a new style to be a Quick Style, and if you don't care about changing any settings related to it, you can save some steps by doing the following:

1. Format and select your example, as described in steps 1–3 of the preceding section.

2. Right-click the text; then click Styles.

3. In the Styles submenu, click Save Selection as a New Quick Style. A smaller version of the Create New Style from Formatting dialog box appears, as shown in Figure 6.10.

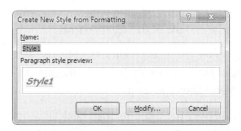

Figure 6.10   *Creating a new Quick Style.*

4. In the Name box, type a *meaningful* name for your style. (Don't make me say that again!)

5. Click OK.

The new style appears in the Quick Style Gallery and in the Styles and Apply Styles panes. By default, however, the style will be available only in the current document.

 SHOW ME   **Media 6.3—Creating a New Style in Word**
Access this video file through your registered Web Edition at
my.safaribooksonline.com/9780132182713/media.

Modifying an Existing Style

Like death and taxes, change is inevitable. And someday, in some way, you'll have to make a change to a style. You can modify just about any aspect of any style. But remember: When you change a style, Word applies the change to all the text formatted with that style. This makes it easy to change the color of all your Heading 2 paragraphs, for example, but change a style only when you want the change to be universal. Otherwise, just change the text locally or create a new style for it.

Renaming a Style

Of all the changes that can be made to styles, renaming is probably the most common because nobody ever listens to me. If you don't give a style a meaningful name when you create it (exactly what I keep telling you), you'll eventually go back and rename it. A style's name also affects how it is sorted in Word's various style listings.

1. In the Styles pane, point to the style you want to rename. A drop-down arrow appears to the right of the style's name.

2. Click the drop-down arrow; then click Modify. The Modify Style dialog box appears, as shown in Figure 6.11. In the Name box, the style's name is highlighted, so you can type over it.

3. Type a new name over the old one; then click OK. The style is renamed in the Styles and Apply Styles panes (and in the Quick Style Gallery, if the style is a Quick Style).

You can't rename any of Word's built-in styles. If you follow the preceding steps for a built-in style, Word just adds the new name to the style's existing name. This extra name is called an "alias."

Figure 6.11   *Renaming a style in the Modify Style dialog box.*

Changing a Style's Definition

If you need to make a lot of changes to a style, you can modify its definition. (Yes, I said it's a pain to deal with style definitions, but sometimes it's necessary. But it's still easier to create a new style from an example.) A style's definition is the collection of formatting settings that, well, *define* the style and its appearance.

When you update a style's definition, you work in the Modify Style dialog box. You can make several changes directly within this dialog box and use it to access other dialog boxes—such as Paragraph, Tabs, Font, and others.

 LET ME TRY IT

Updating a Style's Definition

The Modify Style dialog box's options change according to the type of style you're modifying. If you're working on a paragraph style, the dialog box makes paragraph-level formatting tools and dialog boxes available. If you're updating a character style, only character formatting options are available; the paragraph options are grayed out, so you can't use them.

The following example shows how to make some simple formatting changes to a paragraph style:

1. In the Styles pane, point to the style you want to modify. A drop-down arrow appears to the right of the style's name.

2. Click the drop-down arrow; then click Modify. The Modify Style dialog box appears (refer to Figure 6.11).

3. In the Formatting section, click the Font drop-down arrow, and select a different font.

4. Click the Increase Indent button once to indent the paragraph from the left margin.

5. Click the Format button in the lower-left corner of the dialog box. The button displays a list of dialog boxes, as shown in Figure 6.12. You can open any of these dialog boxes to make further changes to the style.

Figure 6.12   *Accessing other dialog boxes from the Modify Style dialog box.*

6. Click Paragraph to open the Paragraph dialog box. Notice that the Modify Style dialog box stays open in the background.

7. Click the Line and Page Breaks tab.

8. Select the Keep with Next check box. This setting tells Word to keep any paragraph with this style on the same page with the following paragraph.

9. Click OK to return to the Modify Style dialog box.

10. Click OK to close the Modify Style dialog box and save the style's updated definition.

LET ME TRY IT

Updating a Style to Match Selected Text

You can modify a style by example, in much the same way you create a style by example. To do this, find some text formatted with the style you want to update. Make any formatting changes you want to the text; then select it. Right-click the selected text to open the shortcut menu; then click Styles. In the submenu that pops up, click Update [*style name*] to Match Selection, as shown in Figure 6.13.

Figure 6.13   *Updating a style to match selected text.*

SHOW ME   Media 6.4—Modifying a Style in Word
Access this video file through your registered Web Edition at
my.safaribooksonline.com/9780132182713/media.

Deleting a Style

You can delete any style that you have created. To do so, open the Styles pane and point to the desired style. Click the drop-down arrow that appears to the right of the style's name; then click Delete [*style name*].

You cannot delete any of Word's built-in styles, such as Normal or the Heading styles.

Organizing Text into Lists, Tables, and Columns

7 Setting Up Lists **158**

8 Creating Tables **174**

9 Setting Text in Columns **210**

Lists can be an important part of any document—whether it's a letter to Santa or instructions for assembling a bicycle. This chapter shows you how to create lists in Word so you can present any set of items or steps in a neat little package.

7

Setting Up Lists

If there can be a type of document that is indispensable to everyone, it has to be the list. Simple and straightforward (well, most of the time), lists help us organize the details of our daily lives. From a four-line shopping list to a thousand-page phone directory, lists help us find information, remember details, and follow directions.

Lists are often included in long or complex documents, like the step-by-step instructions in this book. Lists can be an essential document feature because they provide information in a concise, structured way that makes information easier to follow and remember.

In Word, a *list* is a series of paragraphs introduced by a special character or a number. You can build several types of lists in Word and make them as simple or complex as necessary. This chapter focuses on the three basic kinds of lists—bulleted, numbered, and nested. The following sections show you how to create, modify, and customize each type of list.

 TELL ME MORE   Media 7.1—Enhancing a Document's Readability with Lists

Access this audio recording through your registered Web Edition at **my.safaribooksonline.com/9780132182713/media.**

Working with Bulleted Lists

A *bulleted list* is a series of paragraphs, each of which is introduced by a special character called a *bullet*. Bulleted lists are typically used to arrange a series of items that don't need to be in any particular order. (If you want to put a list of items in a specific order for the reader to follow, you should use a numbered list, as described later in this chapter.) Figure 7.1 shows a quick example of a bulleted list—a shopping list. This list isn't in any kind of order and probably doesn't need to be, although you could alphabetize it or arrange it to match the layout of your favorite grocery store.

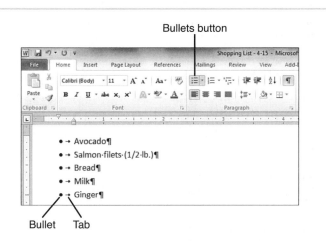

Figure 7.1   *A simple bulleted list. This list uses the default formats from the Blank Document template.*

In Figure 7.1, notice the list's formatting, which is based on the Blank Document template's settings. (Different templates might format lists in different ways.) Each paragraph in the list is indented one-quarter inch from the left margin and is introduced by the default bullet character (•). A tab stop follows the bullet, inserting one-quarter inch of space between the bullet and the text.

Word formats bulleted lists with a hanging indent (as described in Chapter 5, "Paragraph Formatting"). If an item in a list is longer than a single line, the subsequent lines are left-aligned under the first line, as shown in Figure 7.2.

There aren't too many rules about lists, but there is one general guideline worth following—keep the text in a bulleted list as brief as possible. Bulleted lists, in particular, often contain only sentence fragments or a few words. If the items in a bulleted list include multiple complete sentences, consider reformatting the list as body text. This rule-of-thumb doesn't apply in some kinds of documents, such as legal documents.

In Word, you can type the items in the list and then apply the bullet formatting, or you can tell Word to format the items as you type. After you create a bulleted list, you can easily select a different bullet character.

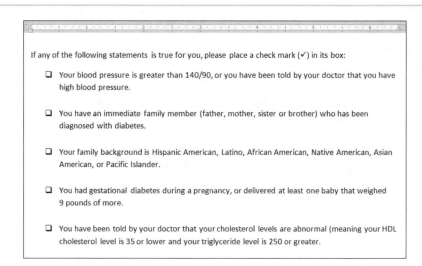

If any of the following statements is true for you, please place a check mark (✓) in its box:

❑ Your blood pressure is greater than 140/90, or you have been told by your doctor that you have high blood pressure.

❑ You have an immediate family member (father, mother, sister or brother) who has been diagnosed with diabetes.

❑ Your family background is Hispanic American, Latino, African American, Native American, Asian American, or Pacific Islander.

❑ You had gestational diabetes during a pregnancy, or delivered at least one baby that weighed 9 pounds of more.

❑ You have been told by your doctor that your cholesterol levels are abnormal (meaning your HDL cholesterol level is 35 or lower and your triglyceride level is 250 or greater.

Figure 7.2   *Lines of a bulleted list, aligned in a hanging indent. In this list, the bullet characters serve as check boxes for the reader.*

Creating a Quick Bulleted List

If you like to type your text before formatting it, that's fine. You can apply bullet list formatting to existing text in a snap. Here's how:

1. Type the items in your list, ending each one with a paragraph return (by pressing Enter).

2. Select the entire list.

3. In the Paragraph group on the Home tab, click the Bullets button. Word applies the default bullet formatting, as shown in Figure 7.3.

Creating a Bulleted List as You Type

If you prefer to do your formatting on the go, you can tell Word to create a bulleted list as you type it. To do this, place the insertion point on an empty paragraph mark (¶), click the Bullets button, and start typing. Word "bulletizes" the current paragraph and each subsequent one you create by pressing Enter. To stop automatic bulleting, press Enter twice after typing the last item in the list.

Here's another fast way to create a bulleted list: Place the insertion point on a blank paragraph, type an asterisk (*), press the spacebar, and start typing the first line of your list. Word's AutoFormat feature replaces the asterisk with a bullet and formats the paragraph as part of a bulleted list.

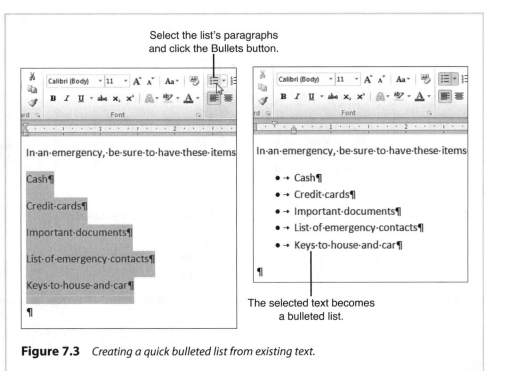

Figure 7.3   *Creating a quick bulleted list from existing text.*

Choosing a Different Bullet Character

The default bullet character (•) is nice, but sometimes you may want your bullets to have a little more...well, *character*. You can use any symbol or letter as a bullet, and selecting a new bullet is as easy as picking an item from a menu. If the menu doesn't offer enough variety, you can define a new bullet by choosing from the thousands of symbols installed on your computer.

 LET ME TRY IT

Using the Bullet Library

1. Select a bulleted list.

2. Click the Bullet button's drop-down arrow. A menu appears, as shown in Figure 7.4. The menu displays the bullets you have used recently, those that have been used in the document so far, and a bullet library (a brief list of available bullets).

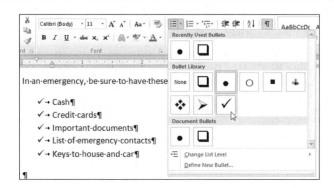

Figure 7.4 *Selecting a different bullet from the Bullet button's drop-down menu.*

3. Point to any bullet on the menu. If Live Preview is enabled, your list changes to show how it will look with this bullet.

4. If you find a bullet you like on the menu, click it. Word applies the new bullet character to your list.

 LET ME TRY IT

Defining a New Bullet

The Bullet Library displays only a tiny portion of the symbols you can use as bullets. If none of the characters in the Bullet Library suits you, you can define a new bullet from the many symbols and alphanumeric characters installed on your system. Here's how:

1. Click Define New Bullet at the bottom of the drop-down menu. The Define New Bullet dialog box opens, as shown in Figure 7.5.

2. Click the Symbol button. The Symbol dialog box opens, as shown in Figure 7.6.

3. Scroll through the menu of symbols and click any character you like; then click OK to return to the Define New Bullet dialog box.

4. Click OK in the Define New Bullet dialog box to apply the new symbol to your list.

To see other symbol sets, click the Font drop-down arrow in the upper-left corner of the Symbol dialog box; then choose a font. Most of the fonts on your computer come with a collection of symbols.

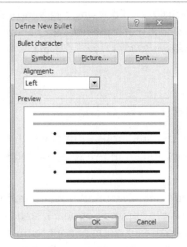

Figure 7.5 *The Define New Bullet dialog box.*

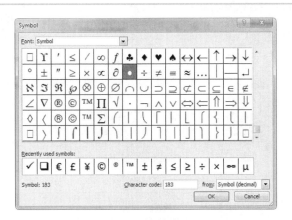

Figure 7.6 *The Symbol dialog box displays all the fonts, symbols, and alphanumeric characters available to you.*

Whenever you select a symbol, Word adds it to the Recently Used Symbols list near the bottom of the dialog box and to the Bullets drop-down menu on the ribbon. This makes it easy to pick the symbol again when you want to reuse it.

You can use a picture as a bullet, too. To do this, click the Picture button in the Define New Bullet dialog box; then select a graphic from the Picture Bullet dialog box. These images are sized for use as bullets and can lend a bit of color and texture to your document. Some of the pictures have 3-D effects, as well.

SHOW ME Media 7.2—Choosing a Different Bullet Character
Access this video file through your registered Web Edition at
my.safaribooksonline.com/9780132182713/media.

Working with Numbered Lists

A *numbered list* is a series of paragraphs, each of which is introduced by a numeral or letter. Numbered lists let you arrange a series of items, such as instructions, in a specific order.

As Figure 7.7 shows, Word's default formatting for numbered lists is identical to bulleted lists—except that Arabic numerals appear instead of bullets. In Figure 7.7, the list's formatting is based on the Blank Document template's settings. (Different templates might format lists in different ways.) Each paragraph in the list is indented one-quarter inch from the left margin and is introduced by the default Arabic numerals (1, 2, 3). A tab stop follows the numeral, inserting one-quarter inch of space between the numeral and the text.

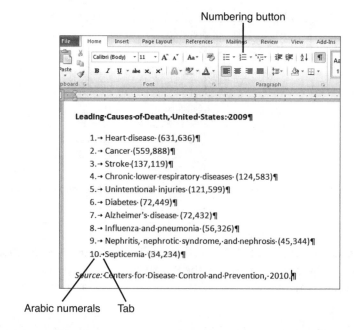

Figure 7.7 *A simple numbered list. This list uses the default formats from the Blank Document template.*

Word formats numbered lists with a hanging indent (as described in Chapter 5). If an item in a list is longer than a single line, the subsequent lines are left-aligned under the first line, as shown in Figure 7.8.

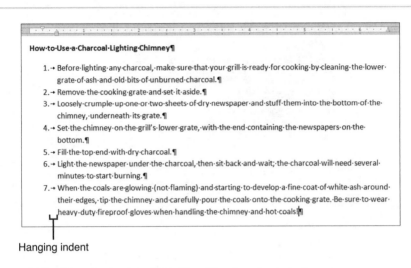

How·to·Use·a·Charcoal·Lighting·Chimney¶

1.→ Before·lighting·any·charcoal,·make·sure·that·your·grill·is·ready·for·cooking·by·cleaning·the·lower·grate·of·ash·and·old·bits·of·unburned·charcoal.¶
2.→ Remove·the·cooking·grate·and·set·it·aside.¶
3.→ Loosely·crumple·up·one·or·two·sheets·of·dry·newspaper·and·stuff·them·into·the·bottom·of·the·chimney,·underneath·its·grate.¶
4.→ Set·the·chimney·on·the·grill's·lower·grate,·with·the·end·containing·the·newspapers·on·the·bottom.¶
5.→ Fill·the·top·end·with·dry·charcoal.¶
6.→ Light·the·newspaper·under·the·charcoal,·then·sit·back·and·wait;·the·charcoal·will·need·several·minutes·to·start·burning.¶
7.→ When·the·coals·are·glowing·(not·flaming)·and·starting·to·develop·a·fine·coat·of·white·ash·around·their·edges,·tip·the·chimney·and·carefully·pour·the·coals·onto·the·cooking·grate.·Be·sure·to·wear·heavy-duty·fireproof·gloves·when·handling·the·chimney·and·hot·coals!¶

Hanging indent

Figure 7.8   *Lines of a numbered list, aligned in a hanging indent.*

In Word, you can type the items in the list first and then apply the number formatting, or you can tell Word to format the items as you type. After you create a numbered list, you can easily select a different number format. You can also control the order of numbering, which is helpful if your list is interrupted by text formatted in a different way.

Creating a Quick Numbered List

You can apply numbered list formatting to existing text. Here's how:

1. Type the items in your list, ending each one with a paragraph return (by pressing Enter).

2. Select the entire list.

3. In the Paragraph group on the Home tab, click the Numbering button. Word applies the default numbered list formatting, as shown in Figure 7.9.

Select the list's paragraphs and click the Numbering button.

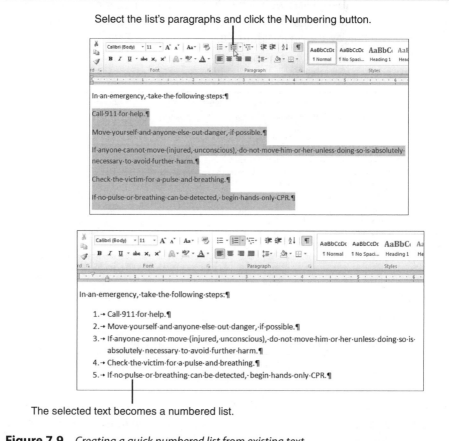

The selected text becomes a numbered list.

Figure 7.9   *Creating a quick numbered list from existing text.*

Creating a Numbered List as You Type

If you prefer to do your formatting on the go, you can tell Word to create a numbered list as you type it. To do this, place the insertion point on an empty paragraph mark (¶), click the Numbering button, and start typing. Word numbers the current paragraph and each subsequent one you create by pressing Enter. To stop automatic numbering, press Enter twice after typing the list's last item.

Choosing a Different Numbering Format

By default, Word uses Arabic numerals (1, 2, 3) in numbered lists. You can use Roman numerals or letters, if you prefer, by picking an item from a menu. If the menu doesn't offer enough variety, you can define a new numbering format.

LET ME TRY IT

Using the Numbering Library

1. Select a numbered list.

2. Click the Numbering button's drop-down arrow. A menu appears, as shown in Figure 7.10. The menu displays the numbering formats you have used recently, those that have been used in the document so far, and a numbering library (a brief list of available numbering formats).

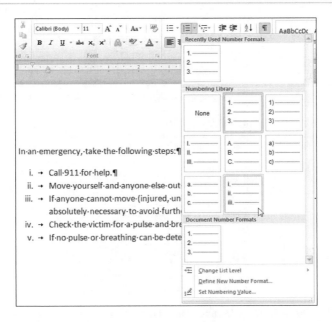

Figure 7.10   *Selecting a different numbering format from the Numbering button's drop-down menu.*

3. Point to any numbering format on the menu. If Live Preview is enabled, your list will change to show how it will look with this format.

4. If you find a format you like on the menu, click it. Word applies the new numbering format to your list.

LET ME TRY IT

Defining a New Numbering Format

The Numbering Library displays only a few of the formats you can use with numbered lists. If none of the options in the Numbering Library appeals to you, you can define a new numbering format. Here's how:

1. Click Define New Number Format at the bottom of the drop-down menu. The Define New Number Format dialog box opens, as shown in Figure 7.11.

Figure 7.11 *The Define New Number Format dialog box.*

2. Click the Number Style drop-down arrow to view a list of numbering styles.

3. Scroll through the menu of styles and click the one you like.

4. If you want to choose a different punctuation mark to follow the numbers, click in the Number Format box, delete the period after the numeral (you can't delete or change the numeral in this box), and then type a new punctuation mark or any other text you might want to appear after the number.

5. Click OK. Word applies the new formatting to your list.

To change other aspects of the numbering format, click the Font button in the Define New Number Format dialog box. The Font dialog box opens. Use any of options you want to change the number's font, size, color, or other characteristics. When you finish, click OK twice to return to your reformatted list.

Whenever you define a new numbering format, Word adds it to the Numbering drop-down menu on the ribbon. This makes it easy to pick the format again when you want to reuse it.

Resuming or Restarting List Numbering

Believe it or not, Word can actually lose track of numbering. This usually happens when a numbered list is interrupted by other paragraphs that aren't part of the list. When this problem arises, you may need to tell Word to resume numbering (that is, pick up where it left off) or to restart numbering (beginning with the number 1).

Suppose, for example, that you create a numbered list of instructions, but one of the instructions is followed by a safety warning that is not numbered. Sometimes (but not always!), Word treats the next item in the list as if it were the beginning of a new list and places the numeral *1* in front of it, as shown in Figure 7.12.

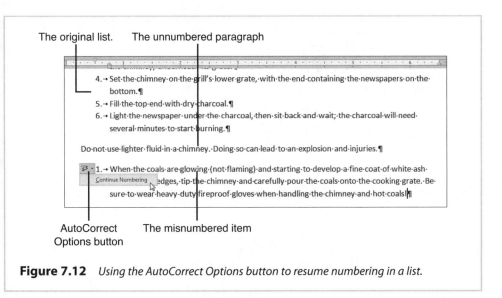

Figure 7.12   *Using the AutoCorrect Options button to resume numbering in a list.*

If this happens, Word should (but won't always!) display an AutoCorrect Options button next to the incorrectly numbered item, as shown in the figure. This happens because Word has made an assumption about what you wanted to do next, and is giving you the chance to fix its potential error.

To correct the problem, point to the AutoCorrect Options button; a drop-down arrow appears next to it. Click the drop-down arrow, and click Continue Numbering. Word updates the item to resume numbering your list where it left off.

Sometimes Word treats a new numbered list as though it's part of a previous list...even when the two lists are separated by other kinds of text. To make matters worse, no AutoCorrect Options button appears to help you sort things out. When this happens, right-click the first item of the new list to open a shortcut menu; then click Restart at 1, as shown in Figure 7.13.

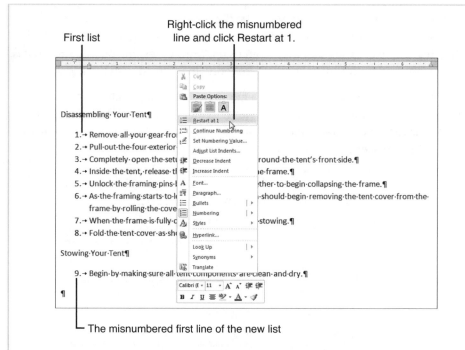

Figure 7.13 *Telling Word to begin numbering a new list with the number 1.*

The preceding example proves an old adage among experienced Word users: "When in doubt, right-click." In many cases, you'll find the solution to a problem by right-clicking the text. It's faster than digging around in the Ribbon and may let you avoid opening one or more dialog boxes.

SHOW ME   Media 7.3—Keeping a List's Numbering on Track in Word
Access this video file through your registered Web Edition at
my.safaribooksonline.com/9780132182713/media.

Creating Nested Lists

A *nested list* is a list within a list, or several lists within a list. A bulleted list, for example, may have primary (level 1) items and some of those may have secondary (level
2) items beneath them. Meeting agendas and resumes are commonly formatted
with nested lists. Word lets you build nested lists with as many as nine different levels. The most basic nested lists, discussed here, use either bullets only or a combination of bullets and numbers.

Word also provides tools for building multilevel lists, like the kind you encounter in
book outlines. We discuss multilevel lists in Chapter 17, "Generating Outlines, Tables
of Contents, and Indexes" (online).

Creating a Nested List with Bullets Only

An item in a bulleted list can include subordinate items. The subordinate items are
indented farther from the left margin and usually use a different bullet than the
primary items use. Here's how to create a nested list with bullets only:

1. Type all the text for the list.

2. Apply the primary bullet format to the entire list.

3. Select the subordinate bullets under one of the primary bullets; then do
   one of the following:
   • Click the Bullets button's drop-down arrow, click Change List Level, and
     then click the desired level for the subordinate bullet points, as shown in
     Figure 7.14.
   • Click the Increase Indent button (in the Paragraph group on the Home
     tab) one time for each level you want to subordinate the selected items.

4. Repeat step 3 for any other steps you want to subordinate.

In the figure, you can see that some items have already been subordinated to the
next level. Compare their appearance to the levels indicated on the Change List
Level submenu.

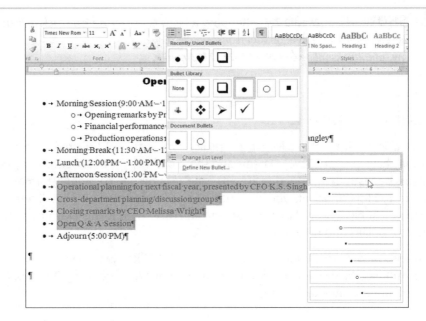

Figure 7.14 *Creating a nested list with bullets.*

Creating a Nested List with Numbers and Bullets

An item in a numbered list can include subordinate items. The subordinate items are indented farther from the left margin and use a bullet rather than a numeral. Here's how to create a nested list with numbers and bullets:

1. Type all the text for the list.

2. Apply the primary numbering format to the entire list.

3. Select the subordinate items under one of the primary items; then do one of the following:

   - Click the Numbering button's drop-down arrow, click Change List Level, and then click the desired level for the subordinate items, as shown in Figure 7.15.
   - Click the Increase Indent button (in the Paragraph group on the Home tab) one time for each level you want to subordinate the selected items.

4. Repeat step 3 for any other steps you want to subordinate.

In the figure, you can see that some items have already been subordinated to the next level. Compare their appearance to the levels indicated on the Change List Level submenu.

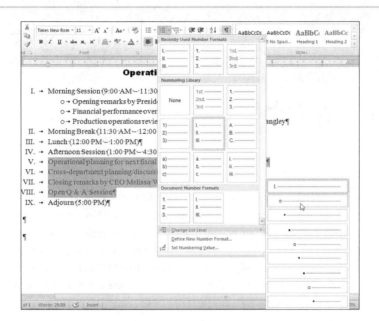

Figure 7.15   *Creating a nested list with numbers and bullets.*

Setting Spacing and Indents in a List

As mentioned earlier in the chapter, Word automatically indents lists from the left margin and places space between the bullet or number and its text. List items are formatted with a hanging indent.

If these settings don't suit you, you can easily change them by using Word's horizontal ruler. By dragging the four Indent markers (First Line, Hanging, Left, and Right) to the right or left, you can give your lists a different shape.

Don't use the Increase Indent or Decrease Indent buttons to change the indents in a list, or you'll wind up changing the list's levels, as described earlier in "Creating Nested Lists."

For a detailed discussion of the ruler, see Chapter 5.

SHOW ME   Media 7.4—Using Word's Ruler to Set Spacing and Indents in a List

Access this video file through your registered Web Edition at
my.safaribooksonline.com/9780132182713/media.

Tables help you arrange information so it's easy to read and understand, while adding visual interest to your documents. This chapter shows you how to create and format tables in your Word documents.

8

Creating Tables

If you flip through magazines, newspapers, and other professionally created publications, you'll see plenty of tables being used in innovative ways. Tables are popular because they are simple yet powerful—they give you fine control over where and how to display pieces of information. They also make data easy to read, interpret, and remember—especially if the data is a combination of text and numbers. And tables add visual variety to a document, with their capability to hold pictures and their nearly limitless formatting possibilities.

In simple terms, a *table* is just a grid of rows and columns. At the point where each row and column intersect is a box, called a *cell*. A table stores information in its cells. You can make a table's cells as neat and uniform as soldiers standing in formation, or you can make each one as unique and distinct as the faces in an audience. A table's text can be formatted just like any other kind of text.

In this chapter, you learn several ways to add tables to your documents. You learn how to resize tables, nest one table within another, format tables and cells, and much more.

Inserting a Table

Word lets you create tables in several ways. The method you choose is largely a matter of preference. The main difference among these table-creating tools is the amount of control they give you in setting up the table before you start entering data into it. But tables are flexible, so you can easily resize and format them before, while, or after you put information in the cells.

When you insert a table from the Table menu or the Insert Table dialog box, Word gives you a barebones grid of rows and columns outlined with thin borders. To make a basic table more visually appealing, you need to use Word's layout and formatting tools to add shading, colors, and other formatting touches to the table. Alternatively, you can skip the formatting tasks by starting with a fully formatted Quick Table.

Inserting a Table from the Table Menu

The Table menu is the fastest and simplest way to set up a table. The result is a perfectly uniform table, which fills the page horizontally from margin to margin, with cells all the same size.

 LET ME TRY IT

Using the Table Menu to Create a Table of a Specific Size

Here's how to use the Table menu to create a 5 x 5 table (a table with five columns and five rows):

1. Place the insertion point on an empty paragraph return.

2. On the Ribbon's Insert tab, click the Table button. The Table menu drops down, as shown in Figure 8.1.

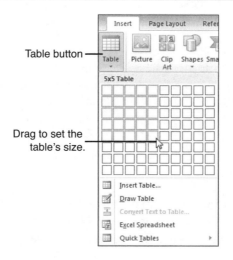

Figure 8.1 *Creating a table from the Table menu.*

3. Point to the first square in the upper-left corner of the Table menu's grid, and notice how the square is highlighted.

4. Without clicking, move the mouse pointer down and to the right, until you have highlighted a grid that contains five rows and five columns of squares (see Figure 8.1).

5. When the last square is highlighted, click it. Word inserts a 5 x 5 table in your document, as shown in Figure 8.2.

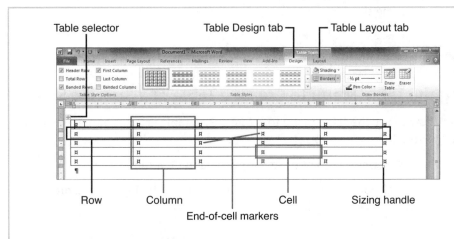

Figure 8.2 *A basic 5 x 5 table.*

It's usually a good idea to insert a new table on a blank paragraph return, and even to have blank paragraphs before and after that one. I suggest this only because it keeps your table nice and separate from the rest of your text while you're working on it. When your table is finished, you can move it to any location in the document.

Notice a few things in Figure 8.2:

- When the insertion point is in the table, two new tabs appear on Word's Ribbon. These are the Table Design and Table Layout tabs, and you use them to format your table as described later in this chapter.

- When the insertion point is resting anywhere on the table, a small square containing a four-way arrow appears by the table's upper-left corner. This tool is called the *table selector*, and you can use it to select the entire table with a single click.

- By the table's lower-right corner is a small box, called a *sizing handle*. You can drag the sizing handle to resize the entire table.

- Because our copy of Word (the one used in the illustrations) is set to show hidden characters, each table cell contains a little square. This square is called the *end-of-cell marker* and shows you where the cell's contents end; nothing can be placed in a cell to the right of this marker.

Inserting a Table from the Insert Table Dialog Box

The Insert Table dialog box lets you specify the number of columns and rows in a table, just like the Table menu. But the Insert Table dialog box also lets you control how the table behaves when you type text into its cells.

 LET ME TRY IT

Using the Insert Table Dialog Box

Here's how to use the Insert Table dialog box to create a simple table:

1. Place the insertion point on an empty paragraph return.

2. On the Ribbon's Insert tab, click the Table button. The Table menu drops down.

3. Click Insert Table. The Insert Table dialog box opens, as shown in Figure 8.3.

Figure 8.3   *The Insert Table dialog box.*

4. Click the Number of Columns box and specify the number of columns for the table.

5. Click the Number of Rows box and specify the number of rows for the table.

6. In the AutoFit Behavior section, choose one of the following options:

- **Fixed Column Width:** This option is selected by default and is set to Auto. When the table is created, it extends from margin to margin and all columns are the same width, but columns automatically (hence the aforementioned *Auto* setting) change their width based on their contents. If you want the columns to maintain an exact width at all times, use the spin control to set a specific width for all the columns, in fractions of an inch.
- **AutoFit to Contents:** When the table is created, the columns are wide enough to display only their end-of-cell markers. As you enter text into a cell, that column will widen as needed to display all your text (or as much as possible) on one line.
- **AutoFit to Window:** This is sort of an odd setting, because it relates to the size of the window your table is viewed in, not to the page. If you choose this option, Word adjusts the table's width based on the space available in the window. This setting is probably more helpful if you use Word to create documents for viewing on the web than for printing.

7. If you want the number of row and columns you set in steps 4 and 5 to be the default setting for future tables, click the Remember Dimensions for New Tables check box.

8. Click OK.

Inserting a Quick Table

Word features a small set of predesigned tables, called *Quick Tables*, that free you from formatting chores. Each table appears with a given number of rows and columns, and uses specific formatting touches (such as colors and fonts) based on your document's current template. If you need to modify the table's appearance, you can resize and reformat a Quick Table like any other table.

 LET ME TRY IT

Using the Quick Table Gallery

You select a Quick Table from the Quick Tables Gallery, which cascades (pops out) from the Tables Menu. Here's how:

1. Place the insertion point on an empty paragraph return.

2. On the Ribbon's Insert tab, click the Table button. The Table menu drops down.

3. Click Quick Tables to open the Quick Tables Gallery, as shown in Figure 8.4.

Figure 8.4   *Selecting a Quick Table from the Quick Tables Gallery.*

4. Scroll through the gallery to view the available Quick Tables.

5. Click a Quick Table to insert it in your document. Figure 8.5 shows the Matrix Quick Table.

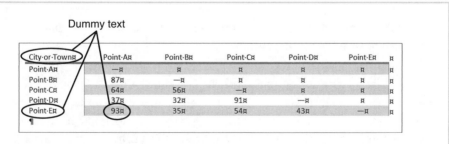

Figure 8.5   *The Matrix Quick Table. Each Quick Table is uniquely formatted and includes dummy text to show you how your text will look.*

Drawing a Table

You can use your mouse pointer to draw a table on the screen. This feature is time-consuming, but it can be helpful if you know that your table won't be perfectly symmetrical. For example, you may need some cells to be different widths than others, or you may need to create a table within a table (a feature called "nested tables," discussed in more detail later in this chapter).

Drawing a table may seem daunting, but it's really easy. And Word is very forgiving; if you make a mistake, you can easily erase it and start again. You begin by drawing a rectangle as the table's exterior border and then draw interior lines within the border to create rows, columns, and individual cells. When the table is drawn, you can edit and format it like any other table you create in Word.

 **LET ME TRY IT**

Using Your Mouse Pointer to Draw a Table

The following steps show you how to draw a simple table; but when you understand the basics, you can use them to draw tables as complex as you need.

1. Place the insertion point on an empty paragraph return.

2. On the Ribbon's Insert tab, click the Table button. The Table menu drops down.

3. Click Draw Table. The insertion point changes to a Pencil icon.

4. Click and drag the pointer down and to the right, creating a rectangle, as shown in Figure 8.6. Release the mouse button when the rectangle is the desired size. This rectangle forms the table's outside border.

5. To draw the table's first row, click a point about one-third of the way down the table's left border; then drag straight to the right. Before you reach the table's opposite edge, the border you're drawing "snaps" into place; you can release the mouse button.

As you drag the Pencil icon, look at Word's horizontal and vertical rulers (if they are open on your screen). A faint dotted line appears on each ruler, showing the pointer's exact location on the page. These indicators are helpful for sizing your table and its features. For example, using these markers, you can make sure that your table's upper-left corner is located 2" from the left and right margins. The indicators can also help you locate the starting and ending points for the table's columns, rows, and cells. Using the rulers this way can save you a lot of guesswork.

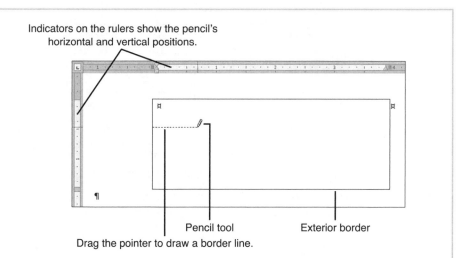

Indicators on the rulers show the pencil's
horizontal and vertical positions.

Pencil tool   Exterior border

Drag the pointer to draw a border line.

Figure 8.6   *Drawing a table. The outside border has been drawn as a rectangle, and the first row's bottom border is now being drawn.*

6. To draw the next row, click a point about two-thirds of the way down the table's right border; then drag straight to the left. Again, the line you're drawing should "snap" into place before you reach the opposite edge of the table.

7. Separate the table into two columns by clicking the mid-point of the table's top border, then drag straight down to the midpoint of the bottom border. You have created a basic two-column-by-three-row table, which should look something like the one shown in Figure 8.7.

8. Suppose you want to divide one of the table's cells into two smaller cells. (This is called "splitting" a cell.) Click the midpoint of a cell's top border; then drag straight down to the midpoint of the cell's bottom border. The cell is split, as shown in Figure 8.8.

9. Suppose you want to erase part of a row's border, to combine two cells into a larger one. (This is called "merging" cells.) Click the Eraser button at the right end of the Table Design tab; the pointer changes shape to resemble an eraser. Click the cell's top border to erase it, as shown in Figure 8.9.

10. Click the Draw Table button on the Table Design tab; then draw a rectangle in the newly merged cell you created in step 9. This rectangle is the exterior border for a nested table, which exists within a cell of the first table (see Figure 8.10). You can repeat any of the preceding steps to create rows, columns, and cells within the nested table.

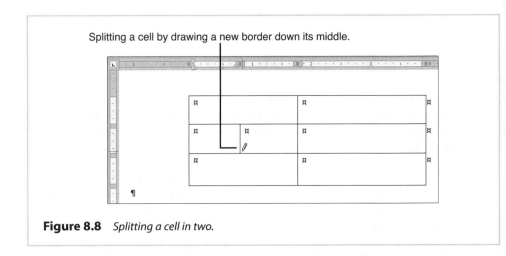

Figure 8.7   *A basic 2 x 3 table, drawn by hand in Word.*

Splitting a cell by drawing a new border down its middle.

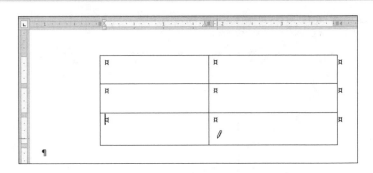

Figure 8.8   *Splitting a cell in two.*

11.   When you finish drawing, click the Draw Table button on the Table Design tab (or press Esc). The mouse pointer returns to normal.

SHOW ME   Media 8.1—Drawing a Table in Word

Access this video file through your registered Web Edition at
my.safaribooksonline.com/9780132182713/media.

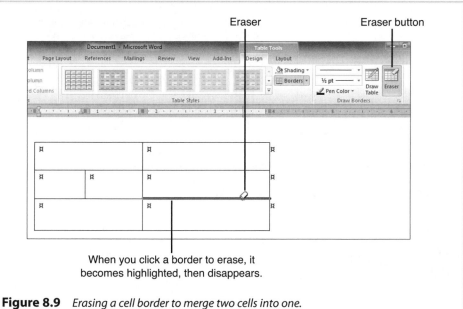

Figure 8.9 *Erasing a cell border to merge two cells into one.*

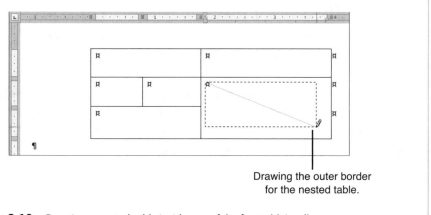

Figure 8.10 *Drawing a nested table inside one of the first table's cells.*

Converting Text to a Table

A relatively difficult but definitely old-fashioned way of creating tables involves setting up lines of text interspersed with tab stops (or a different separator character, such as commas). Each paragraph of tabbed text becomes a row in the table, and each text/tab combo becomes a column. Figure 8.11 shows a few lines of tabbed text and how it might look when converted to an actual table.

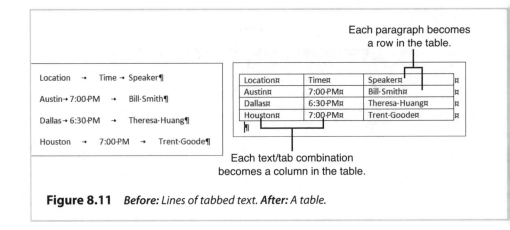

Figure 8.11   *Before: Lines of tabbed text. After: A table.*

 **LET ME TRY IT**

Converting Tabbed Text into a Table

Here's how to convert lines of tabbed text (or text separated by some other character) into a table:

1. Set up the text so that the individual pieces of data are separated by a tab. Make sure that *only one* tab appears between the pieces of data in the paragraph.

2. Select all the paragraphs of tabbed text that you want to include in the table. If any intervening lines of nontabbed text are included in the selection, they will appear in their own rows in your table.

3. On the Insert tab, click the Table button.

4. Click Convert Text to Table. The Convert Text to Table dialog box appears, as shown in Figure 8.12.

5. Make sure the numbers of rows and columns in the dialog box are correct; then do one of the following:

    *   If either of the numbers is wrong, there may be too many or too few tabs hidden somewhere in your text, and this can throw off Word in estimating the numbers of rows and columns. Click Cancel, correct your tabbed text, and then start over with step 1.
    *   If the numbers are correct, go to step 6.

Figure 8.12   *The Convert Text to Table dialog box.*

6. In the Separate Text At section, select the text separator used with your text. (The default is Tabs.) If your text is separated by paragraph marks or commas, click the corresponding option button. If your text is separated by a different character, click the Other option button; then type the character in the text box that appears to the right.

7. Click OK. The dialog box closes, and your tabbed text now appears as a table.

Creating Nested Tables

A *nested table* is a table that resides within another, larger table, as shown in Figure 8.13. Together, these tables are called "nested tables." A table can contain one or more nested tables, and a nested table can contain one or more nested tables within it, and so on until it gets so crowded that nobody can read anything in any of them.

Inserting a Nested Table

You can insert a nested table by using the same table-insertion methods described earlier in this chapter: by using the Table menu or the Insert Table dialog box, or by inserting a Quick Table. To do this, place the insertion point in the cell where the nested table will reside; then use one of the methods described in the section "Inserting a Table."

Professor	Location	Office Hours	Available Dates in January
Dr. Thurman	Cowan 412	9:00 – 11:30 AM; 4:30 – 6:15 PM	Every Tuesday and Thursday
Dr. Smith	Cowan 415	8:30 – 10:45 AM; 5:00 – 6:30 PM	Every Monday, Wednesday and Friday
Dr. Cunningham	Cowan 418	9:00 – 10:45 AM; 4:15 – 6:00 PM	(calendar)
Dr. Wyman	Cowan 420	9:15 – 11:00 AM	Every Monday and Thursday

Calendar (nested table):

M	T	W	T	F	S	S
	1	2	X	4	X	X
7	X	9	X	11	12	X
X	15	16	17	X	X	X
21	X	23	X	25	X	X
28	29	X	31			

The calendar is a nested table.

Figure 8.13   *An example of a nested table. The calendar makes it easy to see which days Dr. Cunningham will be in the office during the month of January.*

Drawing a Nested Table, Redux

The quickest way to add a nested table to an existing table is to draw it. To draw a nested table, do the following:

1. Click inside the original table to place the insertion point there.

2. On the Table Design tab, click Draw Table to activate the pencil pointer.

3. Draw your nested tabled in the desired cell of the original table. Draw a rectangle for the nested table's exterior border; then draw lines for the rows, columns, and cells.

4. When you finish, click Draw Table (or press Esc) to exit drawing mode.

For more details on drawing parts of a table, see the section "Drawing a Table," earlier in this chapter.

Editing a Table

After you create a table, you're ready to start *populating* it (another bit of geek-speak) by adding information to its cells. Before we get into that, however, here's an important point to remember: Word treats the text in a table cell just the way it treats other text, with a few table-specific exceptions. After you type text into a cell, you can do any of the following to it:

*   Select it.

*   Format it with the same tools described in Chapters 4 and 5.

*   Cut, copy, and paste it.

- Create new paragraphs in a cell by pressing Enter.

- Create bulleted or numbered lists in a cell.

And a whole lot more, as well. If you know how to format ordinary text, paragraphs, lists, and such, you can format the text in a table. For that reason, we won't get into specifics about formatting text and paragraphs in tables; just see Chapters 1–7. There a few special formatting tricks for text in tables, however, and we'll describe them as they come up in the following sections.

Be aware that too much text can make a table hard to read. If a table starts to look cramped with text, consider formatting the information in a different way.

Moving Around in a Table

It's easy to move from one cell to another in a table; Table 8.1 tells you how. (Remember: the *current* cell, row, or column is the one holding the insertion point.)

Table 8.1   Table Navigation Methods

To Move from the Current Cell to:	Do This:
Any other cell	Press the desired cell.
Row above	Press the up arrow.
Row below	Press the down arrow.
Next cell	Press Tab
Previous cell	Press Shift+Tab
First cell in the table	Press Ctrl+Home
First cell in the current row	Press Alt+Home
Last cell in the current row	Press Alt+End
First cell in the current column	Press Alt+Page Up
Last cell in the current column	Press Alt+Page Down

Adding Text to a Table

Easy-breezy. To add text to a table, click in the desired cell and start typing. You can also cut or copy text from a different spot (or document) and then paste it into a cell.

Depending on the table's AutoFit setting, a cell will do one of two things when you type in it. The cell will either (a) grow as wide as it can to display as much text as possible on one line, or (b) maintain its current width no matter what. In either case, when the text goes as far to the right as it can, it wraps down to a new line and continues.

You can press Enter inside a cell to begin a new paragraph whenever you need to. A cell's paragraphs can be formatted as bulleted or numbered lists.

Figure 8.14 shows a few of the many ways a table's cells can hold text.

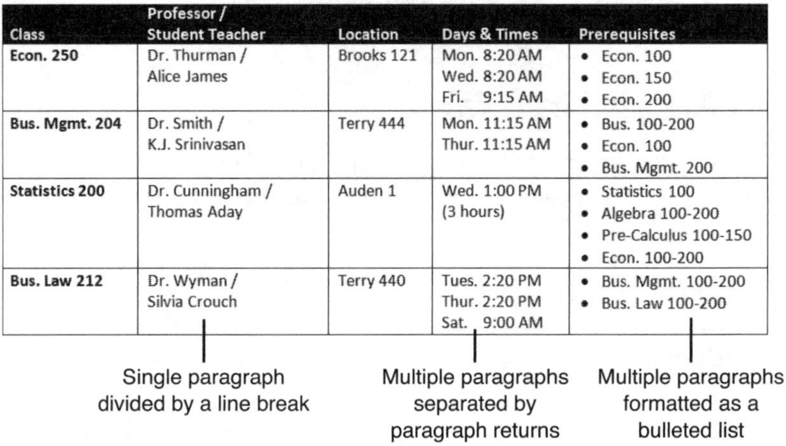

Class	Professor / Student Teacher	Location	Days & Times	Prerequisites
Econ. 250	Dr. Thurman / Alice James	Brooks 121	Mon. 8:20 AM Wed. 8:20 AM Fri. 9:15 AM	• Econ. 100 • Econ. 150 • Econ. 200
Bus. Mgmt. 204	Dr. Smith / K.J. Srinivasan	Terry 444	Mon. 11:15 AM Thur. 11:15 AM	• Bus. 100-200 • Econ. 100 • Bus. Mgmt. 200
Statistics 200	Dr. Cunningham / Thomas Aday	Auden 1	Wed. 1:00 PM (3 hours)	• Statistics 100 • Algebra 100-200 • Pre-Calculus 100-150 • Econ. 100-200
Bus. Law 212	Dr. Wyman / Silvia Crouch	Terry 440	Tues. 2:20 PM Thur. 2:20 PM Sat. 9:00 AM	• Bus. Mgmt. 100-200 • Bus. Law 100-200

Single paragraph divided by a line break

Multiple paragraphs separated by paragraph returns

Multiple paragraphs formatted as a bulleted list

Figure 8.14   *A table's cells are like mini-documents. They can hold text and paragraphs the same way a standard document can.*

Because you use the Tab key to move from one cell to the next in a table, you cannot use it to insert a tab into a cell. You can, however, copy a tab character from another part of the document and paste it into a cell. Then you can use the ruler or the Tabs dialog box to control the tab stop's size and characteristics.

Selecting Parts of a Table

Like other parts of a Word document, parts of a table must be selected (highlighted) before you can perform certain actions on them. For example, if you want to apply shading to a row, you must select the row and then add the shading. You can select an entire table or any single part of it.

There is a difference between selecting a table and selecting its contents. For example, you can select the text in a cell without selecting the cell itself. If a cell contains a sentence and you want to make a word bold, you can select that word without selecting the entire sentence or the entire cell. To select a cell's contents without selecting the cell itself, just select all the text but do not select the end-of-cell marker. All the text-selection tricks described in Chapter 2, "Editing Documents," work in tables.

The following sections show you how to select parts of a table. When you select a table (or any of its cells), any text formatting you do will apply to all the text in all the selected cells. Any table formatting you do will apply to the table, but may or may not affect the text because most table formats deal only with the table itself.

Selecting Table Parts with the Mouse

The easiest way to select a table is by using your mouse. You can use the mouse to select a single cell, multiple adjacent or nonadjacent cells, one or more rows or columns, or the entire table. Table 8.2 and Figure 8.15 show you how to select various parts of a table by using a mouse. Figure 8.16 shows the Select menu on the Table Layout tab; this menu lets you select the cell, column, row, or table that contains the insertion point.

Table 8.2   Selecting Parts of a Table with the Mouse

To Select This:	Do This:
The entire table	On the Table Layout tab, click the Select Table button; then click Select Table. Or...
	Click the table selector. Or...
	Click the table's first cell and drag down and to the right until you reach the table's last cell.
A row	On the Table Layout tab, click the Select Table button; then click Select Row. Or...
	Move the mouse pointer to the left end of the row; when the pointer turns into a right-leaning arrow (without changing color or size), click to select the row. Or...
	Click the row's first or last cell; then drag to the other end of the row.
A column	On the Table Layout tab, click the Select Table button; then click Select Column. Or...
	Move the mouse pointer to the top of a column; when the pointer turns into a small, black, downward-pointing arrow, click to select the column. Or...
	Click the column's top or bottom cell; then drag to the other end of the column.
A cell	On the Table Layout tab, click the Select Table button; then click Select Cell. Or...
	Move the mouse pointer to the lower-left corner of the cell; when the pointer turns into a small, black, right-leaning arrow, click to select the cell.
	Drag the mouse pointer across the cell's contents, including the end-of-cell marker.

Click the table selector to select the entire table.

Date	Location	Leader	Book
May 13	City Library, Room 21	Jill Worthington	*A Catcher in the Rye*
June 15	City Library, Room 21	Kate Epperson	*To Kill a Mockingbird*
July 14	City College, Baker Bldg., Room 114	Mellissa Robinson	*The Wizard of Oz*
August 11	Community Center, Room 3	Shelly Bruce	*The Golden Compass*

Move the pointer to the left end of a row; click to select the row.

Date	Location	Leader	Book
May 13	City Library, Room 21	Jill Worthington	*A Catcher in the Rye*
June 15	City Library, Room 21	Kate Epperson	*To Kill a Mockingbird*
July 14	City College, Baker Bldg., Room 114	Mellissa Robinson	*The Wizard of Oz*
August 11	Community Center, Room 3	Shelly Bruce	*The Golden Compass*

Move the pointer to the top of a column; click to select the column.

Date	Location	Leader	Book
May 13	City Library, Room 21	Jill Worthington	*A Catcher in the Rye*
June 15	City Library, Room 21	Kate Epperson	*To Kill a Mockingbird*
July 14	City College, Baker Bldg., Room 114	Mellissa Robinson	*The Wizard of Oz*
August 11	Community Center, Room 3	Shelly Bruce	*The Golden Compass*

Move the pointer to the lower-left corner of a cell; click to select the cell.

Date	Location	Leader	Book
May 13	City Library, Room 21	Jill Worthington	*A Catcher in the Rye*
June 15	City Library, Room 21	Kate Epperson	*To Kill a Mockingbird*
July 14	City College, Baker Bldg., Room 114	Mellissa Robinson	*The Wizard of Oz*
August 11	Community Center, Room 3	Shelly Bruce	*The Golden Compass*

Figure 8.15   *Selecting a table, a row, a column, and a cell with a single mouse click. The mouse pointer changes to indicate what you can select.*

Figure 8.16   *The Select drop-down menu, on the Table Layout tab.*

When any part of a table is selected, it is highlighted with a blue background.

There are other mouse-based methods for choosing part of a table, too. For example, you can triple-click a cell to select it. You can select multiple adjacent cells, rows, or columns, by selecting the first one you want and then dragging across the next one. If you hold down Ctrl while you click, you can select nonadjacent rows, columns, or cells. Experiment with different methods to find the ones you like best.

Selecting Table Parts with the Keyboard

If you prefer to keep your hands on the keyboard as much as possible, you can select any part or all of a table by using keyboard shortcuts. Here are the major keyboard shortcuts for table selection:

- To select a cell, move the insertion point to the beginning of the cell; then press Shift+End.

- To select a row, move the insertion point to the beginning of the row's first cell; then press Shift+Alt+End.

- To select a column, move the insertion point to the beginning of the column's first cell; then press Shift+Alt+Page Down.

- To select the entire table, move the insertion point to the beginning of the table's first cell; then press Shift+Alt+End to select the entire first row and press Shift+Down Arrow repeatedly to select each of the following rows.

Inserting and Deleting Table Parts

It's common to find that a table is too big or too small. But you can add and remove table parts with ease.

Adding Rows to a Table

To insert a new row into a table, place the insertion point in a row that will be directly above or below the new one. Right-click to open the shortcut menu, as shown in Figure 8.17. Click Insert to open a submenu of options; then do one of the following:

- Click Insert Rows Above to insert a new row above the current row.
- Click Insert Rows Below to insert a new row below the current row.

Instead of using the shortcut menu, you can use the Insert Above and Insert Below buttons in the Rows & Columns group of the Table Layout tab.

Insert options on the Table Layout tab.   Insert options on the shortcut menu

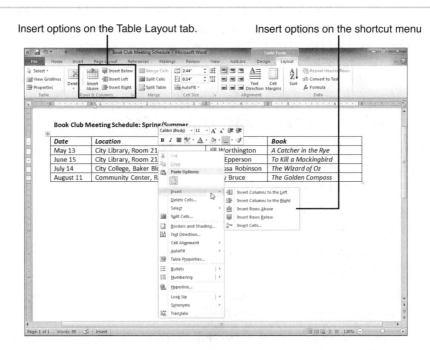

Figure 8.17 *The Insert submenu lets you expand a table with new rows, columns, and cells.*

You can use the Tab key to add a new row to the bottom of a table. To do this, place the insertion point at the end of the table's last cell, then press Tab. A new row appears at the bottom of the table. This feature lets you expand your table on-the-fly, as you are filling it with information.

Adding Columns to a Table

To insert a new column into a table, place the insertion point in a column that will be directly to the right or left of the new one. Right-click to open the shortcut menu (see Figure 8.17). Click Insert and then do one of the following:

- Click Insert Columns to the Left to insert a new column to the left of the current column.

- Click Insert Columns to the Right to insert a new column to the right of the current column.

Instead of using the shortcut menu, you can use the Insert Left and Insert Right buttons in the Rows & Columns group of the Table Layout tab.

Inserting Cells

If you need to add a new cell to a table, Word can accommodate you in several ways. Here's what to do:

1. Click in the cell where you want to insert the new cell.

2. Right-click the cell to open the shortcut menu.

3. Click Insert; then click Insert Cells. (Alternatively, click the dialog box launcher in the Rows & Columns group of the Table Layout tab.) The Insert Cells dialog box opens, as shown in Figure 8.18.

Figure 8.18   *The Insert Cells dialog box.*

4. Choose one of the following options:
   - **Shift Cells Right:** Shifts the remaining cells in the current row to the right to make space for the new cell. This makes the current row one cell longer than the other rows in the table.
   - **Shift Cells Down:** Inserts a new row of empty cells above the current row.
   - **Insert Entire Row:** Inserts a new row of empty cells to the table.
   - **Insert Entire Column:** Inserts a new column of empty cells to the left of the current column.

Deleting Rows, Columns, and Cells

If you decide your table doesn't need one of its rows, columns, or cells, you can delete it. If you delete something from the middle of the table, the rest of the table shifts to fill in the space.

- To delete a row, select it, and then right-click it to open the shortcut menu. Click Delete Rows.

- To delete a column, select it, and then right-click it to open the shortcut menu. Click Delete Columns.

- To delete a cell, right-click it to open the shortcut menu; then click Delete Cells. The Delete Cells dialog box opens, as shown in Figure 8.19. Choose one of the following options:

    - **Shift Cells Left:** Shifts the remaining cells in the current row to the left to fill in the space left by the deleted cell. This makes the current row one cell shorter than the other rows in the table.

    - **Shift Cells Up:** Shifts the contents of the remaining cells in the current column up to fill in the space left by the deleted cell. The cell at the bottom of the column is left blank.

    - **Delete Entire Row:** Deletes the current row.

    - **Delete Entire Column:** Deletes the current column.

Figure 8.19   *The Delete Cells dialog box.*

Instead of using the shortcut menu, you can use the Delete drop-down menu on the Table Layout tab, as shown in Figure 8.20.

Figure 8.20   *The Delete drop-down menu, on the Table Layout tab.*

Merging and Splitting Cells

Cells are not static. In addition to filling them with data, you can format them, resize them, join them together, or split them apart. The following two sections show you how to merge multiple cells into a single cell and how to split a single cell into multiple cells.

Merging Cells

When you *merge* cells, you combine any number of adjacent cells together into a single cell. (You cannot merge nonadjacent cells.) You may decide to merge cells for any number of reasons. A common example involves merging cells in the top row of a table, to allow space for a heading that spans multiple columns, as shown in Figure 8.21.

Districts Reporting			Estimated Q2 Sales	
North	East	South	Gross Units	Gross Revenues
District N1	District E1	District S1	2,890,000	$32,350,000
District N2	District E2	District S2	2,339,000	$31,100,000
District N3	District E3	District S3	2,775,000	$31,900,000
District N4	District E4	District S4	3,110,000	$36,110,000

Figure 8.21 *The first three cells of the first row have been merged for a heading that spans three columns; the same has been done to the row's last two cells. The table's second row contains subheadings.*

To merge cells, take the following steps:

1. Select the adjacent cells you want to merge.

2. Right-click the selected cells to open the shortcut menu; then click Merge Cells. (Alternatively, you can click the Merge Cells button on the Table Layout tab.) Word merges the cells together.

Splitting Cells

When you *split* a cell, you divide it into two or more parts. For example, you may split it into two columns, or into two rows. Word lets you decide how to split the cell. If you split a cell into multiple columns and rows, the result is like creating a nested table, except that the new cells remain part of the original table.

You may decide to split a cell for any number of reasons. A common example involves splitting a cell so that you can insert multiple pieces of data that have a similar meaning or relation to one or more adjacent cells, as shown in Figure 8.22.

Office	Agent(s)	Q4 Gross Units Sold	Q4 Gross Revenues
North	G. Johnson	245,000	$1,550,000
South	S. Suarez	198,000	$1,210,000
East	B. Carr	566,000	$3,250,000
	C. Malone		
	M. Huddleston		
West	J. Gregg	230,000	$1,420,000

Figure 8.22   *The second cell in the table's fourth row has been split into three rows to list all the agents who work in the company's East office.*

To split a cell, take the following steps:

1. Select the cell you want to split.

2. Right-click the cell to open the shortcut menu; then click Split Cells. (Alternatively, you can click the Split Cells button on the Table Layout tab.) The Split Cells dialog box appears, as shown in Figure 8.23.

3. Specify the number of columns and/or rows you want the cell to be split into.

4. Click OK.

Figure 8.23   *The Split Cells dialog box.*

If you select multiple cells for splitting, the Split Cells command is not available on the shortcut menu. Instead, you must use the **Split Cells** button on the Table Layout tab.

SHOW ME   Media 8.2—Merging and Splitting Cells in a Word Table
Access this video file through your registered Web Edition at
my.safaribooksonline.com/9780132182713/media.

Changing a Table's Size

A table can be any size you need it to be, within reason. Otherwise, the sky's the limit. I have seen tables that ran for pages and pages and hope never to see them again. No matter how you format it, too much information is just too much information.

Anyway, you can resize individual parts of a table or the entire thing. You can resize a table by dragging its borders or by specifying exact sizes.

Resizing by Dragging

The simplest way to resize a table or any of its parts is by dragging its borders. Dragging doesn't give you a great deal of precision, but that's OK as long as the table looks pleasing and text doesn't get lost in a sea of white space.

Resizing a Table by Dragging

To resize a table by dragging, rest the mouse pointer on the table until the table selector appears by the upper-left corner and the sizing handle appears by the lower-right corner, as shown in Figure 8.24. Click the sizing handle and drag the lower-right corner in any direction; the entire table resizes as you drag. Word keeps the sizes of the rows and columns in proportion to the table's overall size, as best it can.

Date	Location	Leader	Book
May 13	City Library, Room 21	Jill Worthington	A Catcher in the Rye
June 15	City Library, Room 21	Kate Epperson	To Kill a Mockingbird
July 14	City College, Baker Bldg., Room 114	Mellissa Robinson	The Wizard of Oz
August 11	Community Center, Room 3	Shelly Bruce	The Golden Compass

Sizing handle

Figure 8.24   *You can use a table's sizing handle to resize the table by dragging.*

If you press Shift while dragging a table's sizing handle, Word constrains the operation so that the table can be resized only a certain amount. This prevents the table from getting out-of-whack by being resized in a way that throws things out of proportion.

Resizing a Column by Dragging

To resize a column by dragging, point to its right border. When the pointer changes to a horizontal two-headed arrow, as shown in Figure 8.25, click and drag the border to the right (to widen the column) or left (to narrow the column). As you drag, Word displays a dotted line to show where the border will be dropped when you release the mouse button. Note that any columns to the right of the selected border will change width, too.

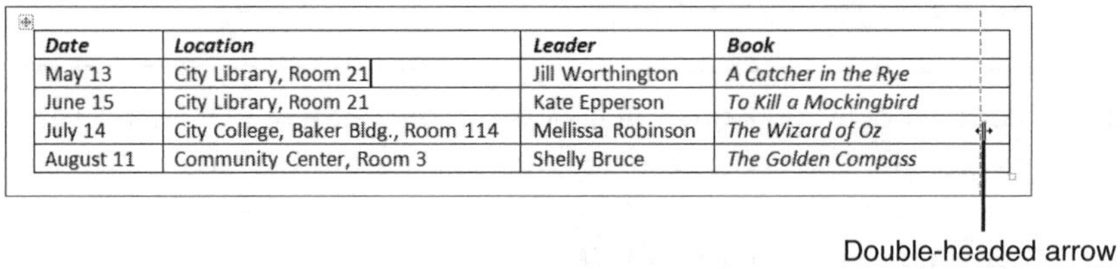

Date	Location	Leader	Book
May 13	City Library, Room 21	Jill Worthington	A Catcher in the Rye
June 15	City Library, Room 21	Kate Epperson	To Kill a Mockingbird
July 14	City College, Baker Bldg., Room 114	Mellissa Robinson	The Wizard of Oz
August 11	Community Center, Room 3	Shelly Bruce	The Golden Compass

Double-headed arrow

Figure 8.25   *Resizing a column by dragging its right border.*

Resizing a Row by Dragging

To resize a row by dragging, point to its bottom border. When the pointer changes to a vertical two-headed arrow, as shown in Figure 8.26, click and drag the border up (to make the row shorter) or down (to make the row taller). As you drag, Word displays a dotted line to show where the border will be dropped when you release the mouse button. Note that a row can be made only so short; if the row contains any text, Word will ensure that the row remains tall enough to display the text. Changing a row's height by dragging does not affect the height of any other rows in the table but does affect the table's overall height.

Resizing a Cell by Dragging

To resize a cell by dragging, select the entire cell, including its end-of-cell marker. Drag the right border to make the cell wider or narrower, as shown in Figure 8.27. (If you drag the cell's bottom border, the entire row's height will change—not just the selected cell's.)

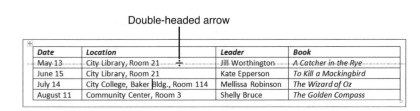

Figure 8.26   *Resizing a row by dragging its bottom border.*

Figure 8.27   *Changing a selected cell's width by dragging.*

Specifying Precise Table Dimensions

If precision is your watchword (whatever *that* means), Word has the tools to set any dimension of a table with laser-like accuracy. So, if you want a table's columns to be exactly 2.5 inches wide, you can do that. Same with row height. Same with the whole table!

You can set precise dimensions by using the Table Properties dialog box or the Ribbon's Table Layout tab.

LET ME TRY IT

Specifying a Table's Overall Width

To set a precise value for a table's total width, you must use the Table Properties dialog box. The Table Layout tab doesn't have a specific tool for this purpose. Here's how to do it:

1. Click anywhere in the table.
2. On the Table Layout tab, click the Properties button. (Alternatively, you can right-click the table to open the shortcut menu and then click Table Properties.) The Table Properties dialog box opens, as shown in Figure 8.28.

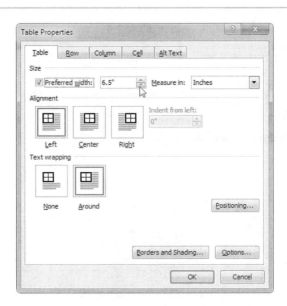

Figure 8.28   *Specifying a table's width in the Table Properties dialog box.*

3. Click the Table tab.

4. Click the Preferred Width check box.

5. In the Preferred Width spinner box, set a precise width for the table, in inches and/or fractions of an inch. Instead of using the arrow buttons, you can select the table's current setting and type a new value in its place.

6. If you prefer to measure the table's width as a percentage of the amount of space available between the right and left margins, click the Measure In drop-down arrow; then click Percent. (If you set an inch value in step 5, Word converts it to a percentage for you.)

7. Click OK. Word adjusts the table's width.

When you set an exact width for a table, Word adjusts the table's column widths accordingly. This may cause the text in some columns to wrap, so some rows may end up being taller than they were before.

LET ME TRY IT

Specifying Column Widths

You can set a precise value for a column's width on the Table Layout tab. Here's how:

1. Click in the column you want to resize.

2. On the Table Layout tab, click the Table Column Width spin control's up or down arrows to set the column's size in inches or fractions of an inch, as shown in Figure 8.29. Instead of using the arrow buttons, you can select the column's current setting and type a new value in its place.

Column Width

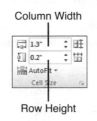

Row Height

Figure 8.29   *Specifying a column's width on the Table Layout tab.*

If you prefer, you can set a column's width on the Column tab of the Table Properties dialog box in the same manner as setting a table's overall width.

> If you have set a specific table width, the total widths of the columns cannot be greater or less than the table's width. If so, Word will readjust the columns after you specify a width. You'll need to do the math to determine how wide each column should be to fit exactly in the table.

LET ME TRY IT

Specifying Row Heights

You can set a precise value for a row's height on the Table Layout tab. Here's how:

1. Click in the row you want to resize.

2. On the Table Layout tab, click the Table Row Height spin control's up or down arrows to set the row's height in inches or fractions of an inch (see Figure 8.29). Instead of using the arrow buttons, you can select the row's current setting and type a new value in its place.

If you prefer, you can set a row's height on the Row tab of the Table Properties dialog box, in the same manner as setting a table's overall width.

Distributing Rows and Columns

Often it's best to allow a table's rows and/or columns to have unequal heights and widths, respectively. This distribution of space within a table's limited confines may present your information in the easiest-to-read manner. If you think it would look better to make all the rows the same height and/or all the columns the same width, Word can even them up with a click. Here's how:

- To distribute all rows equally, so they all have the same height, click the Distribute Rows button on the Table Layout tab, as shown in Figure 8.30.

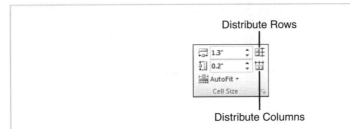

Figure 8.30   *The Distribute Rows and Distribute Columns buttons on the Table Layout tab.*

- To distribute all columns equally, so they all have the same width, click the Distribute Columns button on the Table Layout tab.

Formatting a Table

The look you create for your tables is limited only by your imagination. In addition to Word's table-formatting tools described here, you can use many different font and paragraph formats in your tables. With all these capabilities, you can create table styles that are uniquely yours.

TELL ME MORE   Media 8.3—The Best Ways NOT to Format a Table

Access this audio recording through your registered Web Edition at
my.safaribooksonline.com/9780132182713/media.

SHOW ME   Media 8.4—Formatting a Word Table by Hand

Access this video file through your registered Web Edition at
my.safaribooksonline.com/9780132182713/media.

Using Table Styles

Unless you started with a Quick Table, your table is probably pretty bland. By
default, Word's tables are simple grids surrounded by thin black borders. There's no
shading, no bold or italic, no nothing. But you can transform that table from "blah"
to "WOW!" in seconds with help from Word's built-in Table Styles.

Table Styles completely format a table with complementing fonts, a color scheme,
shading, and borders. There are dozens to choose from, and you can change from
one style to another with no problem. Here's how to apply a Table Style to a table:

1. Click anywhere in the table.

2. On the Ribbon, click the Table Design tab. The Table Styles Gallery takes up
   most of the tab.

3. In the gallery's lower-right corner, click the More button. The gallery
   expands, as shown in Figure 8.31.

4. Scroll through the gallery; then click the Table Style you like. The gallery
   closes and your table is formatted.

Aligning Text in Cells

Sometimes a table can look more "together" if you align its text in certain ways. For
example, if you have a column filled with two-digit numbers, the column may be
easier to read if the numbers are aligned in the center of their cells. If a row has tall
cells, they might look better if their contents are vertically aligned at the bottom of
the cells.

Word lets you align a cell's text in nine different ways. Each alignment is a combination of the text's vertical and horizontal positioning in its cell. For example, text can
be aligned center-left (horizontally aligned along the cell's left margin, and vertically aligned in the cell's center), top-left, bottom-center, and so on.

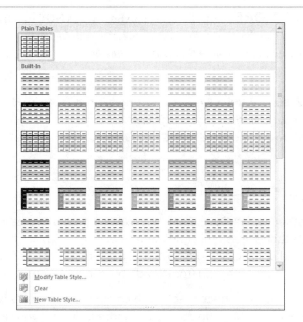

Figure 8.31   *The Table Styles Gallery.*

The Table Layout tab displays the nine alignment options as buttons in the Alignment group, as shown in Figure 8.32. You can also access these alignment options by right-clicking a cell and then clicking Cell Alignment on the shortcut menu.

To align text in a table's cells, select the cell, row, or column you want to align; then click the appropriate Cell Alignment button on the Table Layout tab or on the shortcut menu. You can align the text in each individual cell. But for best results, make sure that the cells in any one row are vertically aligned (top, center, or bottom) in the same way. In columns, headings look best if they are horizontally aligned to the left or center. No matter how you align your column headings, it looks best to horizontally align (left, center, or right) the data in each column the same way.

Choosing Borders for Cells

In most tables, all the cells are surrounded by top, bottom, left, and right borders. Borders delineate the information in the cells, making it easy to see what's what.

But there's no rule that says a table must have borders, or that the borders must be set up in a specific way. If you look at the Table Styles Gallery, you'll see proof of this. A table can look sharp with borders under the rows, or even with just a border under the row of headings at the top. Different combinations of borders can make a table pop, give it a sophisticated edge, and make it easier to read.

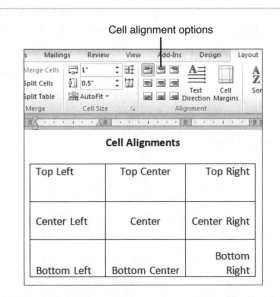

Figure 8.32   *Table cell alignments.*

 LET ME TRY IT

Applying Custom Borders to a Table

You can apply table borders from the Table Design tab. (You can also use the Borders and Shading dialog box, but this task is definitely easiest when performed on the ribbon, so we'll stick with this method.) Here's how:

1. With the insertion point in the table, click the Table Design tab, if it isn't already visible. The bordering tools appear near the right end of the tab, as shown in Figure 8.33.

Figure 8.33   *The bordering tools on the Table Design tab.*

2. Click the Line Style drop-down arrow; then select a line style for the border. You can choose from simple lines, dotted or dashed lines, double lines, and others.

3. Click the Line Weight drop-down arrow; then select a weight for the border.

4. Click the Pen Color drop-down arrow; then select a color for the border.

5. Select the cell(s), row(s), or column(s) that will get the borders, or select the entire table.

6. Click the Borders drop-down arrow, and select the position for your border. You can place a border on one or more sides of the selected cell, row, or column, or place borders around everything, so you may need to repeat this step several times to place borders everywhere you want.

If you choose to have no borders in your table, then no borders will appear on your screen. To see the edges of the table's cells without borders turned on, click the Borders drop-down arrow; then click View Gridlines. Word displays nonprinting dashed lines around every cell in the table.

Adding Shading

In a table, shading is a colored or gray background that appears in one or more cells. You can use shading in nearly as many ways as borders. Properly used, shading adds depth and visual appeal to your tables. If your document includes other colors, be sure the table's shading uses complementary colors or nice, low-key shades of gray.

 LET ME TRY IT

Applying Shading to a Table

You can apply shading from the Table Design tab. (Or from the Borders and Shading dialog box, but as you may have guessed, I don't like that dialog box, so we'll keep using the Ribbon.) Here's how:

1. With the insertion point in the table, click the Table Design tab, if it isn't already visible.

2. Select the cell(s), row(s), or column(s) you want to shade, or select the entire table.

3. Click the Shading drop-down arrow. A menu of shading colors drops down, as shown in Figure 8.34.

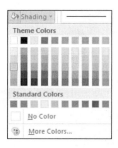

Figure 8.34   *The Shading menu.*

4. Click the color or shade of gray you want to apply.

5. Repeat steps 2–4 for each part of the table you want to shade.

Aligning a Table on the Page

If a table is less than full-width (meaning that it does not extend from the page's left margin to the right margin), you may want to align the table between the margins. This is just like aligning a paragraph: along the left margin, centered between the margins, or along the right margin.

Aligning a table does not affect the alignments inside the table. It only affects the table's positioning between the margins.

 LET ME TRY IT

Setting a Table's Alignment

To align a table on the page, take the following steps:

1. Click anywhere in the table.

2. On the Table Layout tab, click the Properties button. The Table Properties dialog box opens, as shown in Figure 8.35.

3. Click the Table tab, if necessary.

4. In the Alignment section, click the Left, Center, or Right button, depending on your preference.

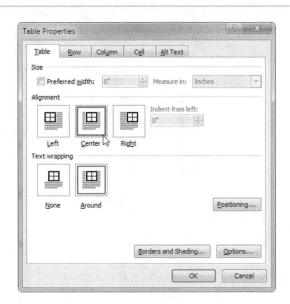

Figure 8.35 *Aligning a table in the Table Properties dialog box.*

5. If you left-align the table, you can use the Indent from Left spin control to indent the table from the left margin by a given distance.

6. Click OK.

Deleting a Table

Believe it or not, you can't just delete a table by selecting it and pressing the Del key. If you do that, Word deletes the table's contents, but the table itself remains.

To completely delete a table, do the following:

1. Click anywhere in the table.

2. Click the Table Layout tab, if it isn't visible.

3. Click the Delete button to open its drop-down menu, as shown in Figure 8.36.

4. Click Delete Table. Word removes the table's structure, contents, and formatting from your document.

Figure 8.36   *Deleting an entire table.*

Word lets you arrange text in columns, so you can create professional-looking multi-column documents, such as brochures and newsletters. This chapter shows you how easy it is to create elegant, easy-to-read multicolumn formats.

9

Setting Text in Columns

Columns were once the exclusive domain of desktop publishing (DTP) programs. In those days, word processors didn't have all the tools required to lay out text in smooth, evenly spaced columns. But things have changed, and Word can set up columns that are both easy to create and nice to look at.

Multi-column layouts are pretty much *de rigueur* in newsletters and brochures, but columns have uses in other kinds of documents, as well. An annual report, for example, might be laid out with page-width (single-column) text for the most part but can include small sidebars formatted with multiple columns.

This chapter teaches you all the basics of columns in Word. You learn how to set up text in a multicolumn layout, change the number of columns and set their widths, control text flow with column breaks, and convert multicolumn text into single-column text.

Understanding Columns

A *column* is simply a section of text set at a given width; its width can be constrained by the page, table cell, or columns (all of which contain their own margins). All text is actually columnar—that is, arranged in one or more columns. The text in this book, for example, is set in a single column.

But text can be arranged in multiple columns, like the text you see in newspapers and magazines. The columns may have the same or different widths, and a page can hold two, three, or more columns, depending on its size. Text "weaves" through columns from top to bottom, left to right, and page to page. Figure 9.1 shows an example of a newsletter with a simple two-column layout; this example is actually a template you can download and install in Microsoft Word.

Just from looking at a multicolumn document, you may get the impression that columns are hard to work with. Not true! Word's column tools are easy to use, and Word can even set up columns automatically, at the click of the mouse. Or you can set up everything yourself...but that actually isn't much harder than letting Word do it for you.

Figure 9.1   *A newsletter template laid out in a two-column format.*

You can apply columns to an entire document or just to part of a document. If you select a portion of a document and format it in columns, Word separates the multi-column text from the rest of the document by inserting one or more breaks—called *section breaks*—as needed. Chapter 10, "Laying Out a Document's Pages," discusses sections and breaks in greater detail, but you will see breaks coming into play later in this chapter.

TELL ME MORE   Media 9.1—Columns: A Simple Way to Get **Professional Results**

Access this audio recording through your registered Web Edition at
my.safaribooksonline.com/9780132182713/media.

Applying a Preset Column Format

Word features several preset column formats. These presets let you arrange text in two or three columns of equal width, or in two unequal columns. If you choose an unequal column layout, Word creates a wide "major" column and a narrow "minor" column. You can decide whether to place the minor column on the left or right side of the page. Column tools are located on the Page Layout tab.

The following examples show you how to apply simple column formatting to a single page of text. Because the entire document is formatted with columns, there is no need for any special breaks at the beginning or end of the text. The text in the example is not already formatted in any special way; paragraphs are formatted with the Normal style, the first line of each paragraph is indented one-quarter inch from the left margin, and there are six points of spacing between paragraphs. Figure 9.2 shows the document in single-column format.

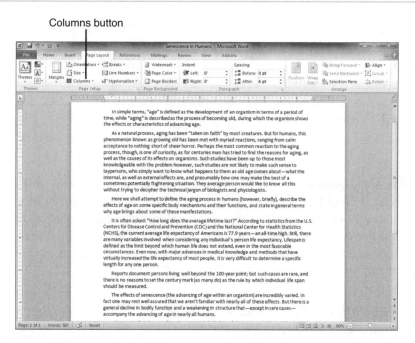

Figure 9.2 *Single-column text, which will be used in the following examples. The Page Layout tab is active on the Ribbon.*

When you convert single-column text to multicolumn text, Word preserves the text's other formatting. This includes fonts, font sizes, line and paragraph spacing, and other formats. However, not all formatting looks as good in narrow columns as it does in page-wide text. After setting text in multiple columns, don't be surprised if you want to make some formatting changes at the character and paragraph levels.

LET ME TRY IT

Choosing a Preset Format from the Columns Menu

Applying a preset column layout is as easy as a mouse click. Word's preset column formats appear on the Columns drop-down menu located on the Page Layout tab.

1. Select the text you want to format in columns, if needed, as follows:
   - To set part of a document in columns, select the text to be formatted.
   - To format an entire document in multiple columns, don't select any text.
2. On the Ribbon, click the Page Layout tab.
3. Click the Columns button. A drop-down menu of preset column formats opens, as shown in Figure 9.3.

Figure 9.3   *The Columns drop-down menu displays preset column formats. Click an option on this menu, and Word automatically formats your text in columns.*

4. Click Two. Word divides the text into two equal columns, as shown in Figure 9.4.

In simple terms, "age" is defined as the development of an organism in terms of a period of time, while "aging" is described as the process of becoming old, during which the organism shows the effects or characteristics of advancing age.

As a natural process, aging has been "taken on faith" by most creatures. But for humans, this phenomenon known as growing old has been met with myriad reactions, ranging from calm acceptance to nothing short of sheer horror. Perhaps the most common reaction to the aging process, though, is one of curiosity, as for centuries man has tried to find the reasons for aging, as well as the causes of its effects on organisms. Such studies have been up to those most knowledgeable with the problem however, such studies are not likely to make such sense to laypersons, who simply want to know what happens to them as old age comes about—what the internal, as well as external effects are, and presumably how one may make the best of a sometimes potentially frightening situation. They average person would like to know all this without trying to decipher the technical jargon of biologists and physiologists.

Here we shall attempt to define the aging process in humans (however, briefly), describe the effects of age on some specific body mechanisms and their functions, and state in general terms why age brings about

does not extend, even in the most favorable circumstances. Even now, with major advances in medical knowledge and methods that have virtually increased the life expectancy of most people, it is very difficult to determine a specific length for any one person.

Reports document persons living well beyond the 100-year point; but such cases are rare, and there is no reasons to set the century mark (as many do) as the rule by which individual life span should be measured.

The effects of senescence (the advancing of age within an organism) are incredibly varied. In fact one may rest well assured that we aren't familiar with nearly all of these effects. But there is a general decline in bodily function and a weakening in structure that—except in rare cases—accompany the advancing of age in nearly all humans.

In humans, after the age of 30, there is a steady decline of about 1-3% per year, in the maximum capacity of many physiological functions. For example, the cardiac index, standard glomerular function, maximum breathing capacity and other significant functions are almost certain to undergo some type of steady, if slow, decline with the passing years. We become more susceptible to death from various infectious diseases and from several mortality factors in which the

Figure 9.4   *The sample text, in a two-column format, with columns of equal width.*

In Figure 9.4, notice that the horizontal ruler is divided to reflect the presence of columns. Each column has its own margins, and on its section of the ruler, each column has its own indent markers. You can set margins, tabs, indents, and other paragraph formats in a column, just as you can in full-width text.

5. Click the Columns button again, and click Three to see how your text looks in three equal columns.

6. Click the Columns button again, and click One. Your text returns to its original single-column format.

 **LET ME TRY IT**

Choosing a Preset Layout from the Columns Dialog Box

Preset column layouts are also available from the Columns dialog box. (You'll learn how to use this dialog box to exercise more control over your column layouts later in the chapter.) Here's how to set up a preset three-column layout using the Columns dialog box:

1. Select the text you want to format, if needed, as follows:
    - To set part of a document in columns, select the text to be formatted.
    - To set the entire document in columns, don't select any text.
2. On the Ribbon, click the Page Layout tab.
3. Click the Columns button.
4. Click More Columns. The Columns dialog box opens, as shown in Figure 9.5.

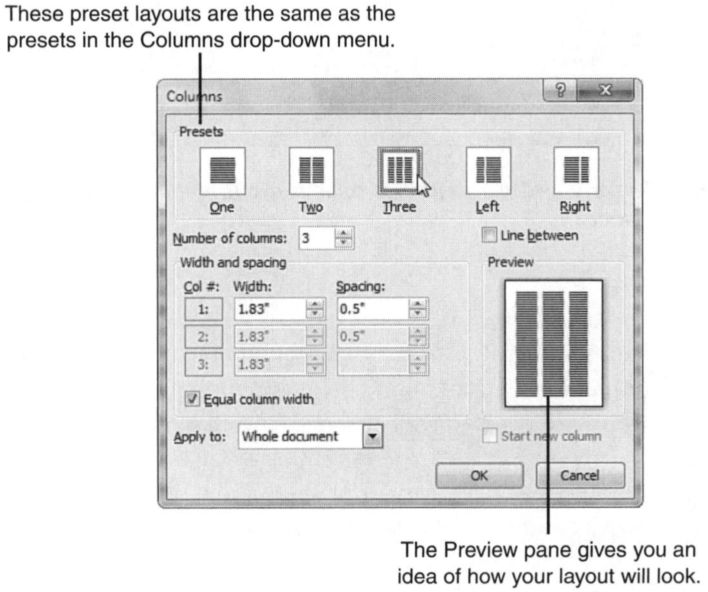

These preset layouts are the same as the presets in the Columns drop-down menu.

The Preview pane gives you an idea of how your layout will look.

Figure 9.5   *The Columns dialog box.*

5. In the Presets section, click the Three icon. If you look at the Width and Spacing section, you see that Word automatically makes all columns the same width and places the same amount of spacing between the columns.
6. Click OK. Figure 9.6 shows text in a simple three-column layout.

Figure 9.6 *Text arranged in a basic three-column layout, formatted with one of Word's preset column formats.*

Because Word adds gaps between columns, your text may take up more pages in multicolumn format than it does in single-column format. If you need to keep the columned text on the same page, try changing the character and paragraph formatting (particularly the line and paragraph spacing) to bring the text back onto the same page. If necessary, you can shrink the column spacing or make columns slightly wider to hold more text. Wide columns with narrow spacing, however, can look jumbled and become hard to read, so be careful when changing these settings. You'll learn more about adjusting column widths later in this chapter.

SHOW ME   Media 9.2—Applying Column Formatting to Existing Text
Access this video file through your registered Web Edition at
my.safaribooksonline.com/9780132182713/media.

Separating Columns with Vertical Lines

A multicolumn layout can look neater, and may be easier to read, if the columns are separated with vertical lines. Here's how to add vertical lines to text that is already set in columns:

1. Click anywhere in the text.

2. On the Page Layout tab, click the Columns button; then click More Columns to open the Columns dialog box.

3. Click the Line Between check box to place a check in it.

4. Click OK. Figure 9.7 shows an example of a three-column layout with vertical lines.

Thin vertical lines separate the columns.

Figure 9.7   *The text from Figure 9.6 with vertical lines inserted between the columns.*

You can add vertical lines while you're setting up a column layout. In the Columns dialog box, just be sure to click the Line Between check box when you select the number of columns.

Creating a Column Layout from Scratch

To take complete control of your column design, you can skip Word's preset layouts altogether and use the other tools in the Columns dialog box. The following sections show you how to specify the number of columns you want and set custom column widths and spacings.

Creating a Custom Column Layout

When formatting columns, remember that the number and widths of columns (and the spaces between them) are limited by the width of your page. For example, on a standard 8.5" x 11" page with one-inch right and left margins, Word enables you to specify up to 13 columns. But each column would be only one-half inch wide, and there would be no spacing between columns. Before creating a custom column layout, be sure to determine how wide your page's margins are set. If you think you'll need more space for your layout, adjust the margins before starting.

 LET ME TRY IT

Setting Up a Complete Multicolumn Layout

The following steps show you how to create a customized three-column layout with columns of different widths. With practice, you can use this procedure to create many different column formats. The following steps assume that you are starting will full-width (one-column) text.

1. Click anywhere in the text.

2. On the Page Layout tab, click the Columns button; then click More Columns to open the Columns dialog box.

3. Use the Number of Columns spin control to specify the number of columns you want; for this example, specify three columns. You can click the up or down arrows to set the number, or select the number in the box and type a new value over it.

4. Click the Line Between check box to place a check mark in it.

5. Clear the Equal Column Width check box to clear it. Clearing this check box lets you set each column's width.

6. Use the Width spin controls to set custom widths for the first two columns. Make these two columns the same width, but make them each narrower than the third column, as shown in Figure 9.8.

7. Use the Width spin control to set a custom width for the third column. In the example shown in Figure 9.8, columns 1 and 2 are each 1.5 inches wide, column 3 is 2.25 inches wide, and the intercolumn spacings are .63" each. That adds up to 6.51 inches, which is just about right for a standard sheet of paper with one-inch margins.

8. Click OK.

Specify the number of columns here.

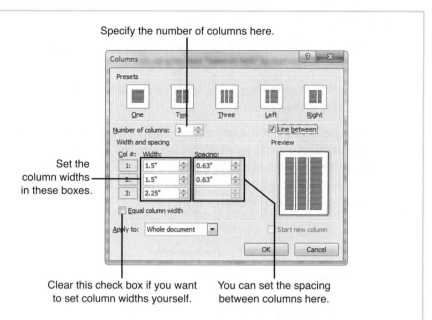

Set the column widths in these boxes.

Clear this check box if you want to set column widths yourself.

You can set the spacing between columns here.

Figure 9.8 *Setting custom column widths for a three-column layout.*

Word automatically calculates the amount of spacing to insert between columns, based on the column widths you set. If you change any of the spacing settings, Word may compensate by making your columns wider or smaller. This is because the total column and spacing widths cannot exceed the amount of space available between the page's margins. Unless you really don't like the result, it's usually best to let Word set the spacing between columns.

In this example, we formatted the entire document in columns, so there was no need to change the setting in the Apply To box of the Column dialog box. However, if you want the column settings to begin at the insertion point's location in the document, click the Apply To drop-down arrow and click This Point Forward; then click OK. Word inserts a section break immediately before the insertion point's location, so text above the insertion point retains its current formatting.

SHOW ME Media 9.3—Creating a Custom Column Layout in Word

Access this video file through your registered Web Edition at
my.safaribooksonline.com/9780132182713/media.

Changing Column Widths

If you don't like the widths of your columns, you can change them. You can change column widths in two ways:

- Open the Columns dialog box, specify new widths in the Widths and Spacing section, and then click OK.

- Drag one or more of the column indicators on the horizontal ruler. A column indicator appears as a small grid of dots on the ruler between the columns, as shown in Figure 9.9. When you point to an indicator, the mouse pointer changes to a two-headed horizontal arrow. Click the indicator and drag it to the left or right to resize your columns.

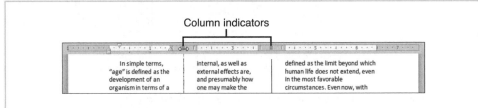

Figure 9.9   *Changing column widths by dragging a column indicator on the ruler.*

Creating Column Breaks

Text automatically flows through columns, sort of like a snake winding its way through a maze. Text starts at the top of the page's first column, flows down to the bottom of that column, and then breaks and resumes its flow at the top of the next column. Word fills every column with text until the text runs out. This is fine, unless you need a column to be "short"—that is, you need the text to stop before it reaches the bottom of a column and then jump to the top of the next column as usual.

To do this, you can insert a special character, called a *column break*, anywhere in a column. Here's how to insert a column break:

1. Place the insertion point where you want to insert the break.

2. On the Page Layout tab, click the Breaks button. A drop-down menu appears, as shown in Figure 9.10, listing the different kinds of breaks you can insert in a document.

3. Click Column. Word inserts the break at the insertion point's location. Any following text is moved to the beginning of the next column, as shown in Figure 9.11.

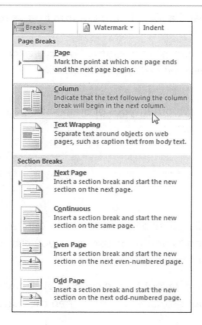

Figure 9.10 *Inserting a column break.*

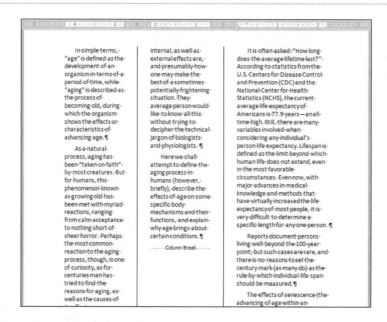

Figure 9.11 *Reflowing columnar text with a column break. With hidden characters displayed, you can see the column break.*

SHOW ME   Media 9.4—Using Column Breaks to Balance Multicolumn
Content
Access this video file through your registered Web Edition at
my.safaribooksonline.com/9780132182713/media.

Column breaks, along with other types of breaks and page-formatting tools, are
covered in detail in Chapter 10.

Converting a Multicolumn Layout to a Single Column

If the whole column thing gets on your nerves (and it can, if you mess with your
columns for hours trying to get them just right), you can bag it all and go back to a
plain old one-column layout.

To convert a multicolumn layout to one column, click anywhere in the columnar
text. On the Page Layout tab, click Columns; then click One.

IV

Formatting Pages and Documents

10 Laying Out a Document's Pages **224**

11 Formatting Documents with Themes and Templates **249**

12 Adding Headers and Footers to a Document **269**

Your text may be a work of art, but it won't be museum-quality unless you carefully prepare your canvas—or, in this case, your page. This chapter teaches you the basics of page formatting, to enhance your entire document's balance, flow, and readability.

Laying Out a Document's Pages

When you're putting together an important document—especially one that other people will read—it's essential to look at the big picture and the little details. In this case, the big picture is the page (or pages) itself. Your cool fonts, brilliant color scheme, and perfectly spaced paragraphs may look great on their own, but the page holds them together. If you neglect page formatting, your document may not have the elegance, coolness factor, or readability you've been aiming for.

This chapter takes you to the 10,000-foot level, away from the details of characters and paragraphs, to look down on your pages from afar. As you learn to appreciate this big-picture view, you also learn how to set and customize your pages' margins; divide a document into sections that can be formatted individually; orient your pages; control hyphenation; and add a background, watermark, or border to a page.

 TELL ME MORE   Media 10.1—Word as a Desktop Publishing Tool
Access this audio recording through your registered Web Edition at
my.safaribooksonline.com/9780132182713/media.

Setting Margins

A page's *margins* are the blank spaces that surround the text on all sides of the page. When we say "sides" here, we don't mean the front and back of the page; we mean the top, bottom, right, and left edges. Margins are like boundaries, holding text back a specific distance from the edge of the page. Figure 10.1 shows examples of two different margin settings. The first example has standard one-inch margins on all sides. The second example has much wider right and left margins, which help keep everything centered and make the short bits of text much easier to read.

We don't generally give much thought to our documents' margins, and that's OK most of the time. If you use one of Word's templates to create a document, you can be sure that the designer put a lot of thought into making the margins just right. And for many kinds of documents, Word's default margin setting (one-inch on all sides) works just fine.

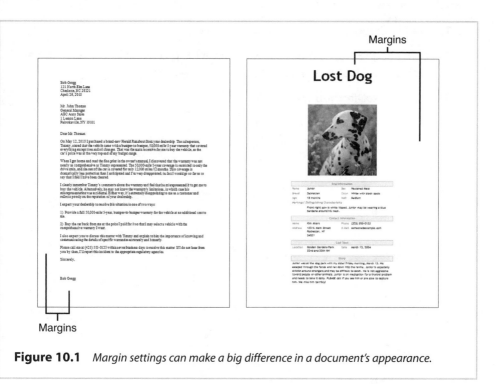

Figure 10.1 *Margin settings can make a big difference in a document's appearance.*

But for some documents, different margins work better. They may make the page look neater overall, focus the reader's attention differently, or create a more professional or even dramatic effect.

You can set margins in two ways. First, you can select one of several preset margin settings. Second, you can create custom margins by setting the width of each margin. You can make all margins the same or different widths.

You'll encounter margin tools in several different places in Word, such as the File tab's Print page and on the View Options menu in Full Screen Reading view. Here, we focus on using the Ribbon's Page Layout tab, the Page Setup dialog box, and Word's horizontal and vertical rulers.

Using Preset Margins

Word 2010 offers six preset margin settings. Select one of the presets, and Word applies it to the entire document. Here's how to apply preset margins:

1. On the Ribbon, click the Page Layout tab.

2. In the Page Setup group, click Margins. A drop-down menu of preset margins opens, as shown in Figure 10.2.

3. Click the setting you want.

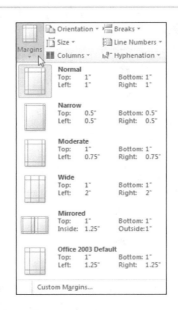

Figure 10.2 *Word's selection of preset margin settings.*

Creating Custom Margins

The quickest ways to set custom margins are through the Page Setup dialog box and the rulers. The Page Setup dialog box gives you precise control over each margin setting. The rulers are much less precise but quick and easy.

 **LET ME TRY IT**

Setting Precise Margins

The Page Setup dialog box lets you control each margin's width, with accuracy down to the hundredth of an inch.

1. On the Ribbon, click the Page Layout tab.

2. In the Page Setup group, click Margins.

3. Click Custom Margins. The Page Setup dialog box opens with the Margins tab visible, as shown in Figure 10.3.

Figure 10.3   *The Margins tab of the Page Setup dialog box.*

4. In the Margins section, click the Top spin control and set a width for the page's top margin. You can click the control's up and down arrow buttons to set a value, or you can select the number in the box and type a new value in its place.

By default, the spin control arrow buttons increase and decrease the margin's value in increments of one-tenth inch. If you want to specify a finer value (in hundredths of an inch), it's easier to select the current setting with the mouse pointer and then type your new setting in its place. Be sure to include a decimal point.

5. Repeat step 4 for the left, bottom, and right margins, as needed.

6. Click OK.

This example assumes you are setting margins for the entire document, so there is no need to change the setting in the Apply To box of the Page Setup dialog box. However, if you want the new margin settings to begin at the insertion point's location in the document, click the Apply To drop-down arrow; then click This Point Forward. Word inserts a section break immediately before the insertion point's location, so text above the insertion point will retain its current formatting. Sections and section breaks are discussed later in this chapter.

 LET ME TRY IT

Setting Margins on the Rulers

You can set a document's margins by dragging the margin indicators on Word's vertical and horizontal rulers. The margin indicators separate the gray and white sections near each end of the rulers. Figure 10.4 shows the margin indicators' locations on the rulers. Both rulers are visible only in Print Layout view.

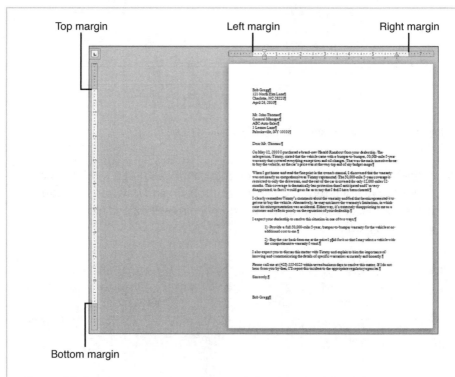

Figure 10.4 *The margin indicators on Word's horizontal and vertical rulers.*

To change one or more margins on the rulers, do the following:

1. In Print Layout view, click the View tab, and then click the Rulers check box to place a check in it, if necessary. This tells Word to display the rulers on the screen.

2. On the View tab, click One Page. Word zooms out so that an entire page of the document fits on the screen. This also makes both the vertical and horizontal rulers visible.

3. Do one or more of the following, as needed:

    - To change the left margin, point to the Left Margin indicator on the horizontal ruler. When the pointer changes to a double-headed arrow, drag the indicator to the left or right and drop it at the desired location.
    - To change the right margin, point to the Right Margin indicator on the horizontal ruler. When the pointer changes to a double-headed arrow, drag the indicator to the left or right and drop it at the desired location.
    - To change the top margin, point to the Top Margin indicator on the vertical ruler. When the pointer changes to a double-headed arrow, drag the indicator up or down and drop it at the desired location.
    - To change the bottom margin, point to the Bottom Margin indicator on the vertical ruler. When the pointer changes to a double-headed arrow, drag the indicator up or down and drop it at the desired location.

This method doesn't give you the precision of the Page Setup dialog box, but you can always use the rulers to create your basic margin settings and then use the dialog box to refine them later.

SHOW ME   Media 10.2—Setting Margins in Word
Access this video file through your registered Web Edition at
my.safaribooksonline.com/9780132182713/media.

Inserting Page Breaks

When a page's contents reach the bottom margin of the page, Word automatically inserts a *page break*. This special character creates a new page after the current one; if you're typing when this happens, the insertion point jumps to the first line of the new page and you can keep typing, as shown in Figure 10.5. Word automatically applies the current margin and other format settings to the newly created page.

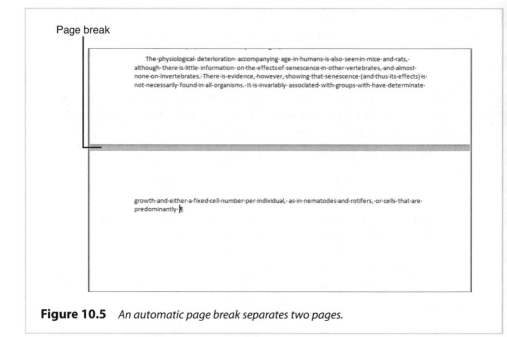

Page break

Figure 10.5   *An automatic page break separates two pages.*

You can force (manually insert) a page break anytime you want at any point on a page. A forced page break works just like an automatic one but ends the current page somewhere above the bottom margin, depending on where you insert the break.

Here's how to insert a forced or manual page break:

1. Place the insertion point where you want to insert the break. To get a clean break, it's usually best to insert the break at the end of a paragraph or on a blank paragraph return.

2. On the Page Layout tab, click the Breaks button. A drop-down menu opens, showing the available types of breaks, as shown in Figure 10.6.

3. Click Page.

> Instead of using the Breaks menu to insert a page break, you can press Ctrl+Enter.

In Print Layout view, a page break appears as a gap between pages. When this gap is visible, you'll notice that Word "jumps" from one page to the next as you scroll through the document. To close the gaps and enable smooth scrolling between pages, double-click the gap. When hidden characters are visible, a manual page break appears as a dotted horizontal line, above the gap between pages.

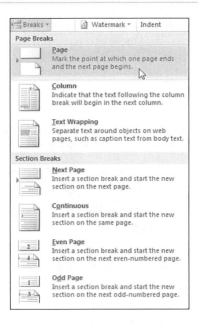

Figure 10.6   *Selecting a page break from the Breaks menu.*

Dividing a Document into Sections

In most general-purpose documents, format settings apply to the entire document, from beginning to end. For example, all pages have the same margins, the same column layouts, the same header and/or footer formats, and so on. Format settings that apply to an entire document may be called *global*, *universal*, or *documentwide* settings.

Sometimes, however, one part of a document has different formatting require-ments than the rest of the document. Most of the document may be laid out in a single column, for example, whereas one page requires a multiple-column design. Or one part of a document may have standard margins and another part may need very wide margins.

Word accommodates these situations by letting you divide a document into *sections*, each of which can be formatted differently from the others. For instance, a document's first section might be formatted as a single column, the second section in multiple columns, and the third section in a single column in the same manner as the first section. You can divide a document into as many sections as you need. A single page can be divided into multiple sections, too.

Word recognizes each section as its own independently formatted "mini-docu-ment," and stores each section's format settings separately from the others. You can give each section its own unique look; you can even assign different paper sizes to different sections.

Understanding Section Breaks

To create a new section, you insert a *section break* at the appropriate point in the document. Word offers four kinds of section breaks:

- **Next Page:** Inserts a page break at the insertion point's location. The new section begins at the top of the new page.

- **Continuous:** Inserts a section break at the insertion point but does not insert a new page. The current page is divided into two sections.

- **Even Page:** Inserts a section break that also acts as a page break. The new section starts on the next even-numbered page. If you insert this type of break on an even-numbered page, Word inserts a blank odd-numbered page before the new section.

- **Odd Page:** Inserts a section break that also acts as a page break. The new section starts on the next odd-numbered page. If you insert this type of break on an odd-numbered page, Word inserts a blank even-numbered page before the new section.

If hidden characters are visible on your screen, you can see section breaks. Each break appears as a dotted, horizontal double line with text that identifies what type of break it is, as shown in Figure 10.7. In the figure, a continuous section break divides the page into two sections; the first section features page-width margins that hold a newsletter's masthead, and the second section holds a three-column layout for the newsletter's articles.

Inserting a Section Break

Here's how to insert a section break:

1. Place the insertion point where you want the break to go.

2. On the Page Layout tab, click Breaks.

3. Click the type of break you want to insert.

 SHOW ME   Media 10.3—Using Section Breaks to Insert a Multicolumn Page in a One-Column Document

Access this video file through your registered Web Edition at
my.safaribooksonline.com/9780132182713/media.

Figure 10.7   *You can identify the breaks in your document when hidden characters are displayed. Here, a continuous section break has been inserted near the top of the page.*

Changing a Section Break

You can change a section break from one type to another. Here's how:

1. Double-click the section break. The Page Setup dialog box appears, as shown in Figure 10.8.
2. Click the Layout tab if it is not already visible.
3. Click the Section Start drop-down arrow; then click the type of section break you want.

In the Section Start drop-down menu, you'll see the New Column option. This type of section break is not available in the Breaks menu on the Page Layout tab. The New Column option places the break at the beginning of a new column, but only in a multicolumn layout.

Removing a Section Break

When you remove a section break from a document, Word must combine two sections that are formatted differently. To do this, Word applies the formatting from the second section (the section after the break) to the first section (the one before the break).

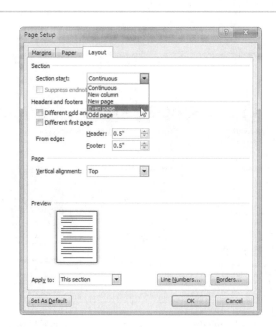

Figure 10.8 *Applying a different section type to a selected section break.*

Be prepared for this; if the sections are drastically different in their formatting, you may need to go back and make some changes after removing the section break. If you want to see how the text will look before removing the break, you can copy some or all of the text from the first section and paste it in at the beginning of the second section. If you like what you see, go ahead and remove the section break.

To remove a section break, click it and then press Del.

Setting Page Orientation

A page's *orientation* refers to the direction in which the document is printed on the page. You can orient a page in either of two ways:

- *Portrait orientation* is the more common orientation and is used for standard documents such as letters, memos, reports, and books. In portrait orientation, text is printed along the page's long edge.

- *Landscape orientation* has specific uses. For example, you would probably print a trifold brochure or a map in landscape orientation. In this orientation, text is printed along the page's short edge.

Figures 10.9 and 10.10 show two sample documents; one is shown in portrait orientation and the other in landscape orientation.

Bob Gregg
121 North Elm Lane
Charlotte, NC 28221
April 26, 2010

Mr. John Thomas
General Manager
ABC Auto Sales
1 Lemon Lane
Paleokaville, NY 10101

Dear Mr. Thomas:

On May 12, 2010 I purchased a brand-new Herald Runabout from your dealership. The salesperson, Timmy, stated that the vehicle came with a bumper-to-bumper, 50,000-mile/5-year warranty that covered everything except tires and oil changes. That was the main incentive for me to buy the vehicle, as the car's price was at the very top end of my budget range.

When I got home and read the fine print in the owner's manual, I discovered that the warranty was not nearly as comprehensive as Timmy represented. The 50,000-mile/5-year coverage is restricted to only the drive train, and the rest of the car is covered for only 12,000 miles/12 months. This coverage is dramatically less protection than I anticipated and I'm very disappointed; in fact I would go so far as to say that I feel I have been cheated.

I clearly remember Timmy's comments about the warranty and feel that he misrepresented it to get me to buy the vehicle. Alternatively, he may not know the warranty's limitations, in which case his misrepresentation was accidental. Either way, it's extremely disappointing to me as a customer and reflects poorly on the reputation of your dealership.

I expect your dealership to resolve this situation in one of two ways:

   1) Provide a full 50,000-mile/5-year, bumper-to-bumper warranty for the vehicle at no additional cost to me.

   2) Buy the car back from me at the price I paid for it so that I may select a vehicle with the comprehensive warranty I want.

I also expect you to discuss this matter with Timmy and explain to him the importance of knowing and communicating the details of specific warranties accurately and honestly.

Please call me at (425) 555-0125 within seven business days to resolve this matter. If I do not hear from you by then, I'll report this incident to the appropriate regulatory agencies.

Sincerely,

Bob Gregg

Figure 10.9   *A letter, in portrait orientation.*

**Wherever you're going,
you're going our way!**

Williams' Travel

Vacation Professionals

With more than 75 years of experience in the travel industry, Williams can help you design your dream getaway in no time at all.

We're the Midwest's leader in planning and booking:

- International vacations
- Cruises
- Eco-tours
- Family-friendly vacations

And much more!

Williams' Travel

**2200 South Boulevard
Suite 14
Prairie View, WY 88888
Phone: 325.555.0125
Fax: 325.555.0145
getaway@williams.com**

**No matter where you
want to go, we'll get
you there!**

Phone: 325.555.0125

Figure 10.10   *A brochure, in landscape orientation.*

To set the orientation for a document or a section of a document, do this:

1. On the Page Layout tab, click Orientation. A drop-down menu opens, as shown in Figure 10.11.

Figure 10.11   *Setting a document's orientation.*

2. Click the desired orientation.

Designating a Paper Size

Word can print on many standard sizes of paper, including letter (8.5" x 11"), legal (8.5" x 14"), and a variety of papers sized for photos, envelopes, and banners. You can also set a custom paper size for a document and tell Word which of your printer's paper trays to use for sheets of different sizes.

Using a Standard Paper Size

Here's how to select one of the standard sheet sizes:

1. On the Page Layout tab, click the Size button. A drop-down menu of paper sizes opens, as shown in Figure 10.12.

2. Scroll through the list; then click the page size you need. If you work in Print Layout view, the page's size and the ruler measurements change to match the selected paper size.

Using a Custom Paper Size

If you need to use a custom paper size or choose a different paper tray, do the following:

1. On the Page Layout tab, click the Size button.

2. Click More Paper Sizes. The Page Setup dialog box opens, with the Paper tab visible, as shown in Figure 10.13.

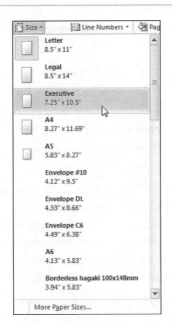

Figure 10.12   *Selecting a standard paper size.*

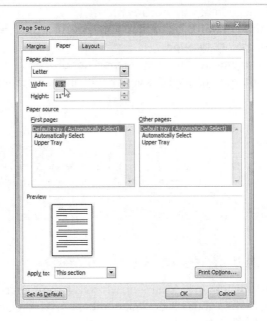

Figure 10.13   *Setting a custom paper size in the Page Setup dialog box.*

3. To set a custom paper size, click the Paper Size drop-down arrow and then click Custom Size. (You can also use this menu to select one of the standard paper sizes.)

4. Click the Width spin control and specify the width of your paper. You can click the up or down arrow buttons or select the number in the box and type a new value in its place.

5. Click the Height spin control and set your paper's height. You can click the up or down arrow buttons or select the number in the box and type a new value in its place.

6. If your printer has more than one paper tray, you can use the Paper Source section to specify which tray to use for the document's first page and for all other pages. This capability is helpful if you want to use a different-size paper for the first page. For example, the document's first page might be an envelope, and the remaining pages might be a letter. The first sheet should be separated from the other sheets by a section break.

7. Click the Apply To drop-down arrow and specify the part of the document to apply the settings to. Choose from the following options:
   - **This Section:** If the document is divided into sections, this is the default option. This option enables you to specify a different size paper and tray for each section of your document.
   - **This Point Forward:** This option applies your selection starting at the insertion point's location.
   - **Whole Document:** If the document is not divided into sections, this is the default option. It applies your paper and tray settings to the entire document.

8. Click OK.

Your printer may limit you to using certain paper sizes. If you need to use an unusual or custom paper size, check your printer's documentation to see if it is supported.

Numbering the Lines in a Document

Word can number the lines in a document, which is a common practice for legal or official documents. When you activate line numbering, Word places a number in front of each line, in the left margin.

Numbering Lines the Fast Way

To number the lines in a document, do this:

1. On the Page Layout tab, click Line Numbers. A drop-down menu of options appears, as shown in Figure 10.14.

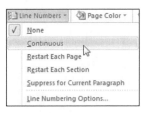

Figure 10.14   *Choosing a line numbering option.*

2. Click one of the following options:

    - **None:** Removes all line numbers from the document.
    - **Continuous:** Numbers all the lines in the document, starting at the first line of the first page and continuing to the last line of the last page.
    - **Restart Each Page:** Numbers all the lines in the document but starts over at the beginning of each page, so each page begins with line 1.
    - **Restart Each Section:** Numbers all the lines in the document but starts over at the beginning of each section, so each section begins with line 1. If the document is not divided into sections, this option has the same effect as Continuous.

If you don't want a certain line of text to be numbered, click that line; then open the Line Numbers drop-down menu and click Suppress for Current Paragraph. Word skips the selected line when numbering.

Setting Up Line Numbers with Precision

For slightly greater control over line numbers, use the Line Numbers dialog box. The following steps assume that lines have not already been numbered:

1. On the Page Layout tab, click Line Numbers.

2. Click Line Numbering Options. The Page Setup dialog box opens with the Layout tab visible.

3. Click the Line Numbers button. The Line Numbers dialog box opens, as shown in Figure 10.15.

Figure 10.15   *Setting line numbering options in the Line Numbers dialog box.*

4. To add line numbers to the document, click the Add Line Numbering check box to place a check in it. The other options in the dialog box become available.

5. Use the Start At spin control box to set the number for the first line. By default, Word starts numbering lines with the number *1*.

6. Use the From Text spin control to set the distance between each line number and the beginning of its line. The default setting (Auto) places the number one-quarter inch to the left of each line.

7. Use the Count By spin control to tell Word to count by 1s, 2s, 3s, and so on when numbering the lines.

8. In the Numbering section, select an option to restart numbering with each page or section, or to number lines continuously throughout the document.

9. Click OK to return to the Page Setup dialog box.

10. Click OK to apply your settings.

Hyphenating a Document

By default, Word does not automatically hyphenate text for you. Instead, if a word is too long to fit at the end of a line, Word moves it down to the next line. This is fine for many documents, but omitting hyphenation can leave the right edge of your paragraphs looking "ragged." (The term "ragged-right" is actually a page layout term, and it means purposely leaving a paragraph's right edge uneven, whether hyphenation is used.)

You can smooth out raggedy-looking text by turning on hyphenation. That way, Word fits as much of a word onto a line as possible before inserting a hyphen and pushing the rest of the word to the next line. You can use either of two hyphenation methods:

- **Automatic:** When you activate automatic hyphenation, Word follows a built-in set of rules for hyphenating words. It's as though your computer is looking up the recommended hyphenation points for each word in a dictionary.

- **Manual:** With manual hyphenation, you have a say in whether and where words get hyphenated. This gives you more control but requires more work on your part.

Automatic Hyphenation

Automatic hyphenation is as easy to use as it sounds. Just turn it on when you want it, and turn it off when you don't. Here's how to activate automatic hyphenation:

1. On the Page Layout tab, click the Hyphenation button. The Hyphenation drop-down menu appears, as shown in Figure 10.16.

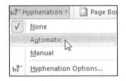

Figure 10.16   *Activating automatic hyphenation.*

2. Click Automatic. Word automatically inserts hyphens wherever it deems necessary throughout the document. As long as automatic hyphenation is active, Word hyphenates text while you type.

To turn off automatic hyphenation, do this:

1. On the Page Layout tab, click the Hyphenation button.

2. Click None. Word stops hyphenating your documents.

If you are still working in the same document that was open when you turned on automatic hyphenation, Word removes the hyphens it originally inserted.

Manual Hyphenation

When you activate manual hyphenation, Word doesn't automatically insert hyphens. Instead, whenever it encounters a word that could be hyphenated, Word displays a dialog box that shows hyphenation options and lets you decide what to do.

To use manual hyphenation, do this:

1. On the Page Layout tab, click the Hyphenation button.

2. Click Manual. Word searches the text for words that could be hyphenated. When it finds such a word, it displays the Manual Hyphenation dialog box, as shown in Figure 10.17. The suggested hyphenation point is highlighted by a blinking black box.

Figure 10.17 *With manual hyphenation, Word displays options instead of automatically hyphenating the text.*

3. If you prefer to use one of the word's other hyphenation points, click it.

4. Do one of the following:

   - Click Yes to hyphenate the word as shown in the dialog box. Word inserts the hyphen and finds another candidate for hyphenation.
   - Click No if you don't want to hyphenate this word. Word skips ahead to the next word that needs a hyphen.
   - Click Cancel to stop manual hyphenating.

 SHOW ME Media 10.4—Hyphenating a Document in Word
Access this video file through your registered Web Edition at
my.safaribooksonline.com/9780132182713/media.

Adding a Watermark to the Page

A *watermark* is a word, symbol, or picture printed lightly, but in a large size, on each page of a document. A watermark is usually added to a document to display a message (such as "Draft" or "Confidential") or to identify the document's creator. When printed, a watermark should be large and dark enough to be visible but not enough to distract the reader or obscure the document's text. Figure 10.18 shows an example of a watermark.

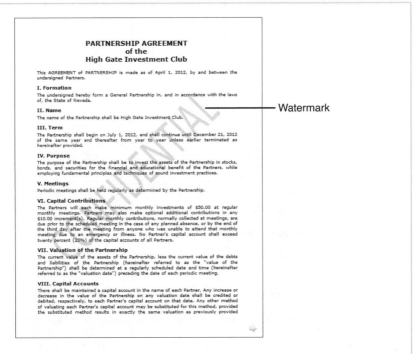

Figure 10.18 *A page with a watermark.*

You can add a preformatted watermark to a document, or you can create a custom watermark.

Inserting a Preformatted Watermark

Word offers a selection of common watermarks, all formatted and ready to add to your document's pages. Here's how to insert a preformatted watermark:

1. On the Page Layout tab, click the Watermark button. The Watermark Gallery drops down, as shown in Figure 10.19.

2. Scroll through the gallery and click a watermark. Word adds it to each page in the document.

Figure 10.19 *Choosing a preformatted watermark.*

Creating a Customized Watermark

You can create a custom watermark that says anything you like. Here's how:

1. On the Page Layout tab, click the Watermark button.

2. Click Custom Watermark. The Printed Watermark dialog box opens, as shown in Figure 10.20.

3. Click the Text Watermark option button.

4. Click the Text drop-down arrow and select a word or phrase. Alternatively, you can select the text in the box and type a different word or phrase in its place.

   You can specify a font, font size, color, and angle for your watermark, but I recommend sticking with the default settings, which are selected based on the document's template, format settings, page size, and so on. The default color and diagonal layout will make the watermark visible but unobtrusive.

5. Click Apply; then click OK.

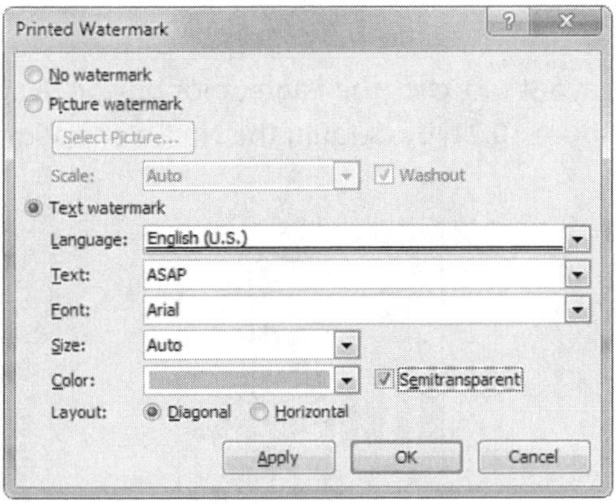

Figure 10.20   *Creating a custom text watermark.*

To use a picture as your watermark, click the Picture Watermark option button. Click Select Picture to open the Insert Picture dialog box, which is just like the Open dialog box. Find and select your picture; then click Insert. When you return to the Printed Watermark dialog box, click OK.

Removing a Watermark

To remove a watermark from a document, go to the Page Layout tab, click the Watermark button, and then click Remove Watermark. Word deletes the watermark from every page.

Adding a Colored Background to the Page

A colored background can add depth and personality to a document's pages. You can choose any color you want, from a calm blue to the hottest of reds.

That said, it's best to go easy on backgrounds, for a couple of reasons. First, a full-page background (especially a solid color) can quickly deplete your printer's ink or toner, which can cause streaky or uneven printing. Second, and at least as important, many people won't take a document seriously if it has *any* kind of background—let alone a hot pink or canary yellow one. If you're preparing a resume, a research paper, or any other document for professional or academic purposes, it's probably best to skip the backgrounds altogether.

Now that you've been warned, here's how to add a colored background to your pages:

1. On the Page Layout tab, click the Page Color button. A color palette opens, as shown in Figure 10.21. By default, the No Color option is selected.

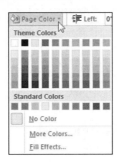

Figure 10.21   *Selecting a color from the Page Colors palette.*

2. If any of the theme or standard colors looks right, click it and you're done. If not, go to step 3.

3. If you want more colors to choose from, click More Colors. The Colors dialog box opens, as shown in Figure 10.22.

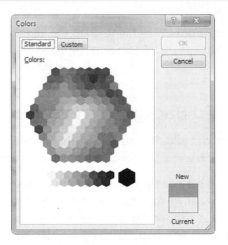

Figure 10.22   *The Colors dialog box lets you choose from thousands of colors.*

4. Select a color on either the Standard or Custom tab; then click OK.

You can also use a special effect (such as a gradient or a texture), a pattern, or a picture as your background. But if a simple colored background can be a turn-off to the reader, imagine one that resembles a blue carpet or streams of confetti. Pictures can also be a huge distraction. I don't recommend using these kinds of backgrounds, ever, unless you're creating a very casual or fun document, such as a party invitation. But, if you insist on it, you can access these backgrounds by clicking the Fill Effects option at the bottom of the Page Color palette.

Placing a Border Around the Page

A border acts like a frame around the margins of the page and can be a nice effect for documents such as certificates, announcements, and invitations. (I'm not as grumpy about borders as I am about backgrounds.)

Here's how to add a simple border to all sides of the page on every page in a document:

1. On the Page Layout tab, click the Page Borders button. The Borders and Shading dialog box opens, with the Page Border tab visible, as shown in Figure 10.23.

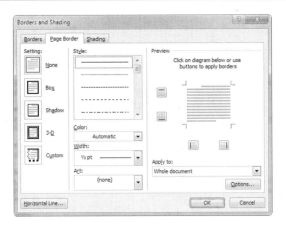

Figure 10.23   *The Page Border tab lets you apply borders to any or all sides of the page.*

2. In the Setting section, click one of the following options:
   - **None:** Leaves the page without any border. This is the default selection.
   - **Box:** Places a plain, straight-line border around the page.

- **Shadow:** Places a "shadow box" border around the page. This type of border has special trim on two sides, creating the impression that the box is floating and casting a shadow down onto the page beneath it.
- **3-D:** Creates the impression that the border is raised or embossed, resulting in a three-dimensional effect.
- **Custom:** Enables you to create different borders for any or all sides of the page.

3. Scroll through the Style list and select the type of border you want.

4. Click the Color drop-down arrow and choose a color for the border. This color palette is similar to the one used for backgrounds; it contains theme-based and standard colors and lets you open the Colors dialog box to choose an exact color.

5. Click the Width drop-down arrow and choose a width for the border. Border widths are measured in points.

6. If you don't want to use plain lines for your border, click the Art drop-down arrow to see a selection of borders made of drawn objects, such as cherries or butterflies. If any of the graphics appeals to you, click it.

7. In the Preview area, click one of the four buttons to remove the border from the corresponding side of the page, if desired.

8. Click the Apply to drop-down arrow; then click Whole Document, if necessary.

9. Click OK to close the dialog box and apply the border.

The Borders and Shading dialog box's Options button lets you set the amount of space between the border and your text. You can specify a different amount of space (measured in points) for each side of the page. You can also align different kinds of borders with one another and choose whether to include the header and footer in the border.

Formatting Documents with Themes and Templates

If you've read (or just flipped through) the last few chapters, you know that Word is a veritable cornucopia of formatting choices. One button after another, devoted to formatting every last detail of your documents. And many Word users—even really experienced ones—spend countless hours doing exactly that: clicking, scrolling, thinking, rubbing their chins, changing their minds, on and on, trying to make a document look just right.

But that's OK. I spend a lot of my own time noodling with formats in Word, and it's a great way to learn some of the program's ins and outs. Even so, it isn't necessary to spend a lot of time nit-picking formatting details, especially when you're up against a deadline and the boss is peeking over the top of your cubicle.

For those times (or any other time, actually), you can quickly format an entire document by applying one of Word's many built-in themes or templates. Using these tools is like visiting a drive-thru beauty parlor, where your document can get an instant, painless header-to-footer makeover. This chapter introduces themes and re-introduces templates, just in case you skipped Chapter 1, "Creating, Saving, and Printing Documents." You'll learn how to apply one of Word's built-in themes or templates to a document, how to modify existing ones, and how to create new ones.

 TELL ME MORE　　Media 11.1—The Truth About Themes and Templates
Access this audio recording through your registered Web Edition at
my.safaribooksonline.com/9780132182713/media.

Using Themes

A *theme* is a predefined set of fonts, colors, and special effects that you can use to completely format or reformat an entire document. Here's what happens when you apply a theme:

- Word replaces the fonts in your document with the theme's fonts, called a *font set*. Typically, this just means the current fonts are replaced with different ones. A theme uses one font for headings and another for body text. Theme fonts have been chosen to complement one another.

- If your document contains any colors (colored fonts or a background, for example), Word replaces them with the theme's colors, called a *color set*.

A theme changes the appearance of your document's text but does not change any styles that you have already applied to the text. You can think of a theme as a "layer" of design characteristics that is simply laid over the document.

- The theme's special graphical effects become available, so you can apply them to certain graphic objects you insert into the document. These effects include lines, fills, and other effects that complement the theme's other elements. A theme doesn't insert any new graphics of its own.

Word has 40 built-in themes. Depending on how your computer is configured to receive updated content from the Office.com website, the Themes menu may also contain additional themes that have been downloaded from the site. You can download other themes from Office.com, too; just visit the site and search on the keyword "theme."

Themes work only with Word documents saved in the DOCX format, meaning files that are created or saved in Word 2007 or Word 2010 format. If you are formatting a document created in an older version of Word, themes aren't available; you can make them available by saving the document in the DOCX format.

After you apply a theme, you can modify and save it as a new one or create an entirely new theme from scratch.

Applying a Theme

Applying a theme is as easy as applying a font. Just pick one from a menu and you're done. Here's how:

1. On the Page Layout tab, click Themes. A drop-down menu of available themes appears, as shown in Figure 11.1. The menu displays a thumbnail view of each theme to give you an idea of its color scheme.

2. Scroll through the menu and click a theme.

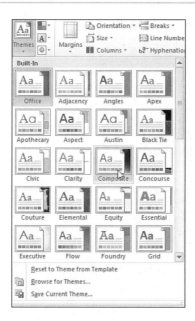

Figure 11.1   *Choosing a theme from the Themes drop-down menu.*

On the Themes menu, notice that every theme has a name. Each name is associated with a specific set of fonts, colors, and effects. Later in this chapter, you'll learn how to select and modify these theme elements individually.

Browsing for a Theme

If the Themes menu doesn't include the theme you want, you can search for it on your computer or network, as follows:

1. On the Themes menu, click Browse for Themes. The Choose Theme or Themed Document dialog box opens, as shown in Figure 11.2. This dialog box looks and functions just like Word's Open dialog box.

2. Navigate to the drive and folder that contain your theme.

3. Click the theme you want; then click the Open button.

Word applies the theme to the document and adds it to the Themes menu so that you can find it more easily in the future.

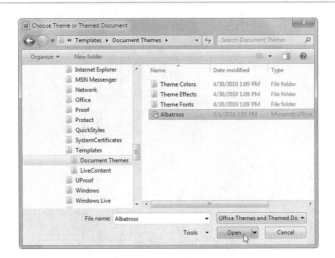

Figure 11.2   *Finding a theme through the Choose Theme or Themed Document dialog box.*

Removing a Theme from a Document

You can remove a theme and restore the document's original formatting. Here's how:

1. On the Page Layout tab, click Themes.

2. At the bottom of the Themes menu, click Revert to Theme from Template.

Modifying a Theme

If you like a theme but would rather use a different font set, color set, or effects, you can change any or all of these elements.

 LET ME TRY IT

Changing a Theme's Color Set

You can change a theme's color set as follows:

1. Open a document that contains the theme you want to modify, or start with a blank document and apply the theme to it.

2. On the Page Layout tab, click the Theme Colors button. A drop-down menu of Word's built-in theme color sets appears, as shown in Figure 11.3.

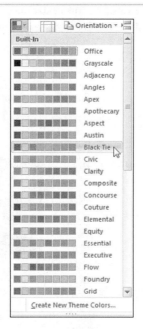

Figure 11.3 *Choosing a new color set for a document's theme.*

3. Scroll through the list of color sets; then click the one you want. Word replaces the current color set with the one you select.

LET ME TRY IT

Creating a Custom Color Set

You can create an entirely new color set, or modify an existing one, and then save it with a new name. The new set can be used to modify an existing theme or as part of a new theme. To create a custom color set, do the following:

1. To start a new color set from scratch, just start with a blank document. If you want to modify an existing color set, apply it to a new, blank document.

2. On the Page Layout tab, click Theme Colors.

3. Click Create New Theme Colors. The Create New Theme Colors dialog box opens, as shown in Figure 11.4. The Theme Colors section contains 12 placeholders, and each placeholder displays the current color for a specific

part of the theme. For example, the Text/Background – Dark 1 placeholder shows the color currently used by the theme for dark text that appears on a light background.

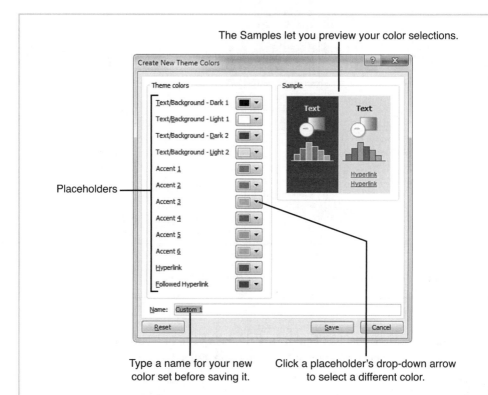

Figure 11.4   *The Create New Theme Colors dialog box enables you to specify new colors for the 12 placeholders in any theme.*

4. Click the drop-down arrow that appears to the right of the first place-holder whose color you want to change. A color palette pops out, as shown in Figure 11.5.

5. Choose a color from the palette. (If you want to see a wider selection of colors, click More Colors to open the Colors dialog box.)

6. Repeat steps 4–5 for any other colors(s) you want to change.

7. Select the text in the Name box, and type a name for your custom color set.

8. Click the Save button.

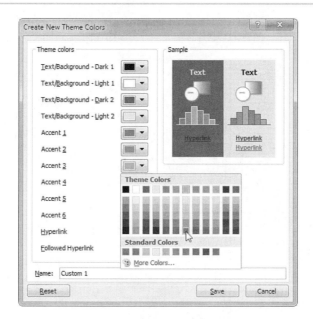

Figure 11.5 *Selecting a new color for the Accent 3 placeholder.*

Unless you specify a different location, Word automatically saves your custom color sets in the C:\Users*username*\\AppData\\Roaming\\Microsoft\\Templates\\Document Themes\\Theme Colors folder if you use Windows Vista or Windows 7. After the set is saved, Word adds it to the Theme Colors menu in a new section named *Custom*.

 LET ME TRY IT

Changing a Theme's Font Set

Here's how to change a theme's font set:

1. Open a document that contains the theme you want to modify, or start with a blank document and apply the theme to it.

2. On the Page Layout tab, click the Theme Fonts button. A drop-down menu of Word's built-in theme font sets appears, as shown in Figure 11.6.

3. Scroll through the list of fonts; then click the one you want. Word replaces the current font set with the one you select.

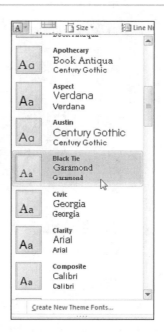

Figure 11.6   *Choosing a new font set for a document's theme.*

 LET ME TRY IT

Creating a Custom Font Set

As with color sets, you can create a new font set or modify an existing one. The new set can be used to modify an existing theme or as part of a new theme. To create a custom font set, do the following:

1. To start a new font set from scratch, just start with a blank document. If you want to modify an existing font set, apply it to the document.

2. On the Page Layout tab, click Theme Fonts.

3. Click Create New Theme Fonts. The Create New Theme Fonts dialog box opens, as shown in Figure 11.7. This dialog box enables you to set the fonts for headings and for body text.

4. Click the Heading Font drop-down arrow; then click a font.

5. Click the Body Font drop-down arrow; then click a font.

6. Select the text in the Name box, and type a name for your custom font set.

7. Click the Save button.

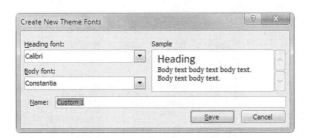

Figure 11.7   *The Create New Theme Fonts dialog box enables you to specify new fonts for a document's headings and body text.*

Unless you specify a different location, Word automatically saves your custom font sets in the C:\Users*username*\AppData\Roaming\Microsoft\Templates\Document Themes\Theme Fonts folder if you use Windows Vista or Windows 7. After the set is saved, Word adds it to the Theme Fonts menu, in a new section named *Custom*.

 LET ME TRY IT

Changing a Theme's Effects Set

If your document contains graphics that use special effects—such as diagrams or organization charts—you can apply a different set of effects to the current theme. Here's how:

1. Open a document that contains the theme you want to modify.

2. On the Page Layout tab, click the Theme Effects button. A drop-down menu of Word's built-in theme effects sets appears, as shown in Figure 11.8.

3. Scroll through the menu of effects; then click the one you want. Word replaces the current set of special graphic effects with the one you select.

You can select a different built-in set of effects for use only in modifying or creating a theme. You cannot create a new set of special effects.

 SHOW ME   Media 11.2—Modifying a Theme in Word
Access this video file through your registered Web Edition at
my.safaribooksonline.com/9780132182713/media.

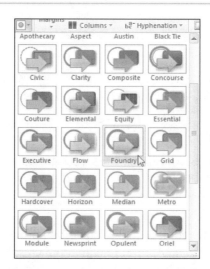

Figure 11.8   *Choosing a new set of special graphical effects for a document's theme.*

Creating a Custom Theme

If you want to create a new theme, you simply modify an existing theme and then save it under a new name. Here's what to do:

1. Open a new document and apply the theme you want to modify. If you plan to change everything in the theme (fonts, colors, and effects), you can just start with a blank document.

2. Select a color set, and/or a font set, and/or a set of special effects, as described in the previous section, "Modifying a Theme."

3. On the Page Layout tab, click the Themes button.

4. At the bottom of the Themes menu, click Save Current Theme. The Save Current Theme dialog box opens, as shown in Figure 11.9. This dialog box looks and functions just like Word's Save As dialog box.

5. In the File Name box, type a name for the new theme.

6. Click the Save button.

Unless you specify a different location, Word automatically saves your custom themes in the C:\Users*username*\AppData\Roaming\Microsoft\Templates\ Document Themes folder in Windows Vista and Windows 7. Remember this location; if you create a lot of custom themes, this is where you'll find them. After the theme is saved, Word adds it to the Themes menu in a new section named *Custom*.

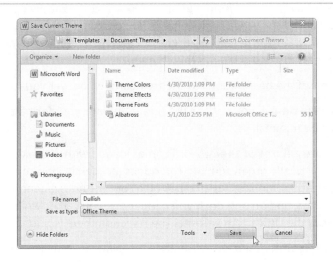

Figure 11.9   *Saving a new theme.*

Deleting a Custom Theme

You can delete a theme that you created, but you cannot delete any of Word's built-in themes or themes that have been downloaded from Office.com.

To delete a custom theme, open the Themes menu, right-click the theme to open a shortcut menu, and then click Delete. Word displays a message box asking if you really want to delete the theme. Click Yes.

Using Templates

In Chapter 1, you learned how to create documents based on templates that come with Word, or that you download from the Office.com website through Word's File tab. Here, we pick up where that discussion left off to help you get the maximum mileage out of Word's templates.

What Templates Are

In case you need a refresher (or skipped Chapter 1), a *template* is a special type of document that has already been formatted. It's special because a template itself isn't actually a document. Rather, a template is like the outer "shell" of a document, which you stuff with text. The template provides all the formatting settings—fonts, styles, margins, color schemes, and so on—that make a document look good. You provide the content.

When you start a document from a template, Word automatically opens a *copy* of the template and displays it as a document. You don't actually see or change the template itself when you're just creating a document. (But you can modify and create templates, as discussed later in this chapter.)

Here are a few of the best reasons to use templates whenever you can:

- **They save time.** If you choose the right template, your formatting chores should be minimal.

- **There are zillions of them.** Word comes loaded with a trunkload of templates, all neatly organized into categories (academic, business, and so on). You can find templates for all types of letters, resumes, agendas, calendars, letterheads, and on and on. If you need more, you can download them for free from the Office.com website. The selection there is huge.

- **They're flexible.** You can customize a template any way you like and save it as a new template. This means you can have multiple versions of a resume template, each one uniquely formatted (and preloaded with your own text, such as contact information and a perfect job-specific "objective") for a different job search. You can also create brand-new templates from scratch.

- **They're easy to use.** Formatting aside, many templates feature placeholder text that helps you use the template and keep your writing on track. Lots of templates include graphics, as well, such as borders, fancy mastheads, clip art, and pictures.

Need more convincing? Just go back to Chapter 1 and learn (or relearn) how to create a document based on a template. While you're at it, browse through the stockpile of templates stored on your PC or network, and take a little time to rummage through the ever-changing collection of templates on Office.com. After you see the variety and design features of templates, you'll probably agree that they're worth using at least part of the time.

Types of Templates

Word 2010 supports three kinds of templates. You can identify a template by its filename extension:

- **Word templates:** These templates have the extension *.dotx*. The *dot* has always been the standard filename extension for Word templates; the *x* is a relatively new addition, which means the template has a lot of XML stuff in it. XML stands for eXtensible Markup Language, which is a document-markup language that enables all kinds of cool stuff (so much cool stuff that there's no way to fit any of it into this book, except for its name). Templates with the .dotx extension work only in Word 2007 and 2010.

- **Word templates with macros:** These templates have the extension *.dotm*. You learned about the *dot* part in the preceding paragraph; the *m* means the template supports macros. A macro is like a mini-program that you can create to make Word perform a set of tasks whenever you want. Once upon a time, macros were fast, easy, and even fun to create, but Microsoft took care of that a few years ago, and now you need to be a junior programmer to create them. For that reason, this is all we're going to say about macros.

- **Templates for older versions of Word:** These templates have the extension *dot*. If you need to create a document that will be opened in a version of Word that predates Word 2007, you should use this kind of template. Older versions don't support all the cool formatting and XML widgets supported by Word 2007 and 2010.

By default, Windows hides filename extensions. Most of the time it isn't necessary to see extensions, but sometimes it helps—like when you're trying to figure out what kind of template you're opening or saving. To make filename extensions visible, open Windows Explorer and click the Organize button; then click Folder and Search Options. When the Folder Options dialog box opens, click the View tab; then clear the Hide Extensions for Known File Types check box. Click OK. Now all your dialog boxes will display extensions.

Figure 11.10 shows Word's Open dialog box, after navigating to the folder where Word's templates are stored. For this figure, the display of filename extensions has been enabled, so you can see them.

Where Templates Are Stored

You may wonder why anyone needs to know where templates are stored. Yep, it sounds geeky, and we avoid this kind of thing because most people really don't care where Word hides any of its junk. But in reality, if you use templates a lot, you WILL need to know where they're stored. Otherwise, you'll waste time rooting around for them on your computer. When you create new templates or download them from the Office.com website, Word saves them as follows:

- In Windows 7:
  C:\Users*username*\AppData\Roaming\Microsoft\Templates

- In Windows Vista:
  C:\Users*username*\AppData\Roaming\Microsoft\Templates

- In Windows XP:
  Documents and Settings*username*\Application Data\Microsoft\Templates

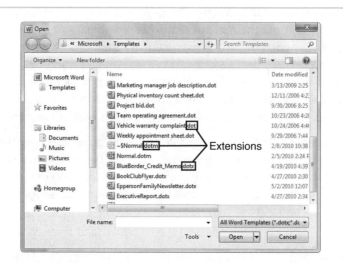

Figure 11.10   *Viewing Word template file, with filename extensions visible.*

(In each case, replace *username* with your name, if you're logged in under your own name. If not, use the name you typically log in under.)

Whenever you save a new or modified template, be sure to save it in the aforementioned folder, depending on your operating system. This way, it'll be easy to find, and all your customized and downloaded templates will be stored in the same place.

Note that Word saves its built-in templates in a different location, typically C:\Program Files\Microsoft Office\Templates\1033.

SHOW ME   Media 11.3—Locating Word Templates on Your PC and Finding Others Online
Access this video file through your registered Web Edition at my.safaribooksonline.com/9780132182713/media.

The Normal Template

Whenever you start a new document from scratch (that is, when you don't start from another template), the document is based on Word's Normal template. This is the template Word uses when you use the "Blank Document" option to create a new, blank document, as described in Chapter 1. Normal—or Normal.dotm, with the filename extension—is special because it contains all the default formatting settings for every document you create that is not based on another template.

You can make changes to the Normal template. For example, you can change the default fonts used for normal text or headings, reset the margins, or whatever. (You'll learn about modifying templates later in this chapter.) However, it isn't a good idea to change the Normal template too much simply because you may regret it later. If you really don't like the Normal template, create a new template that contains all the settings you need, and use it as the starting point for your standard documents.

Determining What Template a Document Is Using

Word doesn't make it obvious when a document has been created from a template. You have to dig around if you want to know which template a document is using.

 LET ME TRY IT

Finding the Name of a Document's Template

If you open a document that you have worked on before but can't remember which template it is based on, here's how to find out:

1. On the File tab, click Info.

2. Click the Properties drop-down arrow.

3. Click Advanced Properties. The Properties dialog box opens.

4. Click the Summary tab, as shown in Figure 11.11. The current template's name appears near the bottom of the dialog box.

5. Click OK.

Applying a Different Template to a Document

If you apply a template to a document and decide you don't like it, you can apply a different one. The process is a little convoluted, but it works.

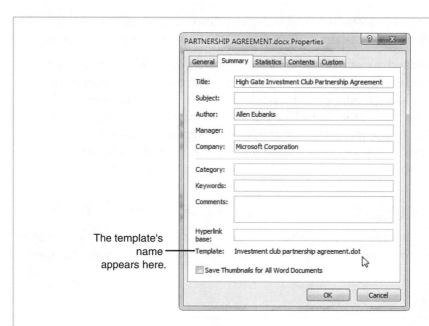

The template's name appears here.

Figure 11.11   *Finding a document's template in the Properties dialog box.*

LET ME TRY IT

Changing a Document's Template

Applying a new template to a document takes several steps that you might not think necessary, but there are no direct methods for changing a template. Here's what to do:

1. On the File tab, click Options. The Word Options dialog box opens. (You'll learn more about the Word Options dialog box in Chapter 22, "Making Word Your Own.")

2. In the left-hand pane, click Add-Ins.

3. At the bottom of the Add-Ins page, click the Manage drop-down arrow; then click Templates.

4. Click Go. The Templates and Add-Ins dialog box opens, as shown in Figure 11.12, with the Templates tab visible. The Document Template box shows the name and location of the document's currently attached template.

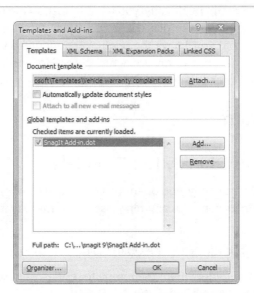

Figure 11.12 *The Templates and Add-Ins dialog box.*

5. Click Attach. The Attach Template dialog box opens. This dialog box looks and works just like Word's Open dialog box. By default, the dialog box shows the contents of the folder where your custom and downloaded templates are stored.

6. Click a template; then click Open.

7. If you want your document's styles to reflect the styles in the new template, click the Automatically Update Document Styles check box to place a check in it. If you don't want the document's styles to change, leave this check box cleared.

8. Click OK. Word attaches the selected template to your document. If the document contains styles with names that match any of the style names in the new template, and if you selected the check box in step 7, those document styles are updated with the template's styles. Styles that don't match any names in the new template are left unchanged.

Modifying a Template

Modifying a template is the same as modifying a regular document in Word. The big difference is how you save it; to make sure you're making changes directly to the template, you need to save it as a template.

When you modify a template directly, you need to make a big decision first. That is, do you want to change that template permanently, or do you want to save it under a different name so that you'll have the original and modified versions? If you save the template with a new name, you are actually creating a new template; that process is described later, in the section "Creating a New Template."

 LET ME TRY IT

Making Changes Directly to a Template

To modify a template directly, you open the template file, modify it, and then save it without changing its name (or anything else about the way it's saved). Here's what to do:

1. On the File tab, click Open. The Open dialog box appears.

2. Navigate to the folder where the template resides, as described in the preceding section, "Where Templates Are Stored."

3. Click the Files of Type button. A list opens, displaying all the types of files Word can open, as shown in Figure 11.13.

4. Click All Word Templates.

Files of Type

Figure 11.13 *Telling Word to list only templates, in the Open dialog box.*

5. Select the desired template; then click Open. The template opens in the Word window.

6. Make any formatting changes you want.

7. To make sure you're saving the file with its original name and as a template, go to the File tab and click Save As. The Save As dialog box opens.

8. Check the dialog box to make sure that you're saving the file back to its original location, with the same name, as a template. If the dialog box confirms this (and it will), click Save.

9. Keep making changes, if necessary. Now that you are sure you're changing the original template, you can save further changes by clicking the Save button on the Quick Access toolbar.

10. Close the file.

It isn't necessary to use the Save As dialog box to confirm that you're actually working with the template file, as described in steps 7–8. If you opened the template itself, that's the file you'll be saving. Even so, it's always better to be safe than sorry. Don't hesitate to check before saving a file if you have any concern that you might be saving it in the wrong place or in the wrong format.

Creating a New Template

To create a new template, you can make changes to an existing template and save it under a different name.

 LET ME TRY IT

Creating a New Template from an Existing One

When you create a new template from an existing one, you have to save it so that you don't change the original template. Here's what to do:

1. On the File tab, click Open. The Open dialog box appears.

2. Navigate to the folder where the template resides, as described in the preceding section, "Where Templates Are Stored."

3. Click the Files of Type button.

4. Click All Word Templates.

5. Select the desired template; then click Open. The template opens in the Word window.

6. Make any formatting changes you want.

7. On the File tab, click Save As. The Save As dialog box opens. It should show that Word is ready to save the template in its original location, with its original name, as a template.

8. Navigate to the folder where Word stores your custom and downloaded templates (as described in the section "Where Templates Are Stored").

9. In the File Name box, type a new name for the template.

10. Don't change the file type.

11. Click Save.

12. Keep making changes, if necessary. You can save further changes by clicking the Save button on the Quick Access toolbar.

13. Close the file.

If you can't find an existing template to start with (for example, if you need to create a template that's totally unique), just start with a new, blank document. Before you make any changes to the document, however, save it as a template, give it a different name, and save it with your other templates, as described in the preceding steps. When that is done, you can be sure you're creating a new template and not making changes to the Normal template, on which the blank document is based.

 SHOW ME Media 11.4—Modifying and Creating Templates in Word
Access this video file through your registered Web Edition at
my.safaribooksonline.com/9780132182713/media.

Headers and footers provide the reader with important information about your document, and make it easier to navigate a document that is long or divided into multiple sections. This chapter shows you how to create and edit headers and footers.

Adding Headers and Footers to a Document

You can think of headers and footers as design elements in a document because they reside in the pages' margins, and because you can format them differently than the rest of a document to make them "pop." But headers and footers are also informational elements that can help guide the reader through a long document by providing page numbers, section titles, and other facts about the document.

Most books have a header and/or a footer on every page that displays the page number along with the title of the current chapter or section. Newspapers almost always display their name and the current page number in a header; magazines often do the same in a footer. You should consider adding headers and/or footers to any multiple-page document you create for professional or academic purposes.

Word makes it easy to create and control headers and footers, so this chapter is pretty short. You learn how to insert headers and footers, edit them, and decide which pages they appear on.

Understanding Headers, Footers, and Field Codes

A *header* is a line or two of text (sometimes with graphics) that occupies the top margin of a page. A *footer* is exactly the same thing but appears in the page's bottom margin. Figure 12.1 shows a page with both a header and a footer. Headers and footers are not considered part of a document's normal text, such as headings or paragraphs of body text. Instead, Word treats headers and footers as special elements of a document because they must appear in exactly the same place and with the same content on every page (unless you decide to use different headers and/or footers on different pages of the document, as we discuss later).

Typically, a header or footer is formatted with a centered tab stop in the middle of the page, and a right-aligned tab stop at or near the right margin. These tabs let you insert text in three places (left-aligned, center-aligned, and right-aligned):

Header ———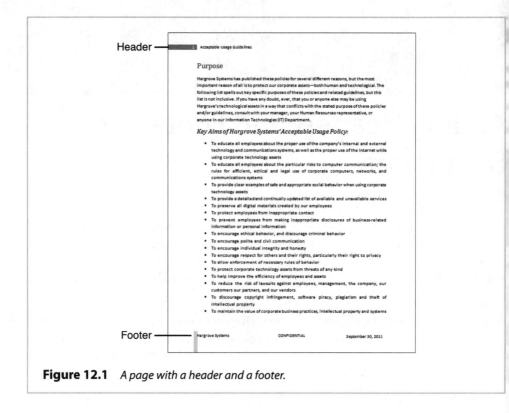

Footer ———

Figure 12.1 *A page with a header and a footer.*

But a header or footer can be even simpler than this. For example, in a multiple-page document, there may be just a footer that displays only the current page number.

On the other hand, headers and footers can be design elements, containing fancy fonts, lines or borders, shading, graphics, and other items. You can format a header or footer with fonts, font sizes, colors, and many of the same tools you use to format a document's body text. You just don't have as much space to work in.

Headers and footers often include little pieces of programming magic, called *field codes*. Field codes can display many kinds of information (such as the current page number and total number of pages, date, or time), which they draw either from your computer or from the document itself. When you tell Word to display page numbers in a footer, for example, it inserts a "Page" field code at the insertion point's location in the footer; the field code automatically updates on each page to display the right number. Word offers dozens of predefined field codes, several of which are suitable for using in a header or footer.

TELL ME MORE   Media 12.1—Why Bother with Headers or Footers?

Access this audio recording through your registered Web Edition at **my.safaribookson-line.com/9780132182713/media**.

nserting Preformatted Page Numbers

A simple header or footer might display only the current page number. Word has a special tool for this: the Page Number button. The Page Number button lets you choose from a variety of preformatted numbers, with different fonts, colors, and alignments. These options free you from formatting your page numbers manually.

Why can't you just type a page number in the footer area and forget about it? Good question! Here's a good answer: Because Word will just repeat the number you typed on every page. If you want each page to display its actual number, you need to use the Page Number button or insert a complete header or footer that contains the page number. That way, Word will insert a Page field code into your header or footer; the field code has to be there if you want your pages to be numbered automatically.

LET ME TRY IT

nserting and Formatting Page Numbers

You can place a page number in either the page's header or footer area in the right or left margin or at the insertion point's location. You just tell Word where to place the page number and which format to use. Here's how:

1. In an open document that does not already have page numbers, click the Insert tab.

2. In the Header & Footer group, click Page Number. A drop-down menu appears, showing different options for inserting a page number.

3. Click one of the following items on the menu:

    *   **Top of Page:** Inserts a Page field code in the document's header area.
    *   **Bottom of Page:** Inserts a Page field code in the document's footer area.
    *   **Page Margins:** Inserts a Page field code in either the right or left margin, either high or low on the page.

- **Current Position:** Inserts a Page field code at the insertion point's location, wherever it may be in the document.

4. When you click any of these options, a menu pops out and displays several preformatted page numbers that can be inserted at that position on the page. Figure 12.2 shows the menu that appears when the Bottom of Page option is clicked.

Figure 12.2   *Selecting a preformatted page number to go on the bottom of the page.*

5. Scroll through the menu to find a page number you like; then click it. Word inserts the formatted Page field code at the appropriate location. Figure 12.3 shows the result after adding the page number to the bottom-right of the page.

In Figure 12.3, notice that the footer area is divided from the document's body by a dashed line that displays the Footer tag. Figure 12.4 shows the document's header area, along with the Header & Footer Tools Design tab, which appears whenever you work with a header or footer.

Page numbers, headers, and footers are visible only in Print Layout view. When the insertion point is located in the header or footer area of a page, Word switches to Header and Footer view. In this view, you can access and edit a header or footer, but the document body is grayed and cannot be accessed until you exit Header and Footer view.

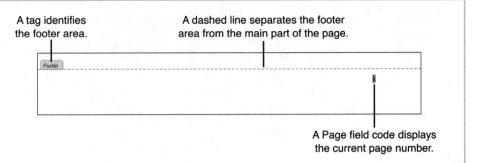

A tag identifies
the footer area.

A dashed line separates the footer
area from the main part of the page.

A Page field code displays
the current page number.

Figure 12.3   *The newly inserted page number, at the bottom-right corner of the page (in the footer area).*

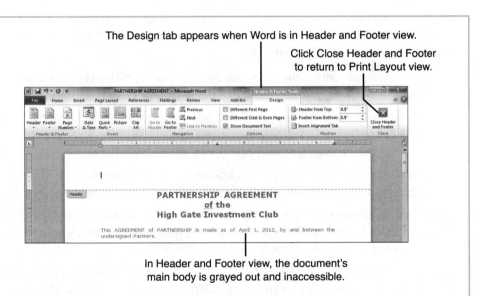

The Design tab appears when Word is in Header and Footer view.

Click Close Header and Footer
to return to Print Layout view.

In Header and Footer view, the document's
main body is grayed out and inaccessible.

Figure 12.4   *The header area and the Design tab that opens when you work with a header or footer.*

Inserting a Preformatted Header or Footer

Preformatted headers and footers contain placeholders where you can insert different kinds of information; the placeholders you get depend on the header or footer you select. Regardless, most of Word's preformatted headers and footers extend the width of the page, and many include a horizontal top or bottom border to separate it from the body of the document.

Word's preformatted headers and footers are special design elements called *building blocks*, which were introduced in Chapter 2, "Editing Documents." You'll learn even more about building blocks in Chapter 15, "Using Advanced Text Features" (online).

If none of Word's built-in headers or footers appeals to you, you can download more from the Office.com website.

 **LET ME TRY IT**

Adding a Preformatted Header to a Document

The following steps show you how to insert one of Word's preformatted headers and fill its placeholders with information. Remember, the process is the same for headers and footers. Here's what to do:

1. In an open document that does not already have a header, click the Insert tab.

2. In the Header & Footer group, click Header. (If you want to add a footer, click Footer instead.) A drop-down menu appears, showing a variety of preformatted headers, as shown in Figure 12.5.

3. Scroll through the menu to find a header you like, and then click it. Figure 12.6 shows the result after choosing the Blank (Three Columns) header.

4. Click a placeholder in the header to select it; then type text in its place. Do this again for any other placeholders in the header. If you decide you don't need one of the placeholders, select it and press Del.

5. When the header is finished, click the Close Header and Footer button on the Design tab to exit Header and Footer view. (Alternatively, you can double-click anywhere in between the header and footer areas to return to Print Layout view.) Notice that when you exit Header and Footer view, the header and footer areas are grayed out so that you cannot access them.

If none of the predefined options in the Header (or Footer) menu looks right, you can download a different one from Office.com. To view downloadable headers, open the Header menu; then click More Headers From Office.com. To view downloadable footers, open the Footer menu; then click More Footers From Office.com.

 SHOW ME Media 12.2—Adding a Header to a Word Document
Access this video file through your registered Web Edition at
my.safaribooksonline.com/9780132182713/media.

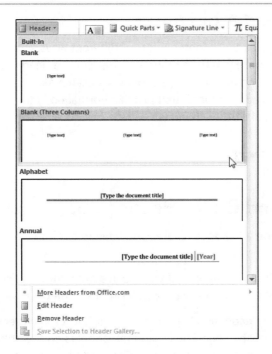

Figure 12.5   *Selecting a preformatted header.*

Many preformatted headers and footers include
a center-aligned and a right-aligned tab stop.

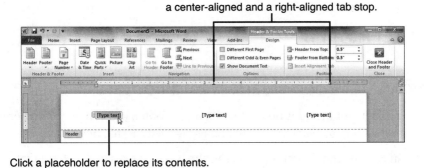

Click a placeholder to replace its contents.

Figure 12.6   *The Blank (Three Column) header, with the first placeholder selected.*

Editing a Header or Footer

You can modify a header or footer in lots of different ways; your only real restriction is the amount of space you have to work in. Generally, a header or footer can (and should) hold only one or two lines, although you can make them bigger. You can edit and format header or footer text just like normal body text, add and delete field codes, and make other changes.

 **LET ME TRY IT**

Getting In and Out of Header and Footer View

Before you can edit a header or footer, you have to get into Header and Footer view. Here's how:

1. Switch to Print Layout view, if you are in a different view. Headers and footers aren't visible in any of Word's other standard working views.

2. To switch to Header and Footer view, double-click in either the header or footer area of any page. The Design tab appears on the ribbon, the header and footer become available for editing, and the document body is grayed out.

3. When you're finished working in Header and Footer view, click the Close Header And Footer button on the Design tab. (Alternatively, you can double-click anywhere on the page between the header and footer areas.)

 **LET ME TRY IT**

Moving Between Headers and Footers

If your document includes both a header and a footer, you can jump from one to the other when you work in Header and Footer view. Here's how:

1. In Header and Footer view, click in the header area. On the Design tab, the Go to Footer button becomes active and the Go to Header button is grayed out.

2. To jump down to the footer, click the Go to Footer button. The insertion point moves to the footer, the Go to Header button becomes active, and the Go to Footer button is grayed out.

3. To return to the header, click Go to Header.

You can use these two buttons to move from header to footer and back as often as you need, as long as you're in Header and Footer view.

LET ME TRY IT

Editing Text

Word enables you to select, edit, format, delete, and cut, copy, and paste header or footer text just as you do in the body of a document. You can set and clear tabs, too, which is helpful for positioning the parts of a header or footer.

Even when a header or footer contains placeholders, it still contains one or two blank paragraphs you can use to insert your own text, field codes, or other objects. Here's how:

1. On the Home tab, click the Show/Hide ¶ button, if necessary, to make hidden characters visible.

2. To remove a placeholder, select it (see Figure 12.7) and press Del. The placeholder vanishes, and the underlying paragraph marks should be visible, as shown in Figure 12.8. Depending on how the header or footer is set up, the paragraph mark may be at the left margin or located elsewhere. (For example, it may have one or more tabs in front of it, pushing the paragraph mark to the right.)

3. Select and delete any other unwanted placeholders, text, or tabs in the header or footer area.

4. Set and clear tab stops as needed, to align your text in the header or footer area.

5. Place the insertion point on the paragraph mark and enter your text and tabs.

6. Format the text using the tools on the Ribbon and the Font and Paragraph dialog boxes.

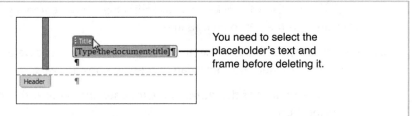

You need to select the placeholder's text and frame before deleting it.

Figure 12.7   *Select a placeholder by clicking it. You may need to click it twice to select both the text and the frame.*

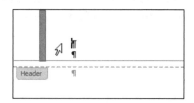

Figure 12.8   *After deleting a placeholder, you should see the underlying paragraph mark(s) in the header or footer area.*

 LET ME TRY IT

Inserting and Deleting Field Codes

Field codes can display all sorts of information—more than you could ever stuff into a header or a footer (or both). If you skim through Word's vast array of field codes, you may find that you wouldn't be interested in using many of them in a header or footer. That's fine, because field codes have a zillion different purposes, such as performing mathematical functions, inserting bar codes, and so on. But they're worth a look, especially the codes that insert a date or time stamp. Here's how to insert a date (or date and time) field code into a header or footer:

1. Click in the header or footer and place the insertion point where you want the field code to appear. You may need to insert tabs or do some other kind of aligning to get the insertion point in the right place.

2. On the Design tab, click the Date & Time button. The Date and Time dialog box opens, as shown in Figure 12.9.

3. In the Available Formats section, click the date (or date and time) format you like.

4. If you want the date (or date and time) to be updated automatically whenever the document is opened or printed, click the Update Automatically check box to place a check in it. Leave this check box cleared if you don't want the information to be updated.

5. If you like the format you selected in step 3, click the Set as Default button; then click Yes when the confirmation message box appears.

6. Click OK. Word inserts the current date (or date and time) at the insertion point's location.

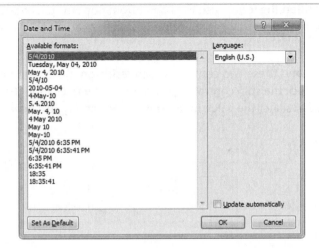

Figure 12.9   *Selecting a date and/or time field in the Date and Time dialog box.*

If you select the Update Automatically option, Word inserts an actual field code in the header or footer. You can manually update the field's value (the date and/or time it displays) by clicking the field and then clicking the Update tag that appears next to it. Otherwise, you can manually update all the fields in a document by pressing F9.

To delete a field code, select it and press Del.

If you want to see all of Word's available fields, click the Quick Parts button (on either the Design tab or the Insert tab); then click Field. The Field dialog box opens, giving you access to dozens of unique fields. Many fields require you to select or set parameters of some type. Sadly (NOT!), the use of these fields is beyond the scope of this book.

 **LET ME TRY IT**

Changing the Position of a Header or Footer

You can move a header or footer up or down to bring it closer to or farther from the edge of the page. Here's how:

- To reposition the header, use the Header from Top spin control to increase or decrease the amount of space between the header and the top of the page.

- To reposition the footer, use the Footer from Bottom spin control to increase or decrease the amount of space between the header and the top of the page.

Figure 12.10 shows these two controls, which reside on the Design tab. In either case, you can click the spin control's up or down arrow to change the value. Alternatively, you can select the value in the spinner box and type a new value in its place.

Figure 12.10   *Use these two spin controls to reposition a header or footer vertically on the page.*

You can insert graphics into a header or footer, such as pictures, rules and borders, clip art, and other types of images. Graphics work the same in a header or footer as they do in the body of a document—but, again, you have a lot less space to work in. To learn all the basics of adding graphics to a document, see Chapter 13, "Adding Graphics to Your Documents."

 SHOW ME   **Media 12.3—Editing a Footer in a Word Document**
Access this video file through your registered Web Edition at
my.safaribooksonline.com/9780132182713/media.

Creating Different Headers or Footers for Odd and Even Pages

You can set up different headers and/or footers for your document's odd and even pages. That way, the odd-numbered pages get their own header or footer, and the even-numbered pages get a different one. Here's how to do it:

1. Create the header or footer for the first (odd-numbered) page.

2. On the Design tab, click the Different Odd & Even Pages check box to place a check mark in it. Word changes the first page's header and footer

tags to read "Odd Page Header" and "Odd Page Footer," as shown in Figure 12.11.

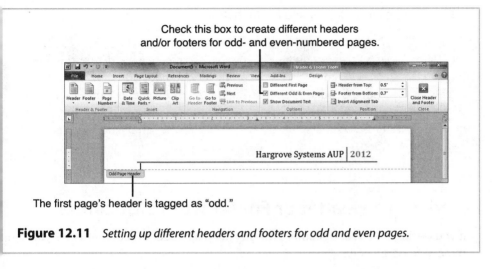

Check this box to create different headers and/or footers for odd- and even-numbered pages.

Hargrove Systems AUP | 2012

Odd Page Header

The first page's header is tagged as "odd."

Figure 12.11   *Setting up different headers and footers for odd and even pages.*

3. Go to the second (even-numbered) page and set up a different header or footer for it, as described earlier in this chapter.

To jump between the header and footer on the same page, use the Go to Header and Go to Footer buttons, as described in the section "Moving Between Headers and Footers." To move from the header or footer on one page (whether odd- or even-numbered) to the next page, click the Next button on the Design tab. To move to the header or footer on the previous page, click the Previous button.

Hiding the Header or Footer on a Document's First Page

It's pretty common for a document to have headers or footers on all but the first page. If you're writing a multipage memo, for example, it may look funny to have a header on the first page along with all the To, From, and other lines that usually reside at the top of the page.

You can hide (suppress) the header and footer on a document's first page. Here's how:

1. Double-click a header or footer to switch to Header and Footer view. The Design tab appears.

2. In the Options group of the Design tab, click the Different First Page check box to place a check mark in it. Word removes the header and/or footer from the document's first page but not from the remaining pages.

3. Click the Close Header and Footer button.

The Different First Page option also enables you to create a header for the first page that is different from the headers on the document's other pages. To create a different first-page header, select the Different First Page check box; then click in the first page's header area. Create a new header as described earlier in the chapter. This header appears only on the first page; the remaining headers remain unchanged.

Removing a Header or Footer from a Document

If you decide that your document doesn't need a header or footer after all, you can remove it. Here's how:

-   To remove a header, go to the Insert tab, click the Header button, and then click Remove Header.

-   To remove a footer, go to the Insert tab, click the Footer button, and then click Remove Footer.

V

Taking Your Documents to the Next Level

13 Adding Graphics to Your Documents **284**

14 Working with Charts and Diagrams **310**

15 Using Advanced Text Features (located online) **335**

16 Citing Your Sources in a Word Document (located online) **355**

17 Generating Outlines, Tables of Contents, and Indexes
(located online) **370**

Photos and other graphical elements can add meaning and depth to many kinds of documents. This chapter shows you how to create visual impact by using Word's graphics tools.

13

Adding Graphics to Your Documents

It's pretty hard to imagine certain kinds of documents without graphics. Can you imagine reading a magazine that had no pictures, or trying to follow the instructions in an assembly manual without diagrams? In an increasingly visual world, people expect to find graphics everywhere, even in routine documents such as term papers and sales reports.

Luckily, Word is more than just a text-generating machine. It offers surprisingly powerful graphics features that enable you to add all sorts of images to your documents. Well-placed, good-looking graphics can punch up any document—whether it's an annual report, a menu, or an invitation—in a way that no amount of fancy text formatting can.

This chapter introduces you to some of Word's most essential graphics features. You learn how to insert photos and clip art images into a document, and how to create basic shapes with Word's drawing tools. Along the way, you learn how to manage and edit graphics so that they add real impact to your documents. This chapter also shows you some basic tricks for getting text and graphics to play together nicely on the same page.

 TELL ME MORE   Media 13.1—Graphics in Word: The Good, the Bad...
Access this audio recording through your registered Web Edition at
my.safaribooksonline.com/9780132182713/media.

Adding a Photo to a Document

Word supports several popular digital photo formats, including TIF, JPG, PNG, and others. Most digital cameras and scanners can save images in all these formats. Different formats provide varying levels of image quality, so if you need a photo to be of a specific quality, be sure to check its file format. If possible, open the photo in a digital photo-editing program such as Photoshop or Paint Shop Pro (or the software that came with your digital camera or scanner) to check its quality before inserting it into your document.

In Word, inserting a photo is easy. When your photo is in place, you can modify it in lots of different ways. The next few pages show you how to add a photo to a document. Later in the chapter, you learn essential techniques for resizing, moving, and changing the appearance of photos and other graphics.

When you insert a picture into a document, Word automatically places the picture at the insertion point's location, sticking it right in line with any text that might already be there. As a result, your photo becomes an *inline picture* (or *inline image*). That means the picture behaves like text, even though it's something else entirely. Inline pictures can be hard to deal with because they can jump around, create a big gap in the middle of the text, and generally just get in the way.

To cause the least disruption to your text, it may be best to place an empty paragraph return where you want to insert the picture. Regardless, you learn how to make text and graphics work together in the section "Wrapping Text Around a Graphic."

 LET ME TRY IT

Adding a Picture to a Document

The following steps show you how to insert a photo from a file stored on one of your computer's disks. You can locate and choose a photo without leaving Word. Here's what to do:

1. Place the insertion point where you want to insert the picture.

2. On the Insert tab, click the Picture button. The Insert Picture dialog box opens, as shown in Figure 13.1. (This dialog box looks and functions just like Word's Open dialog box.)

3. Navigate to the drive and folder that contain the picture; then select the picture.

4. Click **Insert**. Word places the picture in the document. When the picture is selected, the Picture Tools Format tab appears on the Ribbon.

When Word inserts a picture, it maintains the picture's original size. Don't be surprised if the picture is so big that it overwhelms the rest of the document or so small that it looks silly. You learn how to resize (and make other changes to) a picture later in this chapter.

The Type column can tell you
what format your pictures are in.

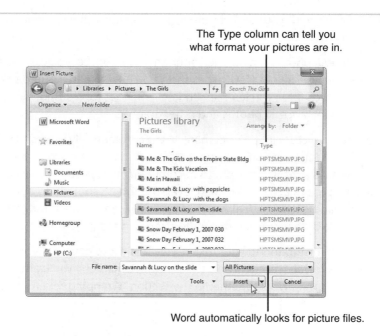

Word automatically looks for picture files.

Figure 13.1 *Selecting a picture to insert into a document.*

Adding Clip Art to a Document

Clip art is a graphic that you select from a collection and insert into a document. People typically think of clip art (also called a *clip*) as a simple line drawing, but clip art can be an illustration, a photo, or even a small video or audio file. Word comes with goodness knows how many built-in clip art images, and you can download many others from the Office.com website.

Like a picture, clip art can go pretty much anywhere in a document. The difference is in how you access clip art images. Because clip art is built into Microsoft Office, you can find images by searching for them in Word's Clip Art pane. Because there are about a bazillion clip art images in Office, you control your searches by using descriptive key words and simple filters.

Finding clip art is a lot like searching the Internet with Google. You type one or more keywords that describe the kind of image you're looking for; then Word displays images that match your description. Depending on how relevant your keywords are, your search can yield hundreds of images or none at all.

A clip art graphic behaves just like a picture when you insert it into a document, so some of the advice from the preceding section on photos also applies here. Be sure to place the insertion point where you want the image to go. Also, clips are inserted full size, so they may be a lot larger than you imagine. And Word inserts the clip as an inline image, so it will behave like text. You learn how to deal with these problems and others in the section "Modifying a Graphic," later in this chapter.

LET ME TRY IT

Finding and Inserting a Clip Art Graphic

Before you launch your search, you can tell Word what kind of clips you want—illustrations, photos, videos, or audio clips. You can also tell Word whether to display matching clips found on the Office.com website. Here's how to find a clip and add it to a document:

1. Place the insertion point where you want the clip to be inserted.

2. On the Insert tab, click Clip Art. The Clip Art pane opens, as shown in Figure 13.2.

Figure 13.2   *The Clip Art pane.*

3. Click in the Search For box and type one or more keywords that describe the type of image you need. If you're writing a holiday letter, for example, a keyword such as "snow" should bring up illustrations of snowmen, snowflakes, and other wintery images.

4. Click the Results Should Be drop-down arrow; then check the types of clips you want to see and clear the ones you don't want to see, as shown in Figure 13.3. If you're interested only in illustrations, for example, select the Illustrations check box and clear all the others. (Selecting the All Media Types check box selects all four types of clips.)

Figure 13.3   *Filtering a clip art search by type.*

5. Make sure that the Include Office.com Content check box contains a check mark; if it doesn't, click it. This option ensures that your search includes clips from the Office.com website and Word's built-in clips (as long as you have an active Internet connection). It also gives you a better chance of finding clips that match your keywords.

6. Click Go. Word searches for matching clips and displays the results in the Clip Art pane.

7. Scroll through the results, and point to a clip you like. A drop-down arrow appears at the clip's right edge, as shown in Figure 13.4.

Figure 13.4 *Choosing a clip from the search results.*

If Word says it can't find any clips that match your keywords, clear the text in the Search For box and try again, using more descriptive keywords.

8. Click the drop-down arrow; then click Insert. Word inserts the image at the insertion point's location in the document.

9. Click the Close button at the right end of the Clip Art pane's title bar.

If you aren't satisfied with the results of your search, you can click the Find More At Office.com link at the bottom of the Clip Art pane. Your web browser opens and takes you to the appropriate page of the Office.com website. Note, however, that if you checked the Include Office.com Content check box in step 5, then clips from the website have already appeared in your search results. In that case, a better strategy is to refine your keyword search and try again.

SHOW ME   Media 13.2—Finding Clip Art in Word

Access this video file through your registered Web Edition at
my.safaribooksonline.com/9780132182713/media.

Modifying a Graphic

Word treats pictures and clip art illustrations (and clip art photos) the same. You can select and modify them in many different ways to get just the look you want. The following sections show you simple methods for resizing, moving, cropping, and adding effects to a graphic, among other things.

> Throughout this section, we use the generic term "graphic" instead of the specific terms "picture" or "illustration." This is because pictures and clip art illustrations are both graphics; Word lets you modify them in essentially the same ways.

Resizing a Graphic

To resize a graphic, you change its width, height, or both. You can resize a graphic in three ways: by dragging, by using the resizing tools on the Format tab, or by opening the Layout dialog box and using the tools on the Size tab.

When changing a graphic's size, you'll probably want to preserve its original *aspect ratio*—that is, its original width-to-height proportions. If you don't maintain the aspect ratio, you will stretch the image vertically and/or horizontally, causing it to look distorted.

LET ME TRY IT

Resizing a Graphic by Dragging

When you click a graphic to select it, Word displays the graphic's *frame*, which is the container for an inserted object; the frame appears as a thin blue border around the image. On the frame's sides and corners is a set of squares and circles, called *selection handles* or *sizing handles*, as shown in Figure 13.5. To resize a graphic by dragging, do one of the following:

- Drag the top or bottom (square) handle to stretch or squash the picture vertically.

- Drag the right or left (square) handle to stretch or squash the picture horizontally.

- Drag any of the corner (circular) handles to resize the picture diagonally.

When you drag a handle, the pointer changes to a double-headed arrow that shows which directions you can drag.

Dragging a corner handle toward the picture's center shrinks the entire picture.

Handles

Because this is an inline image, Word sticks it right in a paragraph.

Figure 13.5 *Reducing a graphic's size by dragging a selection handle.*

When you drag a side, top, or bottom handle, the picture is stretched or squashed in the direction you drag. To preserve the graphic's aspect ratio, drag one of the corner handles. If an image's aspect ratio changes when you drag one of its corner handles, undo the change; then hold down the Shift key while dragging.

 **LET ME TRY IT**

Resizing a Graphic from the Format Tab

When you select a graphic, the Format tab appears on the Ribbon. The Size group contains tools for resizing a graphic, as shown in Figure 13.6. Here's how to use them:

1. Select the image. The Format tab appears on the Ribbon.

Figure 13.6   *Resizing tools on the Format tab.*

2. Click the Shape Height spin control's up- or down-arrow button to increase or decrease the image's height. Alternatively, you can select the dimension in the control's text box and type a new value in its place.

3. Click the Shape Width spin control's up- or down-arrow button to increase or decrease the graphic's width. Alternatively, you can select the dimension in the control's text box and type a new value in its place.

Note that as you change the value in one control, the other control's value updates automatically. These two tools are associated so that the image's aspect ratio always stays the same.

 LET ME TRY IT

Resizing a Graphic in the Layout Dialog Box

The Layout dialog box's Size tab gives you precise control over a graphic's dimensions. The following steps show you how to use this tab:

1. Select the image. The Format tab appears on the Ribbon.

2. Click the dialog box launcher in the Size group. The Layout dialog box opens with its Size tab visible, as shown in Figure 13.7.

3. Click the Lock Aspect Ratio check box, if necessary, to place a check mark in it. This setting ensures that the graphic's aspect ratio stays the same as you resize it.

4. Click the Relative to Original Picture Size check box, if necessary, to place a check mark in it. If you resize the image by changing its scale, this setting ensures that scaling is done in proportion to the graphic's original dimensions.

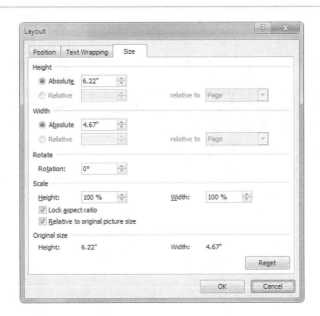

Figure 13.7   *Resizing tools in the Layout dialog box.*

5. Do one of the following:

    - To set exact dimensions for the graphic, use the Absolute spin controls in the Height and Width areas to set them. (If the Lock Aspect Ratio check box is selected, the value in one control updates automatically as you change the other.)

    - To resize the graphic by scaling it, use the Height and Width spin controls in the Scale area to resize the image as a percentage of its current size. For example, if you want to reduce its size by one-half, set both spin controls to 50%.

6. Click OK.

Wrapping Text Around a Graphic

An inline image can be hard to work with because Word basically treats it like text. But you can change this setting and position the graphic wherever you like. This also allows the text and graphic to interact in different ways. For example, you can tell Word to wrap text around a graphic—a common layout technique used in magazines and newsletters.

LET ME TRY IT

Controlling the Way Text Wraps Around a Graphic

The following steps show you how to change the relationship between a graphic and its surrounding text, so the picture is no longer an inline image, and how to set a text-wrapping option. Here's what to do:

1.   Right-click the graphic to open a shortcut menu of editing options.

2.   Click Wrap Text. A submenu opens, displaying several text-wrapping options, as shown in Figure 13.8.

Figure 13.8   *Selecting a text-wrapping setting for a picture.*

3.   Click one of the following options:

   •   **In Line with Text:** Places a graphic in line with the text, essentially making it part of a paragraph.

   •   **Square:** Wraps text around the graphic, creating a square "frame" of text around it.

   •   **Tight:** Works like the Square option but should be used with graphics that aren't square, such as rectangles or parallelograms, which is often the case with geometric shapes. Under this setting, Word places text as close as possible to a tilted or irregular shape.

- **Top and Bottom:** Aligns text along the top and bottom edges of the graphic but leaves the spaces on each side of the graphic empty.
- **Behind Text:** Places the graphic behind the text, so the text appears on top of it.
- **In Front of Text:** Places the graphic in front of the text, so the text is hidden by the graphic.

Each of these settings (except In Line with Text) makes the image a free-floating object, so you can drag it around the screen to place it exactly where you want it. Figure 13.9 shows a picture after the Square setting has been applied to it. You can also drag the picture toward the center of the page, and the text will wrap squarely around it on all sides.

Mom said I should tell you that I have been a very good big sister this year, too. Sometimes it is hard but I do my best! My little sister and I play lots of games, go to the park, and do other fun stuff together. I let her help me set the table and hold my toads while I clean their tank.

My sister's name is Lucy. She is lots of fun. She is in the first grade. I hope she learns to read and write better this year, but mostly she likes to play outside, and paint and color. She is a very good swimmer, and we love to go to the beach together and play in the sea and sand. Sometimes we argue, but we are still good friends. Lucy and I love to play soccer, ride our scooters and play with our friends. Dad built us a tree house last summer, but it's too cold to play in it today. Here is a picture of us at the park. We love to go to the park because there is a lot to do there. We even taught our dog how to go down the slide!

Figure 13.9 *A picture with text wrapped squarely around its edges. With this setting, the text forms a neat frame around the picture.*

You can access the same text-wrapping options on the Format tab, by clicking the Wrap Text button. If you click More Layout Options at the bottom of the Wrap Text menu, the Layout dialog box opens with the Text Wrapping tab visible. On this tab, you can choose the same options listed in the preceding steps, but you can also choose which sides of the object to place text against and set the amount of space between the graphic and the text.

SHOW ME   Media 13.3—Mastering the Art of Text Wrapping in Word
Access this video file through your registered Web Edition at
my.safaribooksonline.com/9780132182713/media.

Changing a Graphic's Position

The easiest way to move a graphic is simply to drag it to a new location on the page and then drop it. If you want to make sure that a graphic always stays with a specific paragraph, you can lock its built-in anchor into place. Every graphic has an anchor, but to see it, you need to turn on the display of hidden characters.

 LET ME TRY IT

Moving a Graphic

When dragging a graphic, be sure to click somewhere in the middle of it. Don't click one of the selection handles, or you'll wind up changing the image's size or shape. Here's the quick way to move and then anchor a graphic:

1. Click the graphic to select it. Point to the middle of the image, and the mouse pointer becomes a four-headed arrow. This symbol means Word is ready for you to drag an object around.

2. Slowly drag the graphic to a new spot in the document. It's a good idea to move slowly, especially if you need to drag the graphic to a different page. Figure 13.10 shows a picture being dragged.

The four-way arrow pointer means you're dragging an object.

Mom said I should tell you that I have been a very good big sister this year, too. Sometimes it is hard but I do my best! My little sister and I play lots of games, go to the park, and do other fun stuff together. I let her help me set the table and hold my toads while I clean their tank.

My sister's name is Lucy. She is lots of fun. She is in the first grade. I hope she learns to read and write better this year, but mostly she likes to play outside, and paint and color. She is a very good swimmer, and we love to go to the beach together and play in the sea and sand. Sometimes we argue, but we are still good friends. Lucy and I love to play soccer, ride our scooters and play with our friends. Dad built us a tree house last summer, but it's too cold to play in it today. Here is a picture of us at the park. We love to go to the park because there is a lot to do there. We even taught our dog how to go down the slide!

Figure 13.10 *Dragging a picture to a different spot on the page.*

When you drag a graphic, a semitransparent (ghostly) version of the image moves with the mouse pointer. The graphic itself stays in its original location until you release the mouse button.

3. Drop the graphic in the desired location. Now you can attach the graphic to the paragraph it is closest to.

4. On the Home tab, click Show/Hide ¶, if necessary, to view hidden characters. The anchor symbol appears next to the graphic's nearest paragraph.

5. Right-click the graphic to open the shortcut menu; then click Size and Position. The Layout dialog box opens with its Position tab visible, as shown in Figure 13.11.

Anchor

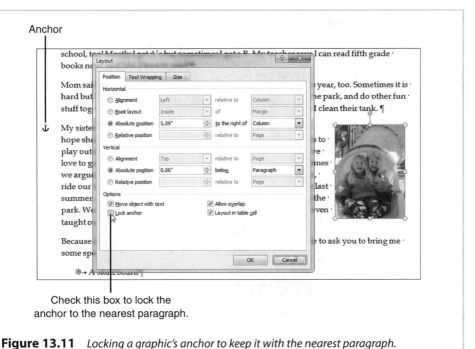

Check this box to lock the
anchor to the nearest paragraph.

Figure 13.11   *Locking a graphic's anchor to keep it with the nearest paragraph.*

6. Click the Lock Anchor check box to place a check mark in it.

7. Click OK. Now, if the paragraph moves, the anchored graphic stays with it.

If dragging a graphic isn't precise enough, you can use the Layout dialog box's Position tab to place the image exactly where you want it. The tab lets you set an absolute position (in inches) for the graphic or to align it in relation to another part of the document, such as a column or the page.

Cropping a Graphic

If a picture or clip isn't composed exactly the way you'd like, you can *crop* (trim off) parts of it. Cropping lets you remove unwanted parts of a graphic and place the focus on a specific area of it. You can even crop a graphic to a different geometric shape, such as a triangle or a circle.

 LET ME TRY IT

Trimming a Graphic's Edges

Here's how to crop a graphic by cutting away one or more of its edges:

1. Select the graphic so that the Format tab becomes active.

2. In the Size group, click Crop. A drop-down menu opens.

3. Click Crop. Word places black cropping handles around the graphic, as shown in Figure 13.12.

Cropping handles

Figure 13.12   *Cropping handles around a picture.*

4. To trim the graphic from the top, the bottom, or a side, click a handle on any of the four edges and drag toward the center of the image. When enough has been trimmed, release the mouse button.

5. Repeat step 4 for any other edge you want to trim.

6. To trim away two edges at once, click one of the corner handles and drag it toward the center of the graphic. For example, to trim the top and right edges at the same time, drag the handle in the image's upper-right corner, as shown in Figure 13.13.

Figure 13.13 *Cropping two sides of a picture at the same time.*

7. Click anywhere outside the graphic to deselect it and turn off the cropping tools.

 LET ME TRY IT

Changing a Graphic's Shape by Cropping

You can give a graphic a completely different shape by cropping. You pick the shape, and Word does the rest. Here's how:

1. Select the graphic so that the Format tab becomes active.

2. In the Size group, click Crop. A drop-down menu opens.

3. Click Crop to Shape. A submenu of shapes appears, as shown in Figure 13.14.

4. Click the desired shape, and Word crops the image to match that shape. Figure 3.15 shows a picture cropped to the shape of a teardrop.

5. Click anywhere outside the graphic to deselect it and turn off the cropping tools.

In Figure 13.15, notice that although the picture's shape has changed, its surrounding frame has not. Word prefers to keep picture frames as squares or rectangles.

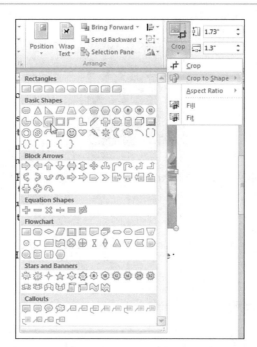

Figure 13.14   *Picking a shape for cropping a picture.*

Figure 13.15   *A photo cropped to a teardrop shape.*

Adjusting Brightness and Contrast

If a graphic's brightness and/or contrast aren't just right, you can adjust them in Word. You can make brightness and contrast corrections by choosing from a menu of preset options, or you can set precise values for both attributes.

LET ME TRY IT

Correcting a Graphic's Brightness and Contrast

Unless you know a lot about image correction, it's probably better (and definitely faster) to choose one of Word's preset correction options. Here's how:

1. Select the graphic so that the Format tab becomes active.

2. In the Adjust group, click Corrections. A drop-down menu opens, as shown in Figure 13.16. The menu's Brightness and Contrast section displays 25 or so different thumbnail versions of the image, each with a slightly different brightness and contrast setting.

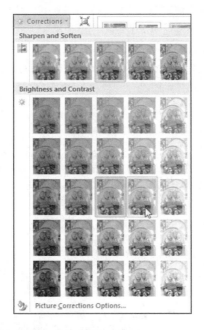

Figure 13.16   *Correcting a picture's brightness and contrast.*

3. Point to any of the thumbnails. If Live Preview is enabled, the image in the document updates to show you how it will look if you select the correction you're pointing at.

4. Click the desired correction.

Adding a Picture Style and Effects

If a plain old picture or illustration isn't exciting enough, you can change its style and add one or more effects to it. For example, you can place a wide border around a picture to make it look like an old-fashioned snapshot from your grandparents' family album. (You know, the kind they had before digital cameras and social networking websites.) You also can add a shadow effect to a graphic to make it look like it's floating over the page, give it a 3-D effect, or skew it in some way.

 **LET ME TRY IT**

Adding a Style and Effect to a Graphic

The following steps show you how to choose a picture style and add a simple effect to an image. This is primarily to show you where these features are located; you can use the same tools to apply many different effects to a graphic:

1. Select the image to open the Format tab. In the Picture Styles group, click the More button to open the Picture Styles Gallery, as shown in Figure 13.17.

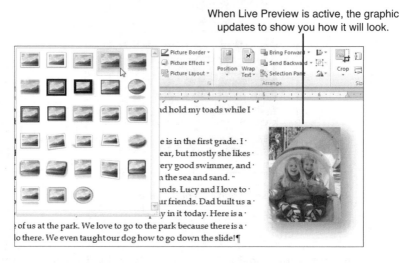

Figure 13.17   *Choosing a picture style from the Picture Style Gallery.*

2. Point to any of the thumbnails in the gallery. If Live Preview is enabled, the image in the document updates to show you how it will look if you select the style you're pointing at.

3. Click the desired style.

4. In the Picture Styles group, click Picture Effects. A menu of effects opens, as shown in Figure 13.18.

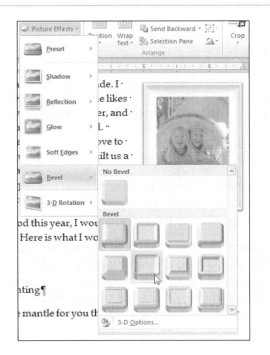

Figure 13.18 *Choosing a picture effect.*

5. Point to any of the effect types to open a submenu that shows variations of that effect. If Live Preview is enabled, the image updates to show you how the effect will look.

6. Click an effect.

Picture styles and effects may not be appropriate for all documents, especially ones meant for business use. In this case, you can place a simple yet dignified border around a graphic. To do this, click the Picture Border button to view a menu of options. From the menu's color palette, pick a color for the border. Open the menu again, click Weight, and then pick a line weight (thickness) for the border. If you want to use dashed lines for the border, open the menu again, click Dashes, and pick a dash style.

 SHOW ME   Media 13.4—Inserting and Modifying a Photo in a Word Document
Access this video file through your registered Web Edition at
my.safaribooksonline.com/9780132182713/media.

Resetting a Picture

If all your attempts at picture formatting leave you feeling unfulfilled, you can remove them and start over. To undo all the formatting changes you have made to the picture, select it, and then click Reset Picture on the Format tab.

Drawing Shapes in Word

Word includes a set of drawing tools that enables you to draw many different geometric shapes directly in a document. These tools are handy for drawing a simple organization chart or diagram, or for adding a quick callout to a photo.

Although it is possible to draw freeform polygons in Word, the freehand tools can be difficult to master. If you need to create freeform graphics such as curves, arcs, or wavy lines, I suggest getting a low-cost drawing program that enables you to create vector graphics and then paste those drawings into your Word documents. (*Vector* graphics are defined as lines, closed shapes, and fills. This is different from photos and some clip art graphics, which are *bitmapped* images, defined as a collection of dots or pixels.)

This section focuses on the most basic geometric shapes—such as lines, boxes, and block arrows—which Word provides as *AutoShapes*. AutoShapes are pre-drawn line art graphics. After inserting an AutoShape into a document, you can modify it in a variety of ways. Many closed AutoShapes (such as boxes and circles) can even hold text.

AutoShapes are flexible but very basic. They're great if you need to add a simple block arrow or a big smiley face to a document, but it can take a lot of formatting to make them real eye-catchers. If you need a text box, org chart, or some other diagram that looks like it was created by a graphic designer, use Word's SmartArt feature. SmartArt is covered in Chapter 14, "Working with Charts and Diagrams."

Drawing an AutoShape

Word has more than 100 built-in AutoShapes, ranging from simple lines to compli-cated 2-D geometric shapes. When you add an AutoShape to document, the shape is surrounded by handles. You can use the handles to resize the object.

Most AutoShapes, such as circles and triangles, are *closed* geometric forms, mean-ing their defining lines come together in some way so that the shape's interior is totally separated from the area surrounding the shape. Lines and arcs are examples of *open* shapes. This is important to understand because you can fill a closed shape with color or a pattern, or even place text within its borders.

 LET ME TRY IT

Inserting an AutoShape

The following steps show you how to insert an open AutoShape (a line) and a closed one (a rectangle) into a document:

1. On the Insert tab, click Shapes. A drop-down menu of available AutoShapes opens, as shown in Figure 13.19.

2. Click the Line icon. The mouse pointer turns into a plus sign (+), so you can draw the line.

3. In your document, click where you want the line to start; then drag in the direction the line should travel.

4. When you reach the point where the line should end, release the mouse button. Word inserts the line, which has a round selection handle at each end (see Figure 13.20). The line is anchored to the nearest paragraph.

5. Click away from the line to deselect it.

6. Return to the Insert tab, click Shapes, and then click the Rectangle icon.

7. In your document, click where you want any corner of the rectangle to appear; then drag in any direction to create a rectangle of any size.

8. When the rectangle is the desired size and shape, release the mouse but-ton. Notice that the rectangle is a solid color. The rectangle isn't actually a solid object. It's actually a thin outline that's filled with color; by default, both the outline and fill are the same color. As shown in Figure 13.21, the rectangle is surrounded by the same kind of selection handles as a photo or a piece of clip art (described earlier in this chapter).

9. Click anywhere outside the rectangle to deselect it.

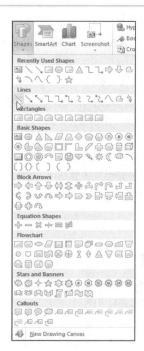

Figure 13.19 *Selecting an AutoShape to insert into a document.*

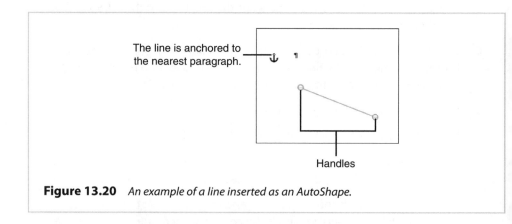

Figure 13.20 *An example of a line inserted as an AutoShape.*

When an AutoShape is selected, the Drawing Tools Format tab appears on the Ribbon. The tab displays some tools for all AutoShapes, but some other tools appear only when a specific type of AutoShape is selected.

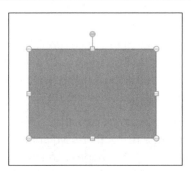

Figure 13.21   *An example of a filled rectangular AutoShape, with its selection handles.*

All AutoShapes have selection handles, but their locations depend on the type of shape you draw. Generally speaking, you can use the handles to resize an AutoShape the same way you can resize a picture or clip art graphic. See the section "Resizing a Graphic" for details.

Modifying an AutoShape

AutoShapes can be formatted in many of the same ways as photos and clip art illustrations. You can find the formatting options on the Drawing Tools Format tab. You can also access shape-dependent formatting options by right-clicking the shape and then clicking Format Shape to open the Format Shape dialog box. Remember, the available formatting options depend on the type of shape you select.

Here's a quick list of modifications you can make to an AutoShape:

- To move a shape, select it. When you point to it, the pointer turns into a four-way arrow, which means Word is ready for you to drag the shape around the screen. Drag the shape wherever you want, and drop it there.

Shapes are not inserted as inline images, so you can drag them around freely without having to set a text wrapping option first. However, you can wrap text around a shape in the same way you wrap it around a picture. See the earlier section, "Wrapping Text Around a Graphic," for details. By default, AutoShapes are assigned the In Front of Text wrapping option.

- To quickly change a shape's appearance, click the More button (on the Format tab) to open the Shape Styles Gallery. The gallery displays different colors and effects for the type of shape you have selected. Styles can include different outline and fill colors, shadows, fonts (for placing text inside a closed shape), and other options.

- To fill a closed shape with a different color, click the Shape Fill button (on the Format tab) and pick a color. This menu also gives you the option of placing a picture, a gradient, or a texture in a closed shape. The Shape Fill button is not available when an open shape is selected.

- To change the color of an outline, click the Shape Outline button and select a color. You can also change the outline's weight or convert the outline from a solid line to a dashed line. If the shape is an arrow, you can select a different line weight and arrowhead from this menu. The Shape Outline button is available for both open and closed shapes.

- To add a preset effect to a shape, click the Shape Effects button. This button's menu offers effects such as shadows, reflections, and 3-D rotations. The options available depend on the type of shape you are editing.

Adding Text to a Shape

Many AutoShapes, but not all, can hold text. When you add text to a shape, Word essentially converts it to a text box. You can format the text in a shape by using the same text formatting tools described in Chapter 4, "Character Formatting," and Chapter 5, "Paragraph Formatting," and the text tools on the Format tab (which are described in detail in Chapter 14, "Working with Charts and Diagrams").

Take these steps to add text to a shape:

1. Right-click a closed shape (such as a rectangle) to open a shortcut menu; then click Add Text. A blank paragraph return and a blinking insertion point appear in the shape, as shown in Figure 13.22.

2. Type your text into the shape. The text can completely fill the shape, if you want.

3. If there is too much text for the shape, you can resize the shape by dragging its sizing handles or using one of the other methods described earlier, in the section "Resizing a Graphic."

Grouping Shapes or Drawn Objects

If you add multiple shapes to a document—for example, to create a diagram or an org chart—you can group them so Word treats them as a single object. Grouping ensures that all the parts of the drawing stay together when you move them.

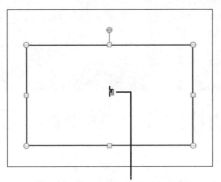

The blank paragraph and insertion point
mean the shape is ready to hold text.

Figure 13.22 *When you add text to an AutoShape, a blank paragraph and insertion point appear.*

Here's how to group multiple drawn objects:

1. Select all the objects. To select multiple objects, hold down the Ctrl key while clicking each object.

2. Right-click the selection to open a shortcut menu, and then click Group.

3. On the Group submenu, click Group.

If you need to change any of the objects in the group, you need to ungroup the objects. To do this, right-click the group, click Group, and then click Ungroup. You can regroup the objects again whenever you want by repeating the preceding steps.

 SHOW ME Media 13.5—Drawing Geometric Shapes in Word
Access this video file through your registered Web Edition at
my.safaribooksonline.com/9780132182713/media.

Deleting a Graphic

To delete a graphic—whether it's a picture, clip art, or an AutoShape—just select the object and press the Del key.

Charts and diagrams can convey complex information in a small space, while making a document more attractive. This chapter introduces Word's built-in charting and diagramming features, and shows you how to build and modify these kinds of graphics.

Working with Charts and Diagrams

Even though you can say and do a lot with text, words alone aren't always the best way to present certain kinds of information. It can take a lot of words to describe the sales results of several business units over a period of time, for example, or to explain a company's workflow process. When you need to convey such information, a chart or diagram can do it concisely while adding visual impact to your document.

Charts and diagrams are very common in business documents (and WAAAAAYYYYY overused in presentations), but they aren't just for business anymore. These graphics appear daily in newspapers, magazines, research papers, white papers, instruction manuals, and many other kinds of documents.

This chapter introduces you to Word's chart- and diagram-building tools. You learn how to create these graphics directly within a document. You also learn how to edit their contents, modify their appearance, and change an existing chart or diagram to a completely different type.

Understanding Charts and Diagrams

If you have worked with charts or diagrams before, you have permission to skip this section and start building one of your own. If charts and/or diagrams are new to you, the next couple of pages can give you a basic understanding of their uses.

Chart Basics

A *chart* is a graphic that presents numerical data visually. Figures 14.1 and 14.2 show two commonly used types of charts (also called *graphs*) and point out their essential elements. Word offers a large selection of chart types, but it's important to remember that each type of chart has a best use. Here are just three examples:

- *Pie charts* are most often used to show how a total amount of something (such as money) can be divided. For example, a pie chart might show $100,000 (the whole pie) being split among three organizations. In this scenario, Organization 1 might get a $50,000 "slice," while Organization 2 and Organization 3 each get a $25,000 "slice."

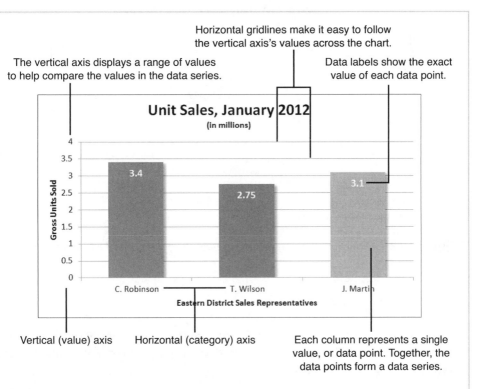

Horizontal gridlines make it easy to follow the vertical axis's values across the chart.

The vertical axis displays a range of values to help compare the values in the data series.

Data labels show the exact value of each data point.

Unit Sales, January 2012
(in millions)

Gross Units Sold

3.4

2.75

3.1

C. Robinson   T. Wilson   J. Martin

Eastern District Sales Representatives

Vertical (value) axis   Horizontal (category) axis   Each column represents a single value, or data point. Together, the data points form a data series.

Figure 14.1   *A simple column chart, showing the performance of three sales reps for a given month.*

- *Bar charts* or *column charts* are typically used to compare values. For example, a bar chart might contain three bars, each representing a salesperson. Each person's bar could show how many units of a product sold in a given period of time.

- *Line charts* enable you to track numerical data over a period of time. For example, you can use a line chart to show your weight every week over the course of a year.

When you create a chart, Word automatically opens a Microsoft Excel worksheet where you enter data for the chart. The data is automatically saved and linked to the Word chart, so you can change the chart's data as needed. Word offers dozens of chart-formatting features.

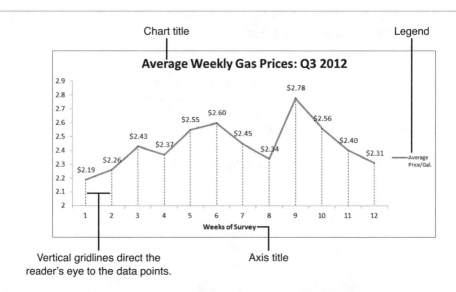

Figure 14.2 *A line chart, showing how the average price of gasoline fluctuated over a three-month period.*

Diagram Basics

A *diagram* is a graphic that depicts relationships (as in an organization chart) or a process (as in a workflow diagram). In Word, you can also use diagramming tools to format a simple list so it really pops.

Word's *SmartArt* feature provides all the tools you need to create great-looking diagrams in minutes. SmartArt provides dozens of different diagrams, preformatted with a variety of colors and geometric shapes. Shapes can be formatted just about any way you like, and they have built-in text boxes so that you can add descriptive or explanatory text to your diagrams.

Figure 14.3 shows a simple organization chart—a diagram that shows the hierarchy of relationships in an organization. Figure 14.4 shows a basic flowchart—a type of process diagram that shows the steps of a process from beginning to end. The diagrams use different shapes and connecting lines to create different looks.

As with charts, different diagrams have different uses. As you peruse the various types of SmartArt diagrams, Word provides a brief description of each one. This information can help you choose the correct type of diagram for the information you need to present.

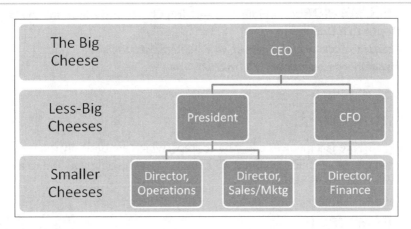

Figure 14.3   *A short organization chart that shows the levels of upper management for a make-believe corporation.*

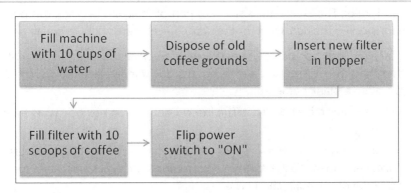

Figure 14.4   *A flowchart that outlines the process of making a pot of coffee.*

If you think any of the charts or diagrams in Figures 14.1–14.4 were hard to create, rest easy. The most difficult one (the line chart in Figure 14.2) took less than five minutes to make. The easiest one (the process chart in Figure 14.4) took about 1 minute. If you already have your data in hand, you're halfway home. The toughest part is picking the right type of chart or diagram; the rest is just filling in the blanks with your data. You don't have to reformat anything unless you really want to.

TELL ME MORE   Media 14.1—Using Charts and Diagrams to Add Depth to a Document

Access this audio recording through your registered Web Edition at
my.safaribooksonline.com/9780132182713/media.

Creating a Chart

Creating a new chart involves a few basic steps, which are basically the same no matter what type of chart you build. Of course, the more data you add to a chart, the longer the process takes.

LET ME TRY IT

Creating a New Chart

When you build a chart, you make choices in Word but type the chart's data in an Excel worksheet. The Excel data is saved as part of the chart in Word; this portion of the chart is called the *datasheet* (or the *data source*). Here's how to create a chart:

1. Place the insertion point where you want to place the chart. To prevent the chart from disrupting any text in the document, place the insertion point on a blank paragraph.

2. On the Insert tab, click Chart. The Insert Chart dialog box opens, as shown in Figure 14.5.

3. In the dialog box's left pane, click a chart type. In the right pane, several subtypes appear. Each chart type has multiple subtypes; each subtype is a variation of the main chart type.

4. In the right pane, click a chart subtype.

5. Click OK. A chart appears in the Word window, and the Chart Tools tabs (named Design, Layout, and Format) appear on the ribbon. At the same time, Microsoft Excel opens in its own window. The two windows resize to fit together on the screen, as shown in Figure 14.6. The Word chart and the Excel worksheet are both populated with "dummy" data.

6. In the Excel worksheet, replace the dummy data with data for your chart. As you enter data in Excel, the chart automatically updates in Word.

   If you need more or fewer rows or columns for the chart's data, you can expand or reduce the size of the data range in Excel by dragging the handle at the range's bottom-right corner.

7. After entering all the data, close the Excel window.

Select a chart type in the left pane.   Select a chart subtype in the right pane.

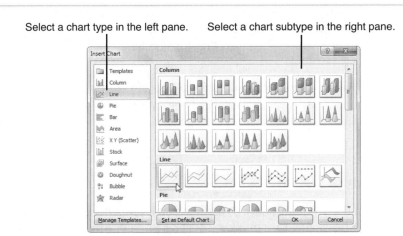

Figure 14.5   *Selecting a chart in the Insert Chart dialog box.*

Chart Tools tabs   "Dummy" data   Data range border

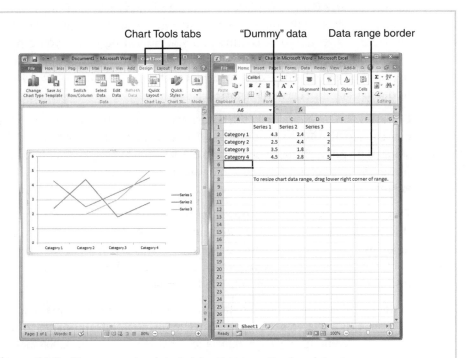

Figure 14.6   *You enter a chart's underlying data in an Excel worksheet.*

Word's charts are based on built-in templates. You can use the templates, but you can't change or delete them. But you can create a new chart, modify it any way you like, and then save it as a user-defined template by clicking Save as Template on the Chart Tools Design tab. (Be sure to save your templates in the default location in the Save Chart Template dialog box.) You can access your templates by clicking Templates in the left pane of the Insert Chart dialog box.

SHOW ME   Media 14.2—Creating a Chart in Word
Access this video file through your registered Web Edition at
my.safaribooksonline.com/9780132182713/media.

Editing Chart Data

At this point in the program, I have to assume you know a thing or two about *Using Microsoft Office Excel 2010*. Hey, that sounds like a good title for another book, doesn't it? (Hint!) Sadly, we don't have space to cover Excel in any detail. However, I can offer a few pointers about working with a chart's data source in Excel:

- To edit a chart's data, right-click the chart, and then click Edit Data. Excel opens and displays the data source, as shown in Figure 14.7. (Well, not *exactly* like Figure 14.7. I did some creative zooming and sizing so that you can see the important stuff.) To change any number or label, click the appropriate cell in Excel and type the new data in its place. Click outside the cell, and your updated data appears in the chart.

- Generally, a numeric value in the datasheet translates to a *data point* in the chart. In Figure 14.7, each number in the range B2:D5 of the datasheet is a single data point. Because our example is a column chart, each data point is presented as a column, and the columns are sized to show their relative values.

- Text in the datasheet usually translates to a *label* that identifies some part of the chart. In Figure 14.7, the quarters in column A of the datasheet are used as labels in the chart to identify the groups of quarters represented by the data points. (Excel treats years as text, even though they are numbers, because years are not commonly used in equations.)

- In the datasheet, each row of data corresponds to a *data series* in the chart. A data series is a related set of data points. In this example, the values for the four "2007" columns make up data series, as do the values for "2008" and "2009."

- The first row in the datasheet is used to create the chart's *legend*. In the figure, the legend appears on the right side of the chart. It shows which data series is represented by each color.

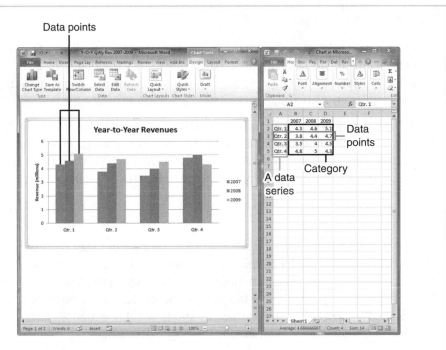

Figure 14.7   *Parts of a data source and corresponding parts of its chart.*

- The first column in the datasheet corresponds to the *category* in the chart. In this example, the category includes the four quarters of a year. Categories are identified by the labels on the horizontal *category axis* of the chart.

- Word applies a vertical *value axis* along the left edge of the chart, according to the values of the data points. The value axis acts as a scale, enabling you to see the relative values of the data points by comparing them to the axis.

- In the datasheet, the *data range* is all the adjacent cells whose data is used in the chart. The data range is surrounded by a blue border; any cells outside this border are not included in the chart. You can expand or reduce the data range by dragging its lower-right corner to include or exclude the cells in a row and/or column.

Simple, huh? Not really, but don't worry. If you aren't familiar with charts yet, just create one as directed earlier; then play with the values in the data sheet. With some practice, you'll see how the Excel data affects the chart.

Modifying a Chart

Charts can be modified in many, many, many different ways, and you can tweak a chart to death (and lose your mind in the process). So, we're going to cover some essential chart-modification techniques here; we won't be messing with fonts, colors, or those minor formatting details.

But I don't want to leave you completely in the dark about those little formatting tweaks. Here's a tip: If you want to change any formatting aspect of any part of a chart, right-click that item, and then click Format [*That Item*] on the shortcut menu. Doing so opens a dialog box of formatting options just for that item.

Resizing a Chart

Because Word treats a chart in much the same way it treats other kinds of graphics, charts have the same sizing options as a picture or a piece of clip art. This means you can resize it by dragging its edges or corners, by using the Shape Height and Shape Width tools on the Format tab, or by using the Layout dialog box's Size tab. For detailed instructions on using these methods, see the section "Resizing a Graphic" in Chapter 13, "Adding Graphics to Your Documents."

There is, however, one rule about resizing graphics that does not apply to charts. That is, Word does not automatically preserve a chart's aspect ratio. If you resize a chart by dragging one of its corner handles, hold down the Shift key while you drag. If you prefer to use the Format tab or the Layout dialog box to set the dimensions in inches, start by opening the Layout dialog box and checking the Lock Aspect Ratio check box.

It pays to be careful when resizing a chart because some chart elements are small, especially the text along the axes, data labels, and gridlines. If you resize a chart, make sure all its elements remain legible at the new size. If not, undo the resizing and try again.

Changing a Chart's Text Wrapping Setting

When you create a chart, Word treats it as an inline image, meaning the chart behaves like a block of selected text when you drag it. To move a chart freely, you need to change the way text wraps around it. Luckily, charts have the same text wrapping options as pictures and clip art images. To learn all about text wrapping, see the section "Wrapping Text Around a Graphic" in Chapter 13.

Moving a Chart

After you change a chart's text wrapping setting so it is no longer an inline image, you can move the chart to any location in your document. As is the case with pictures and clips, it's a good idea to lock the chart's anchor to the nearest paragraph so that it stays in place. For more information, see the section "Changing a Graphic's Position" in Chapter 13.

When you drag a chart, you need to click it somewhere near the edge; just be careful not to click one of the sizing handles. If you click in the middle of a chart and drag, you may wind up moving a piece of the chart instead of the entire thing. If this happens, click Undo (or press Ctrl+Z) to restore the chart.

Changing the Chart Type

Choosing the wrong type of chart can render your data meaningless. No amount of pretty formatting can make up for that kind of mistake. For this reason, it's a good idea to show your chart to other people before settling on a chart type; if it doesn't make sense to someone else, you probably need to choose a different one.

 LET ME TRY IT

Applying a Different Chart Type

Word doesn't lock you in to the first chart type you choose. You can change it anytime. Here's how:

1. Select the chart to activate the Chart Tools tabs.

2. On the Design tab, click Change Chart Type. The Change Chart Type dialog box opens, as shown in Figure 14.8. This dialog box is just like the Insert Chart dialog box.

3. In the dialog box's left pane, click a chart type.

4. In the right pane, click a chart subtype.

5. Click OK. Word updates your chart.

If you choose a chart type that's very different from the current one, you may need to open the datasheet and make adjustments to ensure that all the data points and labels are in the right place.

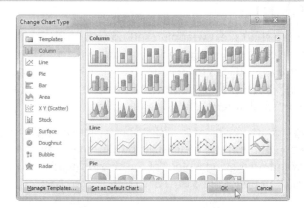

Figure 14.8   *Selecting a different chart type.*

If your chart just needs a makeover, try choosing a subtype that's a different version of the one you're already using. For example, if the chart is currently a clustered column chart, try changing it to a clustered cone, cylinder, or pyramid. These subtypes are functionally the same as the clustered column subtype, but they have cool shapes and 3-D effects.

Applying a Different Chart Layout

Chart layouts are prefabricated variations on a chart type's design. They give you a quick and easy way to add or change certain elements of a chart without changing the chart type or doing a lot of manual formatting. For example, a chart layout may add a title to the top of the chart and move the legend to the bottom. Another may add labels to the category and value axes. If you aren't happy with a chart's balance, a different layout may fix the problem.

 LET ME TRY IT

Picking a Chart Layout

Here's how to apply a different chart layout:

1. Select the chart to activate the Chart Tools tabs.

2. On the Design tab, click the More button in the Chart Layouts group. A small gallery of alternative layouts drops down, as shown in Figure 14.9.

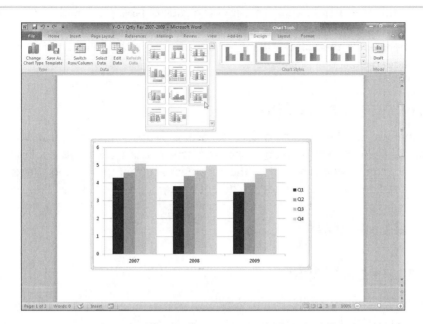

Figure 14.9   *Selecting a different chart layout for a clustered column chart.*

3. Click a layout. Word updates the chart with the new layout's elements, as shown in Figure 14.10.

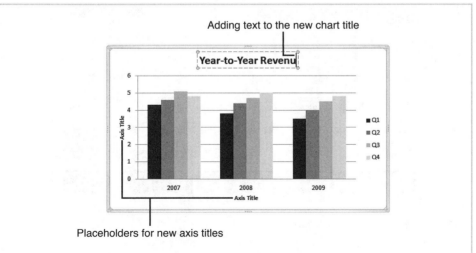

Figure 14.10   *The same chart with a different layout applied.*

4. If the new layout requires it, click in any title or label placeholders, select their generic contents (Chart Title or Axis Title, for example), and type descriptive new text in their place. Figure 14.10 shows this being done to the newly added chart title placeholder.

Applying a Chart Style

Another way to give a chart a quick makeover is by applying a *chart style*. Word provides a selection of chart styles for every type of chart. Each style applies different color combinations (based on the document's current theme) and effects to the chart. Some chart styles add a different background color, as well.

 LET ME TRY IT

Picking a Chart Style

Here's how to apply a different chart style:

1. Select the chart to activate the Chart Tools tabs.

2. On the Design tab, click the More button in the Chart Styles group. A gallery of styles drops down, as shown in Figure 14.11.

3. Click a style.

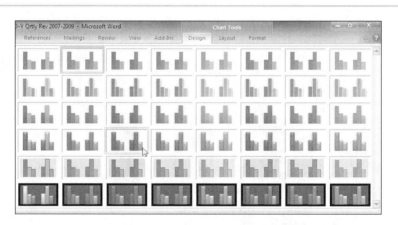

Figure 14.11 *Selecting a chart style.*

Adding Text Elements to a Chart

A chart that shows only numbers doesn't provide the same value as a chart that is labeled. If a chart doesn't have textual elements such as titles and labels, you can—and probably should—add them yourself.

> To format the font in a text element, right-click the element and click Font. Word displays a pared-down version of the Font dialog box. (You can also select the text and point to it to use the mini toolbar's formatting tools.) If you want to format the element's placeholder by adding a border, fill, or other features, right-click the element; then click Format *[Element Name]*. Word displays a dialog box with formatting options specifically for text elements.

 LET ME TRY IT

Adding a Chart Title

A chart title appears at the top of the chart and describes the chart's contents. Here's how to add a title to a chart:

1. On the Layout tab, click **Chart Title**. A menu of options appears.

2. Click one of the following options:

   - **Centered Overlay Title:** Places the title on the chart; does not resize the chart to make room for the title, so the title may cover a portion of the data.

   - **Above Chart:** Places the title above the chart area and resizes the chart to make room for the title.

3. Word inserts an empty placeholder for the chart title.

4. Type the title in the placeholder, as shown in Figure 14.12.

5. Click outside the title placeholder.

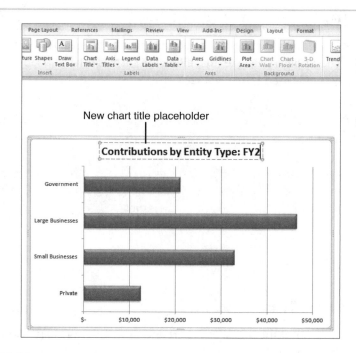

Figure 14.12 *Adding a chart title.*

 LET ME TRY IT

Adding an Axis Title

Most chart types can have two axis titles—one for the horizontal (category) axis and another for the vertical (value) axis. Here's how to add a title for the horizontal axis:

1. On the Layout tab, click Axis Titles.

2. Click Primary Horizontal Axis Title.

3. Click Title Below Axis. Word inserts an empty placeholder for the title, just below the horizontal axis. If needed, Word resizes the chart to make room for the title.

4. Type the title in the placeholder, as shown in Figure 14.13.

5. Click outside the title placeholder.

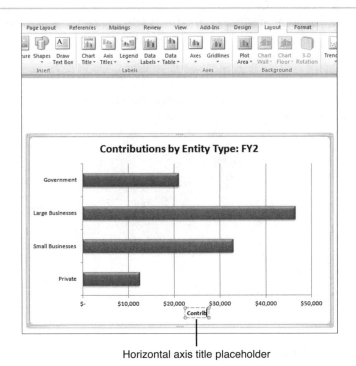

Horizontal axis title placeholder

Figure 14.13   *Adding a horizontal axis title.*

Adding a vertical axis title is the same as described here, but you have three lay-out options to choose from. You can insert the title as rotated text, as vertical text, or as horizontal text. In any case, Word resizes the chart as needed to make room for the title.

 LET ME TRY IT

Adding Data Labels

Data labels display the actual value of each data point in a chart. These labels can help the reader see the values when a chart is crowded or when the values aren't apparent from the chart's axes or gridlines. Here's how to add data labels:

1. On the Layout tab, click Data Labels. A menu of layout options drops down. These options vary depending on the chart type, but the menu pro-vides descriptions to help you select the best location for the labels.

2. Click a layout option. Word inserts the labels. Figure 14.14 shows data labels added to a pie chart, using the Inside End layout option.

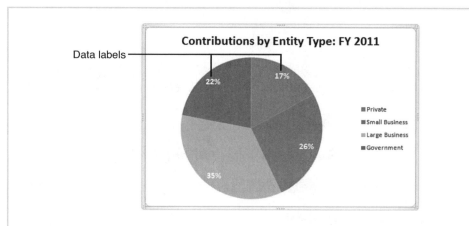

Figure 14.14   *Data labels on a pie chart.*

 LET ME TRY IT

Managing a Chart's Legend

A chart's legend is like a map's key. It tells you what the different data series represent in the chart. In the case of the pie chart in Figure 14.14, the legend identifies the entity represented by each slice, based on the slice's colors. Word automatically inserts a legend when you create a chart, but you can hide it or move it. Here's how:

1. On the Layout tab, click Legend. A menu of options appears, as shown in Figure 14.15.

2. Do one of the following:

    *   To hide the legend, click None.

    *   To move the legend to a different location in relation to the chart, click one of the layout options on the menu. Word displays a description with each option to help you choose the best one.

 SHOW ME   Media 14.3—Changing a Chart's Appearance in Word
Access this video file through your registered Web Edition at
my.safaribooksonline.com/9780132182713/media.

Figure 14.15 *Options for hiding and moving a chart's legend.*

Inserting a SmartArt Diagram

SmartArt diagrams not only look good, but they're easy to create. The same steps are required, regardless of the type of diagram you want to use. As with charts, the more data you add to a diagram, the longer the process takes.

 LET ME TRY IT

Creating a New Diagram

To insert a diagram, select a diagram type, and then pick a layout. When the diagram is in place, you can type text directly into placeholders on the shapes. Here's how to create a new diagram:

1. Place the insertion point where you want to place the diagram. To prevent the diagram from disrupting any text in the document, place the insertion point on a blank paragraph.

2. On the Insert tab, click SmartArt. The Choose a SmartArt Graphic dialog box opens, as shown in Figure 14.16.

3. In the dialog box's left pane, click a diagram type. In the center pane, several layouts appear; each diagram type has multiple layouts.

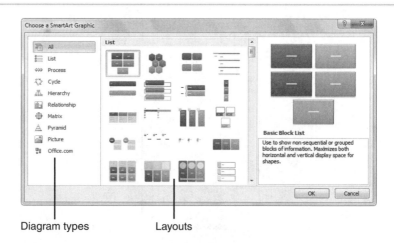

Diagram types   Layouts

Figure 14.16 *Selecting a diagram in the Choose a SmartArt Graphic dialog box.*

4. Click a diagram layout. In the right pane, the dialog box displays an example and description of the selected layout.

5. Click OK. Word inserts the diagram, ready for you to add text, as shown in Figure 14.17. Two SmartArt Tools tabs (Design and Format) appear on the ribbon when the diagram is selected. A pop-out panel, called the *text pane*, opens on the left side of the diagram; the text pane contains placeholders for the diagram's text.

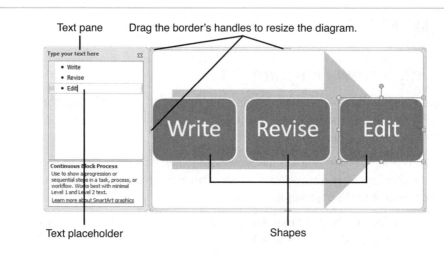

Text placeholder   Shapes

Figure 14.17 *A newly inserted SmartArt diagram (a basic process diagram). Text is being added to the last text placeholder in the text pane.*

If the text pane does not open automatically when you insert a diagram, click the double-arrow icon on left edge of the diagram's border. The icon lets you open the text pane whenever you need it.

6. Click a text placeholder in the text pane or in one of the diagram's shapes; then type the text for that shape.

7. After entering all the text, click the text pane's Close button to close it.

8. Click outside the diagram's border to deselect the diagram.

An important thing to know about diagrams is that some are based on a hierarchy, meaning some shapes are subordinate to others. In an organization chart, for example, the president's title could reside in a top-level (*superior*) shape, and each vice-president's shape would be below (*subordinate* to) the president. If the president has an assistant, that shape would be below the president's shape, but offset to indicate that the assistant reports to the president alone. Figure 14.18 shows an example of a hierarchical organization chart.

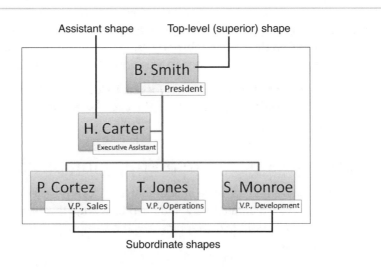

Figure 14.18   *A hierarchical organization chart with superior, subordinate, and assistant shapes.*

In some charts, such as process charts, all the shapes have the same level with no subordinate or assistant shapes.

SHOW ME Media 14.4—Creating a SmartArt Diagram in Word
Access this video file through your registered Web Edition at
my.safaribooksonline.com/9780132182713/media.

Modifying a Diagram

SmartArt diagrams can be changed and formatted in more ways than anyone would care to count. The following sections cover a few of the most basic and common methods of modifying diagrams.

If you really love formatting stuff, follow the same tip I gave you previously, in the discussion of charts. That is: If you want to change the formatting of any part of a diagram (whether it's text, a shape, a line, a background, or anything else), right-click that item; then click Format *[That Item]* on the shortcut menu. Doing so opens a dialog box of formatting options just for that item.

Resizing a Diagram

A diagram has the same sizing options as a chart, a picture, or a piece of clip art. You can resize it by dragging its corners or edges, by using the Shape Height and Shape Width tools on the Format tab, or by using the Layout dialog box's Size tab. For detailed instructions, see the section "Resizing a Graphic" in Chapter 13.

By default, a diagram's aspect ratio is not locked. To lock the aspect ratio, open the Layout dialog box, click the Size tab, check the Lock Aspect Ratio check box, and then click OK.

Changing a Diagram's Text Wrapping Setting

Word inserts a diagram as an inline image, so it acts like any other graphic when you drag it. To move a diagram freely, you need to change the way text wraps around it. To learn all about text wrapping, see the section "Wrapping Text Around a Graphic" in Chapter 13.

Moving a Diagram

You can reposition a diagram the same way you can move a chart, picture, or clip. For more information, see the section "Changing a Graphic's Position" in Chapter 13.

Applying a Different Diagram Layout

Each type of SmartArt diagram has a variety of layouts. Each layout is basically a variation on the primary diagram type and can include different shapes, patterns, and lines. One layout's shapes might even flow in a different direction than another one.

 LET ME TRY IT

Picking a Different Diagram Layout

Here's how to apply a different layout to a diagram:

1. Select the diagram to activate the SmartArt Tools tabs.

2. On the Design tab, click the More button in the Layouts group. A gallery of alternative layouts drops down, as shown in Figure 14.19.

3. Click a layout.

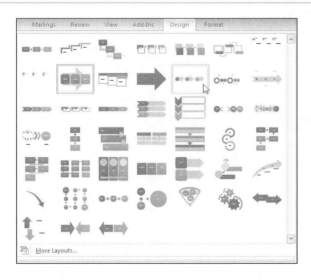

Figure 14.19 *Selecting a different layout for a continuous process diagram.*

Reversing a Diagram's Direction

By default, most diagrams flow from left to right or from top to bottom, but you can reverse a diagram so that it flows in the opposite direction. To change a diagram's direction, click it to active the SmartArt Tools tabs. On the Design tab, click Right to Left. To reverse the diagram again, click Right to Left again.

Applying a SmartArt Style to a Diagram

Like paragraphs of text, diagrams can be formatted with quick styles; in this case, however, they're called *SmartArt styles*. Each style applies different color combinations and effects to the diagram.

 LET ME TRY IT

Picking a SmartArt Style

Here's how to apply a SmartArt style to a diagram:

1. Select the diagram to activate the SmartArt Tools tabs.

2. On the Design tab, click the More button in the SmartArt Styles group. A gallery of styles drops down, as shown in Figure 14.20.

3. Click a style.

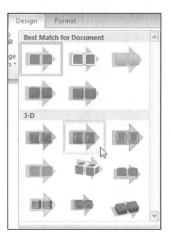

Figure 14.20   *Selecting a SmartArt style for a diagram.*

Adding and Removing Shapes

If a diagram doesn't have the right number of shapes, you can add new ones or remove existing ones. This is helpful if the default layout has too few or too many shapes to hold your text.

Here's how to add a new shape to a diagram:

1. In the diagram, click an existing shape that will be adjacent to (immediately before, after, above, or below) the new one.

2. On the Design tab, click the Add Shape button's drop-down arrow. A drop-down menu of options appears, as shown in Figure 14.21.

Figure 14.21   *Options for adding a shape to a SmartArt diagram.*

3. Click one of the following options:

   • **Add Shape After:** Places a new shape below or to the right of the currently selected one. The new shape has the same hierarchical level as the selected shape.

   • **Add Shape Before:** Place a new shape above or to the left of the currently selected one. The shape has the same hierarchical level as the selected shape.

   • **Add Shape Above:** Places a new shape above or to the left of the currently selected one. The new shape is superior to the selected one.

   • **Add Shape Below:** Places a new shape below or to the right of the currently selected one. The new shape is subordinate to the selected one.

   • **Add Assistant:** Places a new assistant-level shape below the currently selected one.

Some of these options may not be available, depending on the type of diagram and the type of shape you have selected. Some options are available only for hierarchical diagrams or only when a specific hierarchical level is used in the diagram.

To remove a shape from a diagram, select the shape and press Del.

Reorganizing a Diagram

You can move shapes around in a diagram while changing or maintaining their current level in the diagram's hierarchy. Here's how:

1. Click a shape.

2. On the Design tab, click one of the following options in the Create Graphic group (see Figure 14.22):

   - **Promote:** Moves the selected shape to the next higher level in a hierarchy. In a linear diagram where shapes are all the same level, this button moves the selected shape to the right.

   - **Demote:** Moves the selected shape to the next lower level in a hierarchy. In a linear diagram where shapes are all the same level, this button moves the selected shape to the left.

   - **Move Up:** Moves the selected shape forward in the diagram's sequence while keeping the shape on the same level.

   - **Move Down:** Moves the selected shape backward in the diagram's sequence while keeping the shape on the same level.

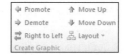

Figure 14.22 *Tools for reorganizing the shapes in a diagram.*

Some of these options may not be available, depending on the selected shape's position. If the shape cannot be promoted any higher, for instance, the Move Up option is not available.

NOTE: Chapters 15-17 of Part V and Chapters 18-22 of Part VI can be found online in your Free Web Edition by going to quepublishing.com/using and registering this product.

The Index that follows this page intentionally begins on page 473 and includes entries for the online chapters.

index

A

accepting revisions, PDF:406-408

accessing paragraph-formatting tools, 112-113

activating reading statistics, 60

adding
bibliographies, PDF:363-364
bookmarks, PDF:444-445
citations, PDF:360-361
clip art to documents, 286-287
colored backgrounds to pages, 245-247
columns to tables, 192
commands to Quick Access toolbar, PDF:454-458
envelopes to letters, PDF:353-354
groups to tabs (Ribbon), PDF:468-469
headings to outlines, PDF:373-374
indexes to documents, PDF:383
photos to documents, 284-285
rows to tables, 191-192
shapes to diagrams, 332-334
sources, PDF:356-359
special characters and symbols, 35-37
style and effects, to graphics, 302-304
table of contents (TOC) to documents, PDF:378-380
text
    to documents, 27-28
    to shapes, 308-309
    to tables, 187-188

address lists, creating for mail merge, PDF:391-394

addressing envelopes, PDF:351-353

adjusting
brightness/contrast in graphics, 300-301
character spacing, 103-105

aligning
paragraphs, 114-115
tables on pages, 207-208
text in cells, 203-204

Apply Styles pane, applying styles, 146-148

applying
different fonts to text, 93-95
font effects, 101-102
font styles, 100-101
Quick Styles, 140
styles
    with Apply Styles pane, 146-148
    to charts, 322-323
themes, 250-251

attaching documents to email, PDF:413-414

AutoCorrect, 78
changing settings, 79-81
creating exceptions to rules, 80-81
creating new entries, 82
deleting entries, 83
disabling, 84
rejecting changes, 78-79

AutoFormat, 108
configuring as you type, 108
Override Formatting Restrictions, PDF:410

AutoShapes, 304
drawing, 305

inserting, 305-307
modifying, 307-308

AutoText, 51

axis titles, adding to charts, 324-326

B

backgrounds, colored backgrounds, adding to pages, 245-247

bibliographies, PDF:363
adding, PDF:363-364

blank pages, inserting, 55

Bookmark dialog box, jumping to bookmarks, PDF:446

bookmarks, PDF:444
adding, PDF:444-445
deleting, PDF:449
inserting, PDF:444
jumping to, PDF:445-446
    with Bookmark dialog box, PDF:446
    with Go To tab, PDF:447-448
    with hyperlinks, PDF:448-449

Border tool, 129

borders
cells, 204-206
paragraphs, 129
    Border tool, 129
    Borders and Shading dialog box, 130-131
placing around pages, 247-248

Borders and Shading dialog box, 130-131
shading paragraphs, 133

brightness, adjusting in graphics, 300-301

browsing
  documents, 38
    Go To command, 40-41
  objects, navigating
    documents, 38-40
  themes, 251-252
building blocks, 50-52
  creating, 53-55
  inserting
    *from Building Blocks
      Organizer, 53*
    *from Quick Parts
      Gallery, 52-53*
  text boxes, creating,
    PDF:336-338
Building Blocks Organizer, 51
  inserting building
    blocks, 53
bullet characters, choosing,
  161-163
bullet library, 161-162
bulleted lists, 158-159
  choosing bullet character,
    161-163
  creating, 160-161
  creating as you type, 160
bullets, nested lists, 171-172

C

capitalization, changing
  AutoCorrect settings, 79-80
cells
  borders, 204-206
  deleting, 193-194
  inserting in tables, 193
  merging, 195
  resizing by dragging,
    198-199
  splitting, 195-196
changing
  AutoCorrect settings,
    79-81
  capitalization,
    AutoCorrect settings,
    79-80
  chart types, 319-320
  font size, 95-96

format of WordArt
    objects, PDF:347-350
  proofing options, 65
  Quick Style sets, 142-143
  section breaks, 233
  style definitions, 153
  text case, 105
character formatting
  clearing, 109-110
  copying and pasting with
    Format Painter, 106-107
character spacing, adjusting,
  103-105
Character styles, 137
charts, 310-311
  adding text elements, 323
    axis titles, 324-326
    data labels, 326
    legends, 326-327
    titles, 323-324
  changing, chart types,
    319-320
  changing text wrapping
    settings, 318
  creating, 314-316
  editing data, 316-317
  layouts, 320-322
  modifying, 318
  moving, 319
  resizing, 318
  styles, applying, 322-323
checking spelling and
  grammar in entire
  documents, 66-69
choosing
  bullet characters, 161-163
  numbering formats,
    166-169
  targets for hyperlinks,
    PDF:440-442
citations, PDF:360
  adding, PDF:360-361
  deleting, PDF:363
  editing, PDF:361-363
clearing
  character formatting,
    109-110
  styles, 148
Click and Type, 33-35

clip art
  adding, to documents,
    286-287
  finding, 287-290
  inserting, 287-290
Clipboard, 45-46
  pasting from, 46-47
closing, documents, 26
collaboration tools,
  PDF:399-400
collapsing parts of outlines,
  PDF:375-377
color, changing font color,
  96-97
  with Colors dialog box,
    98-100
  with Font Color palette,
    97-98
color sets, modifying in
  themes, 252-253
colored backgrounds, adding
  to pages, 245-247
colors, modifying in themes,
  253-255
Colors dialog box, changing
  font color, 98-100
column breaks, creating,
  220-222
column width, specifying for
  tables, 201
columns, 210-211
  adding to tables, 192
  converting multicolumn
    layout to single
    column, 222
  creating, column breaks,
    220-222
  creating custom layout,
    218-219
  deleting, 193-194
  distributing, 202
  layouts, changing, 220
  preset column formats,
    212-213
    *Columns dialog box,
      214-216*
    *Columns menu,
      212-214*
  resizing by dragging, 198

separating with vertical lines, 216-217

Columns dialog box, preset column formats, 214-216

Columns menu, preset column formats, 212-214

comments, PDF:400
  deleting, PDF:405
  editing, PDF:405
  hiding, PDF:404-405
  inserting, PDF:400-402
  navigating, PDF:403-404

contrast, adjusting in graphics, 300-301

converting
  multicolumn layout to single column, 222
  text to tables, 183-184
    tabbed text, 184-185

copying and moving text, 44-45

copying and pasting text, 45

copying character formatting with Format Painter, 106-107

cropping graphics, 298-300

cross-references, PDF:449
  creating dynamic cross-references to headings, PDF:449-451
  deleting, PDF:451
  following, PDF:451

custom paper size, 236-238

custom themes, creating, 258

customized watermarks, inserting, 244-245

customizing
  Quick Access toolbar, PDF:452-453
  Ribbon, PDF:461
  status bar, PDF:459-460

D

data, editing in charts, 316-317

data labels, adding to charts, 326

Decrease Indent button, 117

definitions, looking up, 84-86

deleting
  bookmarks, PDF:449
  cells, 193-194
  citations, PDF:363
  columns, 193-194
  comments, PDF:405
  cross-references, PDF:451
  documents from SkyDrive, PDF:433-434
  field codes, 278-279
  graphics, 309
  indexes, PDF:385-386
  notes, PDF:367-368
  rows, 193-194
  sources, PDF:359-360
  styles, 156
  table of contents (TOC), PDF:382
  tables, 208
  text, 37
  themes, 259

demoting headings in outlines, PDF:374-375

diagrams, 312-313
  creating, 327-329
  layouts, 331-332
  modifying, 330
  moving, 331
  reorganizing, 334
  resizing, 330
  reversing, 332
  shapes, adding/removing, 332-334
  SmartArt style, applying, 331-333
  text wrapping settings, 331

disabling AutoCorrect, 84

distributing
  columns, 202
  rows, 202

dividing documents into sections, 231-232

document properties, 51

document statistics
  finding, 57-58
  viewing, 57

documents
  adding
    indexes, PDF:383
    table of contents (TOC), PDF:378-380
  attaching to email, PDF:413-414
  browsing, 38
    Go To command, 40-41
  clip art, adding, 286-287
  closing, 26
  deleting from SkyDrive, PDF:433-434
  dividing into sections, 231-232
  downloading with SkyDrive, PDF:432-433
  editing with Word Web App, PDF:430-431
  emailing links to, PDF:414-417
  evaluating readability, 58-59
  extending with Click and Type, 33-35
  hyphenating, 240-241
    automatically, 241
    manually, 242
  inserting one Word document into another, 55-56
  mail merge
    adding fields, PDF:394-395
    creating, PDF:389-390
  moving around in, 38
  navigating by browsing objects, 38-40
  numbering lines
    with precision, 239-240
    quickly, 239
  opening, 17-18
    from Open dialog box, 19-20
    from Recent Documents list, 18-19
    with Word Web App, PDF:426-430
  page orientation, 234-236
  photos, adding, 284-285
  preparing for mail merge, PDF:389

printing, 22
   print jobs, setting up,
   23-25
   Quick Print, 22
saving, 12-13
   in custom Windows Live
   folders, PDF:421-424
   with different name,
   location, or file types,
   16-17
   to disk, 13-14
   resaving existing
   documents, 14-15
searching for, in Open
   dialog box, 20-21
section breaks, 232-233
   changing, 233
   inserting, 232
   removing, 233-234
sharing, PDF:417-418
   SkyDrive. See SkyDrive
   Word Web App. See
   Word Web App
starting from scratch, 7-8
starting from templates,
   8-9
   local templates, 10
   online templates, 10-12
text, adding, 27-28
downloading documents
  SkyDrive, PDF:432-433
drag-and-drop, moving
  text, 49
dragging
  resizing
   cells, 198-199
   columns, 198
   graphics, 290-291
   rows, 198
  sizing tables, 197-198
drawing
  AutoShapes, 305
  nested tables, 186
  shapes, 304
  tables, 180
   with mouse pointer,
   180-182
  text boxes, PDF:338-339
drawn objects, grouping,
  308-309

dynamic cross-references,
  creating to headings,
  PDF:449-451

E

editing
  chart data, 316-317
  citations, PDF:361-363
  comments, PDF:405
  documents, Word Web
   App, PDF:430-431
  footers, 276
  headers, 276
  sources, PDF:359
  tables, 186-187
  text, headers and footers,
   277-278
  WordArt text, PDF:347
editing privileges, restricting,
  PDF:408-411
effects, adding to graphics,
  302-304
effects sets, modifying in
  themes, 257
email
  attaching documents to,
   PDF:413-414
  sending links to
   documents,
   PDF:414-417
endnotes, PDF:364-365
  inserting, PDF:366-367
envelopes
  adding to letters,
   PDF:353-354
  addressing, PDF:351-353
errors
  finding and fixing while
   you type, 61-62
  grammar, fixing as you
   type, 63-65
  spelling, fixing as you
   type, 62-63
evaluating document's
  readability, 58-59
exceptions to AutoCorrect
  rules, creating, 80-81

expanding
  parts of outlines,
   PDF:375-377
  Ribbon, PDF:461-462
extending documents, with
  Click and Type, 33-35

F

field codes, 269-271
  deleting, 278-279
  inserting, 278-279
fields, 51
  mail merge, PDF:390-391
   adding to main
   document,
   PDF:394-395
   selecting, PDF:391-394
Find and Replace dialog box
  changing paragraph
   formatting, 134-135
  finding text, 72-76
Find command, 69-72
finding
  clip art, 287-290
  document statistics, 57-58
  errors, while you type,
   61-62
  name of document's
   template, 252-253
  synonyms, 86-87
  text, 69-70
   with Find and Replace
   dialog box, 72-76
finding templates, online, 11
fixing errors while you type,
  61-62
Flesch Reading Ease scale, 59
following
  cross-references, PDF:451
  hyperlinks, PDF:442-443
Font Color palette, changing
  font color, 97-98
Font dialog box, 91-92
font effects, applying,
  101-102
font sets, modifying themes,
  255-257

ont Size list, 96

onts
applying different fonts, 93-95
applying font effects, 101-102
applying styles, 100-101
changing color, 96-97
  with Colors dialog box, 98-100
  with Font Color palette, 97-98
changing size, 95-96
character spacing, adjusting, 103-105
selecting different, 92-93
text case, changing, 105

ooter view, 276

ooters, 269-271
changing position of, 279-280
creating different footers for odd and even pages, 280-281
editing, 276
  text, 277-278
hiding on document's first page, 281-282
moving between headers and footers, 276-277
preformatted footers, inserting, 273-274
removing, 282

ootnotes, PDF:364-365
inserting, PDF:365-366

Format Painter, copying character formatting, 106-107

Format tab, resizing graphics, 291-292

ormatting, 90
character formatting, copying with Format Painter, 106-107
manual formatting, 148
page numbers, 271-272
tables, 202-203
  aligning tables on pages, 207-208

aligning text in cells, 203-204
borders for cells, 204-206
shading, 206-207
Table Styles, 86
text
  with Quick Styles, 140-142
  in text boxes, PDF:342
text boxes, PDF:341

Free Web Edition, 5

G

generating indexes, PDF:384-386

Go To command, browsing documents, 40-41

Go To tab, jumping to bookmarks, PDF:447-448

grammar, 60-61
checking entire documents, 66-69
errors, fixing as you type, 63-65

graphics
adding, style and effects, 302-304
adjusting, brightness/contrast, 300-301
creating hyperlinks, PDF:438-440
cropping, 298-300
deleting, 309
modifying, 290
moving, 296-297
resizing, 290
  by dragging, 290-291
  with Format tab, 291-292
  in Layout dialog box, 292-293
wrapping text around, 293-295

grouping shapes, 308-309

groups, renaming on Ribbon, PDF:465-466

H

Header view, 276

headers, 269-271
changing position of, 279-280
creating different headers for odd or even pages, 280-281
editing, 276
editing text, 277-278
hiding on document's first page, 281-282
moving between footers and headers, 276-277
preformatted headers, inserting, 273-274
removing, 282

headings
adding to outlines, PDF:373-374
creating dynamic cross-references, PDF:449-451
demoting in outlines, PDF:374-375
promoting in outlines, PDF:374-375

hidden characters, viewing, 29-30

hiding
comments, PDF:404-405
headers and footers, 281-282
tabs, Ribbon, PDF:462-464

highlighting
occurrences of search text, 74-75
text, 106

hyperlinks, PDF:435-436
choosing targets, PDF:440-442
creating
  graphics, PDF:438-440
  text, PDF:436-438
following, PDF:442-443
jumping to bookmarks, PDF:448-449
modifying, PDF:443
removing, PDF:443

hyphenating documents, 240-241
 automatically, 241
 manually, 242

I

images. *See* graphics
Increase Indent button, 117
indenting
 lists, 173
 paragraphs, 115-116
 Paragraph dialog box, 118-119
 from Ribbon, 116-117
 rulers, 117-118
index entries, marking, PDF:383-384
indexes
 adding to documents, PDF:383
 deleting, PDF:385-386
 generating, PDF:384-386
 marking index entries, PDF:383-384
 updating, PDF:385
information, looking up with Research pane, 87-88
Insert Mode, 30-32
Insert Table dialog box, inserting tables, 177-178
inserting
 AutoShapes, 305-307
 blank pages, 55
 bookmarks, PDF:444
 building blocks
 from Building Blocks Organizer, 53
 from Quick Parts Gallery, 52-53
 cells in tables, 193
 clip art, 287-290
 comments, PDF:400-402
 endnotes, PDF:366-367
 field codes, 278-279
 footnotes, PDF:365-366
 nested tables, 185
 nonalphanumeric characters, 35-37

one Word document into another, 55-56
 page breaks, 229-230
 page numbers, 271-272
 preformatted headers, 273-274
 preformatted page numbers, 271
 section breaks, 232
 table of contents (TOC), customized, PDF:381-382
 tables, 174
 with Insert Table dialog box, 177-178
 Quick Tables, 178-179
 from Table menu, 175-177
 text boxes, PDF:336
 watermarks
 customized watermarks, 244-245
 preformatted watermarks, 243-244
 WordArt text, PDF:346-347

J

jumping
 to bookmarks, PDF:445-446
 with Bookmark dialog box, PDF:446
 with Go To tab, PDF:447-448
 with hyperlinks, PDF:448-449
 to and between notes, PDF:367

K

keyboard, selecting parts of tables, 191
 selecting text, 43
keyboard shortcuts, creating, PDF:469-471

L

Layout dialog box, resizing graphics, 292-293
layouts
 charts, 320-322
 columns, changing widths, 220
 creating custom column layout, 218-219
 diagrams, 331-332
legends, adding to charts, 326-327
letters, adding envelopes to, PDF:353-354
libraries
 bullet library, 161-162
 numbering libraries, 167-168
limiting what others can do to documents, PDF:408-411
Line and Paragraph Spacing tool, 125
 paragraph spacing, 127-128
line spacing, paragraphs, 124-125
 Paragraph dialog box, 126
lines, 28
Linked styles, 137
linking text boxes, PDF:343-344
links to documents, emailing, PDF:414-417
list numbering, restarting, 169-170
List styles, 137
lists, 158
 bulleted lists, 158-159
 choosing bullet character, 161-163
 creating, 160-161
 creating as you type, 160
 nested lists, 171
 with bullets only, 171-172

with numbers and bullets, 172-173
numbered lists, 164-165
choosing numbering formats, 166-169
creating, 165-166
creating as you type, 166
restarting list numbering, 169-170
spacing and indents, 173

local templates, starting documents, 10

M

mail merge
creating documents for printing, PDF:397-398
documents, creating, PDF:389-390
fields, adding to main document, PDF:394-395
fields, setting up, PDF:390-391
selecting fields and creating address lists, PDF:391-394
preparing main documents, PDF:389
previewing, PDF:396

managing sources, PDF:355-356

manual formatting, 148

margins, 224-225
creating custom margins, 226-229
precise margins, 226-228
preset margins, 226
setting on rulers, 228-229

marking index entries, PDF:383-384

merging cells, 195

Microsoft SharePoint, PDF:434

mini toolbar, 90-91

minimizing Ribbon, PDF:461-462

Modify Style dialog box, 153-155

modifying
AutoShapes, 307-308
charts, 318
diagrams, 330
graphics, 290
hyperlinks, PDF:443
styles, 152
templates, 265-267
themes, 252
color sets, 252-253
creating custom color sets, 253-255
effects sets, 257
font sets, 255-257

mouse, selecting parts of tables, 189-191

mouse pointer, drawing tables, 180-182

moving
around in documents, 38
around in tables, 187
charts, 319
diagrams, 331
graphics, 296-297
between headers and footers, 276-277
Quick Access toolbar, PDF:453-454
text, 45
drag-and-drop, 49
text boxes, PDF:340

N

navigating
comments, PDF:403-404
documents by browsing objects, 38-40

nested lists, 171
with bullets only, 171-172
with numbers and bullets, 172-173

nested tables, 185-186
drawing, 186
inserting, 185

nonalphanumeric characters, inserting, 35-37

nonprinting characters, viewing, 29-30

Normal style, 137

Normal template, 262-263

notes
deleting, PDF:367-368
jumping to and between, PDF:367
switching from one type to another, PDF:368-369

numbered lists, 164-165
choosing numbering formats, 166-169
creating, 165-166
creating as you type, 166
restarting list numbering, 169-170

numbering formats, choosing, 166-169

numbering libraries, 167-168

numbering lines
with precision, 239-240
quickly, 239

O

objects, browsing documents, 38-40

online chapters, 5

online templates, starting documents from, 10-12

Open dialog box
opening documents, 19-20
searching for documents, 20-21

opening documents, 17-18
from Open dialog box, 19-20
from Recent Documents list, 18-19
with Word Web App, PDF:426-430

Outline view, PDF:372-373

outlines, PDF:370
creating, PDF:370-371, 373
expanding and collapsing, parts, PDF:375-377

headings
  adding, PDF:373-374
  promoting and
    demoting,
    PDF:374-375
  Outline view, PDF:372-373
  reorganizing, PDF:376-378
Overtype Mode, 30-32

P

page breaks, 229-230
page numbers
  inserting and formatting,
    271-272
  preformatted page
    numbers, inserting, 271
page orientation, 234-236
pages, borders, 247-248
paper size
  custom paper size,
    236-238
  standard paper size,
    236-237
Paragraph dialog box
  indenting paragraphs,
    118-119
  line spacing, 126
  paragraph spacing, 128
paragraph formatting,
  changing with Find and
  Replace dialog box,
  134-135
  tools, accessing, 112-113
paragraph spacing, 127
  Line and Paragraph
    Spacing tool, 127-128
  setting in Paragraph
    dialog box, 128
Paragraph styles, 137
paragraphs, 28, 111-112
  aligning, 114-115
  borders, 129
    Border tool, 129
    Borders and Shading
      dialog box, 130-131
  finding and replacing
    paragraph formatting,
    134-135

indenting, 115-116
  Paragraph dialog box,
    118-119
  from Ribbon, 116-117
  with rulers, 117-118
line spacing, 124-125
  Paragraph dialog
    box, 126
paragraph-formatting
  tools, accessing, 112-113
shading, 132
  Borders and Shading
    dialog box, 133
  Shading tool, 132-133
tab stops
  setting, 119-122
  setting on rulers,
    122-123
  setting with Tabs dialog
    box, 123-124
Paste Options, 47-48
pasting from Clipboard,
  46-47
photos, adding to
  documents, 284-285
pictures. See also graphics
  resetting, 304
precise margins, 226-228
preformatted headers,
  inserting, 273-274
preformatted page numbers,
  inserting, 271
preformatted watermarks,
  243-244
preparing, documents for
  mail merge, PDF:389
preset column formats,
  212-213
  Columns dialog box,
    214-216
  Columns menu, 212-214
preset margins, 226
previewing mail merge,
  PDF:396
print jobs, setting up, 23-25

printing
  documents, 22
    print jobs, setting up,
      23-25
    Quick Print, 22
  merge documents,
    PDF:397-398
  from Word Web App,
    PDF:429
promoting headings in
  outlines, PDF:374-375
proofing, 57
proofing options,
  changing, 65

Q

Quick Access toolbar, 49-50
  adding commands,
    PDF:454-458
  customizing, PDF:452-453
  moving, PDF:453-454
  removing commands,
    PDF:458
  reorganizing,PDF: 458
  restoring, PDF:459
Quick Access Toolbar menu,
  PDF:454-455
Quick Parts Gallery, inserting
  building blocks, 52-53
Quick Print, 22
Quick Style Gallery, removing
  Quick Styles, 143
Quick Styles
  applying, 140
  changing sets, 142-143
  creating, 150-152
  formatting text, 140-142
  removing from Quick
    Style Gallery, 143
  versus styles, 139
Quick Styles Gallery, Styles
  pane, 144
  applying styles, 144-146
Quick Table Gallery, 178-179
Quick Tables, 178-179

R

readability of documents, evaluating, 58-59

reading statistics, activating, 60

Recent Documents list, opening documents, 18-19

Redo button, 50

refining text searches, 71-72

rejecting
AutoCorrect changes, 78-79
revisions, PDF:406-408

removing
character formatting, 109-110
commands from Quick Access toolbar, PDF:458
footers, 282
headers, 282
hyperlinks, PDF:443
Quick Styles from Quick Style Gallery, 143
section breaks, 233-234
shapes from diagrams, 332-334
tab stops, 123
themes, 252
watermarks, 245

renaming
groups, Ribbon, PDF:465-466
styles, 152
tabs, Ribbon, PDF:465-466

reorganizing
diagrams, 334
outlines, PDF:376-378
Quick Access toolbar, PDF:458
Ribbon, PDF:464-465

replacing text, 76-77

resaving, existing documents, 14-15

Research pane, looking up information, 87-88

research tools, 84
definitions, looking up, 84-86
synonyms, finding, 86-87

resetting pictures, 304

resizing
cells by dragging, 198-199
charts, 318
columns by dragging, 198
diagrams, 330
graphics, 290
by dragging, 290-291
with Format tab, 291-292
in Layout dialog box, 292-293
rows by dragging, 198
tables by dragging, 197-198
text boxes, PDF:339

restarting list numbering, 169-170

restoring
Quick Access toolbar, PDF:459
Ribbon, PDF:469

restricting, editing privileges, PDF:408-411

reversing diagrams, 332

revisions
accepting and rejecting, PDF:406-408
limiting what others can do, PDF:408-411

Ribbon, 10
adding groups to tabs, PDF:468-469
customizing, PDF:461
expanding, PDF:461-462
indenting paragraphs, 116-117
minimizing, PDF:461-462
renaming tabs/groups, PDF:465-466
reorganizing, PDF:464-465
restoring, PDF:469
showing/hiding tabs, PDF:462-464
tabs, creating, PDF:466-468

right-clicking, adding commands to Quick Access toolbar, PDF:455-456

row height, specifying in tables, 201-202

rows
adding to tables, 191-192
deleting, 193-194
distributing, 202
resizing by dragging, 198

rulers
indenting paragraphs, 117-118
setting margins, 228-229
tab stops, setting, 122-123

S

sans serif fonts, 95

saving documents, 12-13
in custom Windows Live folders, PDF:421-424
in default Windows Live folders, PDF:419-421
with different name, location, or file types, 16-17
to disk, 13-14
resaving existing documents, 14-15

searching
for documents in Open dialog box, 20-21
for special characters, 75-76
for specific text, 70-71

section breaks, 231-233
changing, 233
inserting, 232
removing, 233-234

selecting
fields, mail merge, PDF:391-394
fonts, different fonts, 92-93
parts of tables, 188-189
with the keyboard, 191
with the mouse, 189-191
text, 41-43

separating columns with vertical lines, 216-217

serif fonts, 95

shading
paragraphs, 132
Borders and Shading dialog box, 133
Shading tool, 132-133
tables, 206-207

Shading tool, 132-133

shapes
adding to diagrams, 332-334
drawing, 304
grouping, 308-309
removing from diagrams, 332-334
text, adding to, 308-309

SharePoint, PDF:434

sharing documents, PDF:417-418
SkyDrive. *See* SkyDrive
Word Web App. *See* Word Web App

shortcuts, creating blank documents, 7

showing tabs, Ribbon, PDF:462-464

sizing tables, 197, 199
by dragging, 197-198
specifying column widths, 201
specifying row heights, 201-202
specifying width, 199-200

SkyDrive, PDF:417-419
documents, deleting, PDF:433-434
downloading documents, PDF:432-433
saving
documents in custom Windows Live folders, PDF:421-424
documents in default Windows Live folders, PDF:419-421

SmartArt diagrams, 327-329

SmartArt style, applying to diagrams, 331-333

sources
adding, PDF:356-359
deleting, PDF:359-360
editing, PDF:359
managing, PDF:355-356

spacing lists, 173

special characters
adding, 35-37
searching for, 75-76

spelling, 60-61
checking entire documents, 66-69
errors, fixing as you type, 62-63

splitting cells, 195-196

standard paper size, 236-237

status bar, customizing, PDF:459-460

storing templates, 261-262

styles, 136-138
adding, to graphics, 302-304
advantages of, 138-139
applying
with Apply Styles pane, 146-148
to charts, 322-323
from Styles pane, 144-146
changing definitions, 153
Character styles, 137
clearing, 148
creating, 148-151
deleting, 156
font styles, applying, 100-101
Linked styles, 137
List styles, 137
modifying, 152
Normal style, 137
Paragraph styles, 137
Quick Styles. *See* Quick Styles
versus Quick Styles, 139
renaming, 152
Table styles, 137

updating
definitions, 153-155
to match selected text, 155-156

Styles pane, Quick Styles Gallery, 144
applying styles, 144-146

switching
from one type of note to another, PDF:368-369
to Word from Word Web App, PDF:431-432

symbols, adding, 35-37

synonyms, finding, 86-87

T

tab stops
removing, 123
setting, 119-122
on rulers, 122-123
with Tabs dialog box, 123-124

Tab Type button, 122

tabbed text, converting to tables, 184-185

Table menu, inserting tables, 175-177

table of contents (TOC), PDF:378
adding to documents, PDF:378-380
deleting, PDF:382
inserting customized, PDF:381-382
updating, PDF:382

Table styles, 137

tables, 174
adding text to, 187-188
cells
deleting, 193-194
inserting, 193
merging, 195
splitting, 195-196
columns
adding, 192
deleting, 193-194
converting text to, 183-184

deleting, 208
distributing rows and
   columns, 202
drawing, 180
   with mouse pointer,
      180-182
editing, 186-187
formatting, 202-203
   aligning tables on
      pages, 207-208
   aligning text in cells,
      203-204
   borders for cells,
      204-206
   shading, 206-207
   with Table Styles, 86
inserting, 174
   with Insert Table dialog
      box, 177-178
   Quick Tables, 178-179
   from Table menu,
      175-177
moving around in, 187
nested tables, 185-186
   drawing, 186
   inserting, 185
rows
   adding, 191-192
   deleting, 193-194
selecting parts of, 188-189
   with the keyboard, 191
   with the mouse,
      189-191
sizing, 197
   by dragging, 197-198
   specifying column
      widths, 201
   specifying row heights,
      201-202
specifying
   dimensions, 199
   width, 199-200
Tables Styles, 86
tabs
adding new groups
   (Ribbon), PDF:468-469
creating, for Ribbon,
   PDF:466-468
renaming on Ribbon,
   PDF:465-466
showing/hiding, on
   Ribbon, PDF:462-464

Tabs dialog box, setting tab
   stops, 123-124
targets, choosing for
   hyperlinks, PDF:440-442
templates, 259-260
   applying different
      templates to
      documents, 263-265
   creating new, 267-268
   finding name of, 252-253
   modifying, 265-267
   Normal template, 262-263
   for older versions of
      Word, 261
   starting documents, 8-9
      local templates, 10
      online templates, 10-12
   storing, 261-262
   types of, 260-262
text
   adding
      to documents, 27-28
      to shapes, 308-309
      to tables, 187-188
   aligning in cells, 203-204
   converting to tables,
      183-184
      tabbed text, 184-185
   copying and moving,
      44-45
   copying and pasting, 45
   creating hyperlinks,
      PDF:436-438
   deleting, 37
   editing, in headers and
      footers, 277-278
   finding, 69-70
      with Find and Replace
         dialog box, 72-76
   formatting
      with Quick Styles,
         140-142
      in text boxes, PDF:342
   highlighting, 106
   moving, 45
      drag-and-drop, 49
   refining text searches,
      71-72
   replacing, 76-77
   searching for specific
      pieces of text, 70-71

selecting, 41-43
   wrapping around
      graphics, 293-295
text boxes, PDF:335
   creating from building
      blocks, PDF:336-338
   drawing, PDF:338-339
   formatting, PDF:341
      text, PDF:342
   inserting, PDF:336
   linking, PDF:343-344
   moving, PDF:340
   resizing, PDF:339
text case, changing, 105
text elements, adding to
   charts, 323
   axis titles, 324-326
   data labels, 326
   legends, 326-327
   titles, 323-324
text wrapping settings
   changing in charts, 318
   diagrams, 331
themes, 249-250
   applying, 250-251
   browsing, 251-252
   creating custom
      themes, 258
   deleting, 259
   modifying, 252
      color sets, 252-253
      creating custom color
         sets, 253-255
      effects sets, 257
      font sets, 255-257
   removing, 252
titles, adding to charts,
   323-324
toggling between Insert and
   Overtype Modes, 30-32
toolbars
   mini toolbar, 90-91
   Quick Access toolbar,
      49-50
      adding commands to,
         PDF:454-458
      customizing,
         PDF:452-453
      moving, PDF:453-454

*removing commands,
PDF:458
reorganizing, PDF:458
restoring, PDF:459*

tools
Border tool, 129
Line and Paragraph
Spacing tool, 125
*paragraph spacing,
127-128*
Shading tool, 132-133

Track Changes feature,
PDF:405-406
accepting and rejecting
revisions, PDF:406-408

U

Undo, 49-50

updating
indexes, PDF:385
style definitions, 153-155
styles to match selected
text, 155-156
table of contents
(TOC), PDF:382

V

vertical lines, separating
columns, 216-217

viewing
document statistics, 57
hidden characters, 29-30

W

watermarks, 242-243
inserting
*customized
watermarks, 244-245
preformatted
watermarks, 243-244*
removing, 245

Web Apps, PDF:417

widths, changing column
widths, 220

Windows Live, PDF:417-418

Windows Live folders
saving documents,
PDF:419-421
saving in custom folders,
PDF:421-424

Word, switching to from
Word Web App,
PDF:431-432

Word options dialog box,
adding commands to,
Quick Access toolbar,
PDF:456-458

Word templates, 260
with macros, 261

Word Web App, PDF:426
documents, editing,
PDF:430-431
opening documents,
PDF:426-430
switching to Word,
PDF:431-432

WordArt, PDF:345
creating, PDF:346-347

WordArt objects, changing
format of, PDF:347-350

WordArt text
editing, PDF:347
inserting, PDF:346-347

wrapping text around
graphics, 293-295